Syntax-Based Collocation Extraction

T0142035

Text, Speech and Language Technology

VOLUME 44

For further volumes:
http://www.springer.com/series/6636

Syntax-Based Collocation Extraction

by

Violeta Seretan
University of Geneva, Switzerland

 Springer

Violeta Seretan
University of Geneva
Department of Linguistics (Office L706)
Rue de Candolle 2
1211 Geneva
Switzerland
violeta.seretan@unige.ch

ISSN 1386-291X
ISBN 978-94-007-3471-5   ISBN 978-94-007-0134-2 (eBook)
DOI 10.1007/978-94-007-0134-2
Springer Dordrecht Heidelberg London New York

Printed on acid-free paper

Springer is part of Springer Science+Business Media (www.springer.com)

To Vincenzo

Preface

This book is based on my doctoral dissertation research carried out at the Department of Linguistics, University of Geneva under the supervision of Eric Wehrli. I wish to express my heartfelt gratitude to my thesis committee members, Christian Boitet, Ulrich Heid, Paola Merlo and Jacques Moeschler as well as to the anonymous Springer reviewers for their comments and suggestions. I am especially grateful to Eric Wehrli both for his input on the dissertation and the present volume and for providing me the opportunity to carry out my work in such a stimulating environment during the eight years I spent in Geneva. My work received the support of several organisations, which are gratefully acknowledged: the Swiss Network for International Studies for sponsoring the project that formed the foundation of the present work; the Swiss National Science Foundation for financing my postdoctoral activity; and the Latsis Foundation for awarding me the 2010 Geneva University Latsis Prize for my dissertation.

I am extremely grateful to the many people that have also contributed, directly or indirectly, to making this book a reality: Anamaria Benţea, Chris Biemann, Dan Cristea, Stephanie Durrleman, Thierry Fontenelle, Nikhil Garg, Maria Georgescul, Jean-Philippe Goldman, François Grize, Ileana Ibănescu, Eric Joanis, Alexis Kauffmann, Christopher Laenzlinger, Antonio Leoni, Gabriele Musillo, Luka Nerima, Vivi Năstase, Mar Ndiaye, Simona Orzan, Olivier Pasteur, Sebastian Padó, Genoveva Puskas, Lorenza Russo, Tanja Samardžić, Yves Scherrer, Gabriela Soare, Valentin Tablan, Bernard Testa, Marco Tomassini, Lonneke van Der Plas, among many others. I also wish to thank my editor, Helen van der Stelt, for practical assistance.

I owe a special debt to Livia Polanyi, who cast an expert eye to parts of the manuscript and helped me rephrase my (often too unidiomatic or anti-collocational) turns of phrase. Finally, I wish to express my gratitude to my husband Vincenzo for his constant support, encouragement, advice and original ideas on the most diverse topics, particularly those related to NLP. This book is dedicated to him.

Geneva   Violeta Seretan
June 2010

Contents

Chapter 1
Introduction

1.1 Collocations and Their Relevance for NLP

A large part of the vocabulary of a language is made up of *phraseological units* or *multi-word expressions*, complex lexical items that have "idiosyncratic interpretations that cross word boundaries" (Sag et al., 2002, 2). The importance of these units has been widely recognized both in theoretical linguistics, in which phraseology was recently established as an independent field of research (Cowie, 1998), and in computational linguistics, where growing attention is currently being paid to recognizing and processing multi-word units in various applications (Baldwin and Kim, 2010).

Phraseological units cover a wide range of phenomena, including compound nouns (*dead end*), phrasal verbs (*to ask out*), idioms (*to lend somebody a hand*), and collocations (*sharp contrast, daunting task, widely available, to meet a requirement*). According to numerous authors (Kjellmer, 1987; Howarth and Nesi, 1996; Stubbs, 1995; Jackendoff, 1997; Mel'čuk, 1998; Lea and Runcie, 2002; Erman and Warren, 2000), phraseological units, in general, and, collocations, in particular, are pervasive in texts of all genres and domains, with collocations representing the highest proportion of phraseological units.[1]

While an agreed-upon definition of collocations does not yet exist, they are generally understood as typical combinations of words that differ from regular combinations in that their components co-occur in a short span of text more often than chance would predict. Unlike idioms, collocations have a rather transparent meaning and are easy to decode. Yet, like idioms, they are difficult to encode—in fact, they are said to represent "idioms of encoding" (Makkai, 1972; Fillmore et al., 1988) since

---

[1] For example, it is claimed that "in all kinds of texts, collocations are indispensable elements with which our utterances are very largely made" (Kjellmer, 1987, 140); "most sentences contain at least one collocation" (Pearce, 2001a; Howarth and Nesi, 1996); "no piece of natural spoken or written English is totally free of collocation" (Lea and Runcie, 2002, vii); "collocations make up the lion's share of the phraseme inventory, and thus deserve our special attention" (Mel'čuk, 1998, 24). According to Stubbs (1995, 122), "a significant proportion of language use is routinized, conventionalized and idiomatic". Jackendoff (1997) estimates the number of phraseological units in a lexicon of the same order as the number of single words. Similarly, Erman and Warren (2000) estimate that about half of fluent native text is constructed using ready-made units.

V. Seretan, *Syntax-Based Collocation Extraction*, Text, Speech and Language Technology 44, DOI 10.1007/978-94-007-0134-2_1,
© Springer Science+Business Media B.V. 2011

Table 1.1 Collocations across languages

French	Literal translation (anti-collocation)	English (correct translation)
Accuser retard	*Accuse delay	Experience delay
Établir distinction	*Establish distinction	Draw distinction
Gagner argent	*Win money	Make money
Relever défi	*Raise challenge	Take up challenge
Poser question	*Put down question	Ask question

they are unpredictable for non-native speakers and, in general, do not preserve the meaning of (all of) their components across languages. For illustration, consider the French collocations listed in Table 1.1. The verbal component of these collocations cannot be translated literally to English; a literal translation would lead to unnatural if not awkward formulations, called *anti-collocations* (Pearce, 2001a, 43). Instead, completely different verbs must be used to encode the meaning of these collocations in English.

The past decades have witnessed significant advances in the work of automatic acquisition of collocations from text corpora, most of which aimed at providing lexicographic support. Boosted by the advent of the computer era and the development of corpus linguistics, but also by the present emphasis on the study of words in context—"You shall know a word by the company it keeps!" (Firth, 1957, 179)—this work led to the development of corpus-based dictionaries including collocations; a representative example is COBUILD, the Collins Birmingham University International Language Database (Sinclair, 1995). From the list of dictionaries in Appendix A it is easy to see the recent expansion of lexicographic work devoted to collocations in many languages. As the compilation of such resources is increasingly corpus-based, automatic collocation extraction methods are being heavily used in many lexicographic projects for collecting the raw material to include in dictionaries, for validating the intuition of lexicographers, and for complementing collocation entries with additional corpus-based information such as frequency of use or usage samples.

In Natural Language Processing (NLP), collocational information derived from corpora is crucial for applications dealing with text production. For instance, collocations are considered to be not only useful, but a key factor in producing more acceptable output in machine translation and natural language generation tasks (Heylen et al., 1994; Orliac and Dillinger, 2003). The importance of collocations lies in their prevalence in language,[2] whereas the difficulty in handling them comes, principally, from their ambiguous linguistic status, their equivocal position at the intersection of lexicon and grammar, and the lack of a precise and operational definition.

There is also a marked interest in collocations in NLP from the opposite perspective, that of text analysis, where they also prove useful in a variety of tasks. For

---

[2] As put by Mel'čuk (2003, 26), "L'importance des collocations réside dans leur omniprésence" [The importance of collocation lies in their omnipresence].

instance, in parsing collocations have been used to solve attachment ambiguities by giving preference to analyses in which they occur (Hindle and Rooth, 1993; Alshawi and Carter, 1994; Ratnaparkhi, 1998; Berthouzoz and Merlo, 1997; Pantel and Lin, 2000; Wehrli, 2000; Volk, 2002). In word sense disambiguation, collocations have been used to discriminate between senses of polysemous words (Brown et al., 1991; Yarowsky, 1995) by relying on the "one sense per collocation" hypothesis, according to which words have a strong tendency to exhibit only one sense in a given collocation (Yarowsky, 1993). Analogously, collocations have been used in information retrieval (Ballestros and Croft, 1996; Hull and Grefenstette, 1998), text classification (Williams, 2002), and topic segmentation (Ferret, 2002). They are also helpful for a wide range of other applications, from speech recognition and OCR, where homophonic/homographic ambiguity can be resolved by taking their collocates into account (Church and Hanks, 1990), to context-sensitive dictionary look-up where collocations can be used to find the specific dictionary subentry that best matches the context of the target word (Michiels, 2000).

1.2 The Need for Syntax-Based Collocation Extraction

Traditionally, in the absence of more powerful linguistic analysis tools, collocation extraction work relies on the criterion of word proximity in text in order to identify potential candidates. Thus, in so-called *n-gram methods* collocations are modelled as sequences of consecutive words, possibly filtered according to their Part of Speech if POS tagging is available. Alternatively, in *window-based methods* they are modelled as interruptible word pairs found in a short window of text.

Although many researchers (Smadja, 1993; Heid, 1994; Pearce, 2002; Krenn, 2000a; Evert, 2004b) postulate that collocation extraction should ideally rely on the syntactic analysis of the source corpora, the syntactic structure of the source text has been taken into account in extraction work only in rare cases; mostly for languages, like German, for which traditional methods are recognized to be inefficient due to systematic long-range dependencies. Usually, syntax-based alternatives are discarded because researchers argue that large-scale parsers are unavailable for many languages and that these methods lack robustness and deliver insufficient precision on unrestricted text, as well as being computationally intensive. Even though significant advances in parsing have meanwhile been achieved, most collocation extraction work still relies on conventional syntax-free methods. However, we believe that the time is right for a methodological shift. We will demonstrate why we think so by means of a series of examples.[3]

Consider, first, the pair *[to] solve – problem* occurring in the corpus excerpt shown in Example 1.

(1) The *problem* is therefore, clearly a deeply rooted one and cannot be *solved* without concerted action by all parties.

---

[3] As all the examples provided thorough this book, the following are naturally-occurring (rather than invented) examples.

As illustrated by this pair, collocations allow for virtually unrestricted morpho-logical and syntactic transformations, leading to surface realizations that are sub-stantially divergent from the base word form and the expected word order (e.g., the verb preceding the object in an SVO language like English). Syntactic analysis is necessary to capture the collocation instances that occur in text in a different form, or for cases in which the collocated words are not found in the immediate vicinity of each other.

Furthermore, even if some pairs of words have a tendency to co-occur in the same form and within a short span of text, a syntactic analysis is required to ensure that they are actually syntactically related, and that they do not constitute extrac-tion noise. For example, a pair like *human – organisation*, although apparently well-formed, is not a valid result if extracted from contexts like the one in (2); only *human rights* and *human rights organisation* are valid collocation candidates in this example.

(2) *human* rights *organisations*

Finally, we argue that syntactic analysis is a real necessity if the extraction results are to be used in other applications. Without explicit syntactic information, extrac-tion results are highly ambiguous and difficult to interpret outside their original context. For instance, for a pair like *question – asked*, both a passive interpretation ("the question asked by somebody") and an active interpretation are possible ("the question asks if"). In Example 3, deep parsing is necessary to identify that *question* and *asked* are in a subject-verb relation rather than in a verb-object relation. Shallow parsers typically fail to analyse such pairs correctly because, lacking a global inter-pretation for the whole sentence, they may favour wrong local attachments.

(3) The *question asked* if the grant funding could be used as start-up capital to develop this project.

Although it may be argued that the goal of automatic extraction is to identify collocation types rather than particular instances, we argue that it is important to identify instances accurately for several reasons: (a) most linguistic phenomena observed in a corpus are infrequent, therefore for each collocation type it is impor-tant to detect the maximum number of instances to allow for statistical inference; (b) some collocations, particularly for languages exhibiting a high degree of word order freedom, occur systematically in long-range dependencies (Goldman et al., 2001); therefore, capturing these dependencies is the only means to capture a col-location type; and (c) ignoring difficult extraction cases prevents the description of results in terms of morpho-syntactic variation potential, which is actually one of the main aims pursued in theoretical and lexicographic work devoted to collocations.

1.3 Aims

The main objective of the work described in this book is to take advantage of recent advances achieved in syntactic parsing to propose a collocation extrac-tion methodology that is more sensitive to the morpho-syntactic context in which collocations occur in the source corpora. Given the encouraging results obtained by syntax-based approaches to other NLP tasks—for instance, term extraction (Maynard and Ananiadou, 1999), semantic role labelling (Gildea and Palmer, 2002) and semantic similarity computation (Padó and Lapata, 2007)—we will demonstrate the extent to which such an approach is feasible and appropriate for the task of collocation extraction.

To this end, we rely on detailed syntactic information provided by a multilingual syntactic parser[4] to design an extraction method in which collocation candidates are identified in text according to their syntactic relatedness. By using the syntactic proximity criterion instead of the linear proximity criterion in choosing candidate pairs, we will show that a substantial improvement can be gained in the quality of extraction results. We test this hypothesis by evaluation experiments performed for several languages which compare the precision obtained against a traditional syntax-free method. In addition, we show that the use of a syntactic filter on the candidate data has a positive impact on the statistical measures of association strength which are used to rank the candidate pairs according to their likelihood to constitute collocations. We will argue that improvement in collocation identification can thus be achieved, by applying association measures on syntactically homogeneous material, and by providing these measures with accurate frequency information on pairs selected by syntax-based methods, as shown by a series of case-study evaluations in which we compare the ranks proposed by the two methods and investigate the causes that lead the syntax-free method to artificially promote erroneous pairs to high positions in the results list at the expense of interesting pairs.

In addition to collocation pairs, our work focuses on the extraction of collocations made up of more than two words. We will show that our syntax-based method which extracts binary collocations can be extended to efficiently identify complex collocations (i.e., collocations containing nested collocations, like *draw a clear distinction*, *reach a joint resolution*, *proliferation of weapons of mass destruction*). We also attempt to broaden as much as possible the set of syntactic configurations (patterns) allowed for the extraction of binary collocations, and, for this purpose, we provide a way to detect all collocationally relevant patterns in a language. In addition to patterns like verb-object or adjective-noun which are the most representative for collocations, other patterns involving functional categories are also relevant and arguably very important—for instance, patterns including prepositions, determiners, and conjunctions (compare the preposition-noun collocation *on page* with the anti-collocation **at page*).[5]

Another practical investigation described in this book is directed towards the acquisition of bilingual collocation resources for integration into a rule-based machine translation system (Wehrli et al., 2009). We propose an efficient method

---

[4] The parser Fips developed at the Language Technology Laboratory of the University of Geneva (Wehrli, 1997, 2007).

[5] See Baldwin et al. (2006) for a detailed account of the idiosyncratic syntax and semantics of preposition-noun expressions in particular.

for finding translation equivalents for collocations in parallel corpora, and, to this end, we employ our syntax-based collocation extraction method on both the source and target versions of the corpus.

1.4 Chapters Outline

In this chapter, we introduced *word collocation*, the central concept to which the book is devoted. We discussed the relevance of word collocation for NLP and provided arguments for a syntax-based approach to collocation extraction. We also outlined the main research directions pursued in our study. The remainder of the book is organised as follows.

Chapter 2: On Collocations

Chapter 2 looks further into the complex phenomenon of collocation and guides the reader through the maze of the numerous, and often conflicting, descriptions that have been provided in the literature on this topic. We identify the most salient defining features, which will serve as the basis for the discussion in the rest of the book.

Chapter 3: Survey of Extraction Methods

Chapter 3 sets the stage for the practical explorations described in following chapters. We start with a discussion of the extent to which theoretical descriptions have been taken into account in the practical work on collocation extraction. We then describe the basics of extraction methodologies relying on statistical association measures, discuss the role of linguistic preprocessing of source corpora, and provide an extensive review of existing extraction work.

Chapter 4: Syntax-Based Extraction

In Chapter 4, we first take a closer look at the existing syntax-based extraction work then state the specific requirements that our method satisfies. We continue by presenting the syntactic parser which is used in our work and by describing and evaluating our extraction method. We present a monolingual and a cross-lingual evaluation experiment in which we compare the syntax-based approach against the traditional syntax-free approach represented by the window method. We also provide a qualitative analysis of the results and a comparison of the two approaches at a more abstract level.

Chapter 5: Extensions

Chapter 5 extends the proposed extraction methodology in three different directions. The first two aim to ensure that a broader spectrum of collocational phenomena in the source text is covered—thus, we propose solutions for the extraction of complex collocations, and for the detection of all syntactic configurations appropriate to collocations in a given language. The third direction explores the topic of automatic acquisition of bilingual collocation correspondences. The solution proposed relies on the application of the monolingual extraction method on both the source and target versions of a parallel corpus.

Chapter 6: Conclusion

In the last chapter, we summarize the main findings of our work and point to directions for further research, including the portability of the proposed methodology to new languages and parsing tools; the exploration of the complex interplay between syntactic parsing and collocation extraction; and the use of complementary resources and tools for improving extraction results and their subsequent processing by human users or NLP applications.

Chapter 2
On Collocations

2.1 Introduction

The phenomenon of collocating words was brought to the attention of linguists in the 1930s by the British contextualist John R. Firth, who actually popularized the term *collocation*, derived from the Latin word *collocare* ("to place together, to assemble"). But long before that, pedagogical studies on first and second language acquisition were already concerned with collocations, seen as language chunks which are memorized by speakers as whole units and which constitute the major means for achieving language fluency (Pawley and Syder, 1983). According to some researchers, amongst whom Gitsaki (1996), collocations have even been known and studied by the ancient Greeks.

At the beginning of the twentieth century, Harold Palmer, who pioneered the study of English as a Foreign Language (EFL), also noted the presence of so-called *polylogs*, or *known units* in language. He built a list of over 6,000 frequent collocations which he included in his teaching, so that students could learn them in block. The same concern for phraseological units led his successor, Albert Sydney Hornby, to include collocational information in the dictionaries from the series that he initiated with the *Idiomatic and Syntactic English Dictionary* (1942) and that continued with *A Learner's Dictionary of Current English* (Hornby et al., 1948b), *The Advanced Learner's Dictionary of Current English* (Hornby et al., 1952), and the *Oxford Advanced Learner's Dictionary* (Hornby et al., 1948a), reprinted multiple times. This pedagogical trend was continued, most notably, by Anthony P. Cowie, Peter Howarth, and Michael Lewis. As for Lewis (2000, 173), he considers collocations as the "islands of reliability" of speakers' utterances. The recent years have shown a continued interest in studying collocations in the context of Foreign Language and Teaching (Meunier and Granger, 2008), paralleled by sustained efforts of compiling collocation dictionaries for many languages (see Appendix A).

Thus, it can be stated that collocations unveiled primarily from pedagogical observations on language acquisition that associated them with a high level of proficiency, which can only be achieved by speakers through memorization and which is seen as a privilege reserved to native speakers. The pedagogical interest in collocations provided a strong motivation for their study, collection and analysis in the perspective of language teaching.

V. Seretan, *Syntax-Based Collocation Extraction*, Text, Speech and Language Technology 44, DOI 10.1007/978-94-007-0134-2_2,

2.2 A Survey of Definitions

The most general understanding of the term *collocation*—as introduced in the framework of contextualism or described in earlier linguistic studies—is that of a relation of *affinity* which holds between words in a language, and which is revealed by the typical co-occurrence of words, i.e., by the recurrent appearance of words in the context of each other. Contextualists consider that in characterizing a word, its context plays the most important role: "You shall know a word by the company it keeps!" (Firth, 1957, 179). Earlier, Bally (1909) used the expression "groupements usuels" ("usual phrases") to refer to words that show an affinity for each other, while preserving their autonomy: "conservent leur autonomie, tout en laissant voir une affinité évidente qui les rapproche" (Bally, 1951, 70–72).[1] In order to describe this affinity, Coseriu (1967) later used the metaphor "lexical solidarity".

The lexical affinity cannot be accounted for by regulatory language processes, since it is not explainable on the basis of grammar rules applied to word classes. As Mel'čuk (1998) points out,

> [the phraseme—in particular, the collocation] cannot be constructed (...) from words or simpler phrases according to general rules of [language] L, but has to be stored and used as a whole (Mel'čuk, 1998).

While the characterisation in terms of affinity provides a good intuition for the concept of collocation, these definitions remain quite vague, as nothing is said about its linguistic status and properties. Lacking a precise definition, the term *collocation* was constantly accompanied over the time by confusion, and was used in different places for denoting different linguistic phenomena. The confusion was only augmented by the examples provided by various researchers, which are highly inconsistent and reflect the divergence of points of view.

As stated many times in the collocation literature (Hausmann, 1989; Bahns, 1993; Lehr, 1996), the understanding of the term varied with researchers' point of view. In NLP, the precise understanding is often subject to the desired usage of collocations in an application: "the definition of collocations varied across research projects" (McKeown and Radev, 2000, 523); "the practical relevance is an essential ingredient of their definition" (Evert, 2004b, 17).

As Bahns (1993, 57) points out, "collocation is a term which is used and understood in many different ways". But despite the diversity of understandings and points of view, it is still possible to identify two main perspectives on the concept of collocation: one which is purely statistical, and one which is more linguistically motivated. In what follows, we survey the most representative definitions of each group in chronological order.

---

[1] Bally distinguishes between "groupements passagers" (free combinations), "groupements usuels" (collocations), and "séries phraséologiques" (idioms).

2.2.1 *Statistical Approaches*

Both the pedagogical and contextualist definitions of collocation mentioned so far imply a statistical component. In order to be acquired by speakers through memorisation in block, collocations must be identifiable on the basis of their frequency—that is, they must recur enough times to be perceived as usual word combinations. Similarly, in contextualism collocations are described in terms of typical word co-occurrence, or as words that show the "tendency to occur together" (Sinclair, 1991, 71). The notions of *frequency, typicality* or *tendency* refer to features that are modelled in statistics.

As a matter of fact, the majority of collocation definitions adopt a statistical view. Although the phenomenon described has an implicit linguistic connotation, the linguistic aspects are often ignored; thus, in the purely statistical approaches to collocations, definitions are almost exclusively given in statistical terms. For instance, Firth (1957) gives the following definition:

(1)   Collocations of a given word are statements of the habitual and customary places of that word (Firth, 1957, 181).

Among the examples he provides, we find word pairs like *night – dark, bright – day*, or *milk – cow* (Firth, 1957, 196). As can be noted, the understanding adopted for the collocation concept in contextualism is a broad one, since, in addition to syntagmatic associations that may indeed constitute phraseological units (*dark night* and *bright day*), it also covers non-syntagmatic associations (*milk – cow*) which are semantically motivated.

The statistical view is predominant in the work of Firth's disciples, M.A.K. Halliday, Michael Hoey, and John Sinclair. The collocation is again understood in a broad sense, as the frequent occurrence of one word in the context of another (where the context represents either the whole sentence, or a window of words called *collocational span*):

(2)   Collocation is the cooccurrence of two or more words within a short space of each other in a text. The usual measure of proximity is a maximum of four words intervening (Sinclair, 1991, 170).

Even later definitions, like the following which are among the most widely used by NLP practitioners, are exclusively given in statistical terms:

(3)   The term *collocation* will be used to refer to sequences of lexical items which habitually co-occur (Cruse, 1986, 40).
(4)   A collocation is an arbitrary and recurrent word combination (Benson, 1990).
(5)   Natural languages are full of collocations, recurrent combinations of words that co-occur more often than expected by chance and that correspond to arbitrary word usages (Smadja, 1993, 143).
(6)   We reserve the term *collocation* to refer to any statistically significant cooccurrence (Sag et al., 2002, 7).

   In particular, the definition provided by Smadja (1993) rests on work by Church and Hanks (1990), in which collocations are modelled using the statistical notion of *significance*, that helps distinguish genuine word associations from associations due to chance alone: collocations are those associations whose probability of co-occurrence, estimated on the basis of their co-occurrence frequency observed in a corpus, is "much larger than chance" (Church and Hanks, 1990, 23).

   A peculiarity of statistical approaches is that they regard collocations as symmetrical relations, paying no attention to the relative importance of the words involved. Thus, Firth (1957, 196) describe collocations in terms of mutual expectancy:

> One of the meanings of *night* is its collocability with *dark*, and of *dark*, of course, its collocation with *night* (...) The collocation of a word or a 'piece' is not to be regarded as mere juxtaposition, it is an order of mutual expectancy (Firth, 1968, 181).

   Cruse (1986, 40) also considers that in a collocation, "the constituent elements are, to varying degrees, mutually selective". Similarly, Sinclair (1991, 173) notes that "collocation is one of the patterns of mutual choice". Still, he distinguishes between *upward* collocations, in which the *node word* (i.e., the word under examination) co-occurs with a word that is more frequent, and *downward* collocations, in which it combines with a less frequent word (Sinclair, 1991, 116). For example, when the word *back* is examined, *back from* is an upward collocation since *from* is more frequent than *back*, while *bring back* is a downward collocation, since *bring* is less frequent than *back*.

2.2.2 Linguistic Approaches

While in the contextualist (and similar) approaches the structural relation between items in a collocation is ignored—as Sinclair (1991, 170) puts it, the collocation refers to "lexical co-occurrence, more or less independently of grammatical pattern or positional relationship"—in other approaches the syntactic relationship between these items is a central defining feature. As compared to the statistical account, the linguistically-motivated one adopts a more restrictive view. In this view, collocations are seen, first of all, as expressions of a language. This account emphasizes the linguistic status of collocations, considering them as syntactically-motivated combinations; consequently, the participating words must be related syntactically. This structural condition prevails over the proximity condition requiring them to appear within a short space of each other. The definitions below (which are less popular in the NLP community) emphasize the condition that collocations are syntactically well-formed constructions:

   (7)   co-occurrence of two or more lexical items as realizations of structural elements within a given syntactic pattern (Cowie, 1978, 132).
   (8)   a sequence of words that occurs more than once in identical form in a corpus, and which is grammatically well structured (Kjellmer, 1987, 133).
   (9)   On appellera collocation la combinaison caractéristique de deux mots dans une des structures suivantes : (a) substantif + adjectif (épithète); (b) substantif + verbe;

(c) verbe + substantif (objet); (d) verbe + adverbe; (e) adjectif + adverbe; (f) substantif + (prép.) + substantif. [We shall call collocation a characteristic combination of two words in a structure like the following: (a) noun + adjective (epithet); (b) noun + verb; (c) verb + noun (object); (d) verb + adverb; (e) adjective + adverb; (f) noun + (prep) + noun.] (Hausmann, 1989, 1010).

(10) A collocation is a sequence of two or more consecutive words, that has characteristics of a syntactic and semantic unit whose exact and unambiguous meaning or connotation cannot be derived directly from the meaning or connotation of its components (Choueka, 1988).

(11) A collocation is an expression consisting of two or more words that correspond to some conventional way of saying things (Manning and Schütze, 1999, 151).

(12) lexically and/or pragmatically constrained recurrent co-occurrences of at least two lexical items which are in a direct syntactic relation with each other (Bartsch, 2004, 76).

One of the most complete linguistic definitions of collocations has been provided by Mel'čuk in the framework of the Meaning-Text Theory, by means of the lexical functions formalism (Mel'čuk, 1998, 2003). This definition, presented later in Section 2.4.3, also considers the collocation as a syntactically-bound word combination.

In the linguistically-motivated approaches, the condition for the participating words to occur in the context of each other is no longer explicitly stated. Obviously, some proximity limitation persists, since the syntactic well-formedness criterion implies that the collocational span is the phrase, clause or, at most, the sentence containing these words. The statistical component is still present in the linguistically-motivated definitions, and is expressed, for instance, by attributes like "conventional", "characteristic", or "recurrent".

In contrast with the statistical approaches, the collocation is seen here as a directed (asymmetrical) relation, in which the role played by the participating words is uneven, and is mainly determined by the syntactic configuration of the collocation. Thus, as will be later discussed in Section 2.5.1, Hausmann (1979, 1985) and Mel'čuk (1998, 2003) use distinct terms, such as *base* and *collocate*, in order to account for the distinct role played by the items in a collocation pair. Hausmann (2004) further specifies that the base is *autosemantic*, whereas the collocate is *synsemantic*, i.e., it can only be interpreted with reference to the whole collocation. In addition, Kjellmer (1991) introduces the notion of *left* and *right predictive collocations* to indicate that an item in a collocation is predicted by the other.

Several authors have attempted to provide a more precise characterisation of collocations from a linguistic point of view, i.e., to capture their intrinsic syntactic and semantic properties in order to distinguish them from other phraseological units and to allow for their more adequate processing in various NLP applications. These attempts are reviewed later in Section 2.5.

2.2.3 Collocation vs. Co-occurrence

As indicated in Section 2.2.1, the term *collocation* has originally been used in a broad sense, for describing the general event of recurrent word co-occurrence.

This purely statistical view was later contrasted by a more restricted, linguistically-motivated view, which explicitly states that the items in a collocation are syntactically related. The second view has recently gained in popularity, and some authors have suggested to use distinct terms to distinguish between the two understandings.[2]

More precisely, it has been proposed to use the term *association* or *co-occurrence* for the general statistical understanding, and to reserve the term *collocation* for the restricted understanding corresponding to the linguistically-motivated approach. For example, Manning and Schütze (1999) and Evert (2004b) state:

> It is probably best to restrict the collocations to the narrower sense of grammatically bound elements and use the term *association* and *co-occurrence* for the more general phenomenon of words that are likely to be used in the same context (Manning and Schütze, 1999, 185)

> In order to make a clear distinction between the two approaches to collocations,[3] I refer to the distributional notion as *cooccurrences* (...) I reserve the term *collocation* for an intensionally defined concept (Evert, 2004b, 17).

The distinction between *co-occurrences* and *collocations* seems to be nowadays unanimously accepted (Bartsch, 2004), and will also be adopted in our work.

2.3 Towards a Core Collocation Concept

As emerges from the review in Section 2.2, a multitude of collocation definitions exist in the literature; some of the most well-known are presented in Appendix B. These are often divergent and may therefore lead to confusion, in spite of the fact that a main distinction can be drawn according to the underlying approach (i.e., a purely statistical one vs. a linguistically-motivated one). This section describes our attempt to provide a unified view, by trying to capture what seems to constitute the essential defining features of the collocation concept. Despite the marked divergence of points of view, several defining features can be identified that are recurrently mentioned and that seem to be accepted by most authors.

We consider that these features denote a core collocation concept, and this concept may be further refined by adding more specific elements to the basic definition. In accordance with Smadja (1993) and Evert (2004b), we consider that the variations brought to the basic definition may be motivated by theoretical and practical considerations: "Depending on their interests and points of view, researchers have focused on different aspects of collocation" (Smadja, 1993, 145); "I use collocation thus as a generic term whose specific meaning can be narrowed down according to the requirements of a particular research question or application" (Evert, 2004b, 17).

---

[2] For instance, Wanner et al. (2006, 611) notes that the second notion "is different from the notion of collocation in the sense of Firth (1957) (...) who define a collocation as a high probability association of lexical items in the corpus".

[3] A statistical approach, called *distributional*, and a phraseological (linguistic) approach, called *intensional* (Evert, 2004b).

In the remainder of this section, we present the features which we identified as potentially relevant to the definition of a core collocation concept.

Collocations are prefabricated phrases. As mentioned in Section 2.1, collocations emerged from studies on language acquisition showing that children memorize not only words in isolation, but also, to a large extent, groups (or *chunks*) of words. These chunks are viewed as the building blocks of language. They are available to speakers as ready-made, or prefabricated units, contributing to conferring fluency and naturalness to their utterances.

As pointed out in many places in the literature, speakers' collocational knowledge does not derive from their awareness of the individual words or grammar rules of a language; on the contrary, collocations are acquired as such, through experience: "We acquire collocations, as we acquire other aspects of language, through encountering texts in the course of our lives" (Hoey, 1991, 219).

According to Sinclair (1991), language is governed by two opposed principles (see also Section 2.4.1): the *open principle*, which refers to the regular choices in language production, and the *idiom principle*, which refers to the use of prefabricated units already available in block. Collocations correspond to the second principle; they are:

(13)   semi-preconstructed phrases that constitute single choices, even though they might appear to be analysable into segments (Sinclair, 1991, 110).

The idea that collocations make up prefabricated units was earlier expressed by Hausmann (1985, 124), who calls them "semi-finished products" of language and associates them with a "déjà-vu" effect in language. The same idea of unity is suggested by Coseriu's metaphor of "lexical solidarity" (Coseriu, 1967).

Collocations are arbitrary. Another collocation feature that is mentioned by most definitions is the arbitrariness—also, peculiarity, or idiosyncrasy—as opposed to regularity (i.e., conformance to rules). Collocations are not regular productions of language, but "arbitrary word usages" (Smadja, 1993), "arbitrary (. . .) word combinations" (Benson, 1990), or "typical, *specific and characteristic* combination of two words" (Hausmann, 1985). A high number of other definitions note this aspect, e.g., Fontenelle (1992), van der Wouden (1997), and Mel'čuk (2003) (see Appendix B).

The availability of collocations as prefabricated units in the lexicon of a language implies that they are to be learned and used as such, and prevents their reconstruction by means of grammatical processes. There might be no clear reason for a particular choice of words in a collocation, but once this choice is made and conventionalized—or, in Sag's terms, *institutionalized* (Sag et al., 2002)—other paraphrases are blocked, as stipulated by Sinclair's *idiom* principle.

Arbitrariness of a collocation may refer not only to the choice of a particular word in conjunction with another in order to express a given meaning (Kahane and Polguère, 2001), but also to its syntactic and semantic properties. As Evert (2004b) states,

(14)   A collocation is a word combination whose semantic and/or syntactic properties
         cannot be fully predicted from those of its components, and which therefore has
         to be listed in a lexicon (Evert, 2004b, 17).

Collocations are unpredictable. Closely related to the two properties mentioned so
far, unpredictability is another main feature that is often cited in collocation definitions (Choueka, 1988; Evert, 2004b). Since the "institutionalization" of a collocation as a prefabricated unit does not depend on clear linguistic reasons, it is
impossible to predict that collocation. First, the affinity of a word for a particular
collocate, which is strongly preferred over other words from the same synonymy
set, is unpredictable.[4] As put by Cruse, "these affinities can not be predicted on
the basis of semantic or syntactic rules, but can be observed with some regularity
in text" (Cruse, 1986).

Second, the morpho-syntactic properties of the collocation cannot be predicted
on the basis of the properties of the participating words. Due to their arbitrariness,
collocations cannot be accounted for by the grammatical prescriptions of a language.

Collocations are recurrent. The property of collocations that is most usually mentioned in the various definitions is, undoubtedly, their frequent recurrence. It is the
frequent usage of collocations that determines their "institutionalization". At the
same time, their recurrence enables their recognition and learning based on experience: "we acquire collocations (...) through encountering texts in the course
of our lives" (Hoey, 1991, 219). A collocation "springs readily to mind; it is
psychologically salient" (Benson et al., 1986b, 252).

As mentioned in Section 2.2.1, the vast majority of collocation definitions
indicate the recurrent nature of collocations. Collocations are "habitual and
customary" (Firth, 1957, 181), "actual words in habitual company" (Firth,
1968, 182), "recurrent word combination" (Benson, 1990), "combinations of
words that co-occur more often than expected by chance" (Smadja, 1993, 143),
"groupements usuels" ("usual phrases") (Bally, 1909), "typical combination"
(Hausmann, 1985), "conventional way of saying things" (Manning and Schütze,
1999, 151), "institutionalized phrases" (Sag et al., 2002, 3).

Collocations are made up of two or more words. Despite the fact that the practical
work is concerned almost exclusively with collocations made up of exactly
two lexical items, in theory there is no length limitation for collocations. As
Sinclair (1991) points out,

In most of the examples, collocation patterns are restricted to pairs of words, but there is
no theoretical restriction to the number of words involved (Sinclair, 1991, 170).

As a matter of fact, the majority of definitions stipulate that collocations may
involve *more* than two items: "co-occurrence of two or more lexical items"
(Cowie, 1978); "sequence of two or more consecutive words" (Choueka, 1988),
"collocation is the cooccurrence of two or more words within a short space

---

[4] See also Manning and Schütze's (1999) *non-substitutability criterion* mentioned in Section 2.5.

of each other" (Sinclair, 1991, 170); "an expression consisting of two or more words" (Manning and Schütze, 1999, 151). Complex collocations, like *major turning point, play a central role, conduct a comprehensive study, abolish the death penalty, become an increasingly important concern*, are massively present in language.

Only in rare cases (Hausmann, 1985; Mel'čuk et al., 1984, 1988, 1992, 1999), theoretical studies explicitly mention the presence of exactly two lexical items in a collocation. However, these items may in turn be composed of more words, and, in particular, of other collocations. The recursive nature of collocations has been noted, for instance, by Heid (1994, 232); our previous examples are clear instances of recursion.

> An additional problem for the interaction between syntactic and collocational description is the recursive nature of collocational properties: the components of a collocation can again be collocational themselves: next to the German collocation *Gültigkeit haben* (n + v), we have *allgemeine Gültigkeit haben*,[5] with *allgemeine Gültigkeit*, a collocation (n + a), as a component (Heid, 1994, 232).

2.4 Theoretical Perspectives on Collocations

This section discusses the main theoretical frameworks within which the collocation phenomenon has been addressed so far in the linguistic literature.

2.4.1 Contextualism

The concept of word collocation plays a central role in contextualism, the linguistic current that brought collocations to the attention of linguists. Contextualists consider that the study of language cannot be done without considering the words' context. In particular, they argue that the meaning of words is defined by their co-occurrence (or collocation) with other words. As Firth (1968, 180) states, the words are "separated in meaning at the collocational level". Firth talks about "meaning by collocation", that he defines as "an abstraction at the syntagmatic level (. . .) not directly concerned with the conceptual or idea approach to the meaning of the words" (Firth, 1957, 196).

The description of collocations within the framework of contextualism passed through several stages. Initially given in terms of habitual co-occurrence of words within a short space of each other in a text (Firth, 1957; Sinclair, 1991), it was then elaborated by Sinclair, who paid less importance to the distance between collocation items in text. These items were no longer required to be in the strict proximity of each other: "On some occasions, words appear to be chosen in pairs or groups and these are not necessarily adjacent" (Sinclair, 1991, 115).

---

[5] Literally, "general validity have".

As we have already mentioned in Section 2.3, Sinclair (1991) considers that language obeys two opposed principles, the *open-choice* and the *idiom principle*. The first refers to the regular choices in language and accounts for the utterances produced by the application of grammatical prescriptions. The second stipulates that these regular choices are further restricted by the presence of prefabricated phrases that are already available to speakers:

> The principle of idiom is that a language user has available to him or her a large number of semi-preconstructed phrases that constitute single choices, even though they might appear to be analysable into segments (Sinclair, 1991, 110).[6]

Collocations illustrate the idiom principle, since "the choice of one word affects the choice of others in its vicinity" (Sinclair, 1991, 173).

2.4.2 Text Cohesion

The problem of collocations has also been addressed, though only to a limited extent, from the perspective of *text cohesion*, which refers to the "relations of meaning that exist within text" (Halliday and Hasan, 1976, 4). Cohesion contributes to the semantic unity of a passage of the language, about which a speaker "can normally decide without difficulty whether it forms a unified whole or is just a collection of unrelated sentences" (Halliday and Hasan, 1976, 1).

Halliday and Hasan distinguish between two types of text cohesion, one of grammatical nature, and one of lexical nature. The collocation, along with the reiteration (a general term encompassing lexical phenomena like repetition, synonyms, and hypernyms) is considered an important element of lexical cohesion. The collocation is basically understood in the same way as in contextualism:

> (15)   the association of lexical items that regularly co-occur (Halliday and Hasan, 1976, 284).

The cohesive effect of collocations derives precisely from words' "tendency to share the same lexical environment" (Halliday and Hasan, 1976, 286). Some examples provided by the authors are: *laugh – joke, blade – shape, ill – doctor, try – succeed*, and *sky – sunshine – cloud – rain*. It is explicitly stated that collocations refer not only to pairs, but also to longer "chains of collocational cohesion" (Halliday and Hasan, 1976, 287). The authors also note "a continuity of lexical meaning" in a collocation, through which the cohesion effect is achieved (1976, 320), but they state that the meaning relations involved are not easy to systematically classify in semantic terms.

---

[6] An analogy can be found between the idiom principle and the *Elsewhere Principle* in linguistics, concerned with the opposition between regularity and specificity. This principle states that whenever two rules can be applied, the more specific one overwrites the more general one. An account for idioms based on this principle was proposed by Zeevat (1995).

2.4.3 Meaning-Text Theory

Collocations received a formal characterization within the Meaning-Text Theory (hereafter, MTT) (Mel'čuk et al., 1984, 1988, 1992, 1999; Mel'čuk, 1998, 2003) by means of *lexical functions*, a language modelling tool that aims to associate a given meaning with the language utterances expressing that meaning.

Lexical functions (henceforth, LFs) are relations that are established between lexical items on the basis of the meaning to express; this meaning is denoted by the name of the LF itself. For instance, the *Magn* LF represents the meaning of intensity, and relates a noun like *rain* with the adjective *heavy*.

MTT distinguishes between two main types of LFs:

- paradigmatic LFs, that capture lexical relations generated by morphological derivations (e.g., *surprise – surprising*), as well as basic semantic relations such as synonymy and antonymy (e.g., *timid – shy, like – dislike*);
- syntagmatic LFs, that describe the semantics of lexical combinations, and are used to model collocations (this category comprises a relatively higher number of functions, i.e., more than 60).

The authors indicate that a LF can be seen as a function in the mathematical sense, which maps arguments onto values. For instance, a syntagmatic function maps a lexical item (called *headword* or *base*) onto the typical lexical item (called *collocate*) which is used to convey the meaning represented by the LF:

$$Magn(rain) = heavy$$

The argument-value combination corresponds to the language utterance that represents the appropriate means for expressing the required meaning (*heavy rain*).

Unlike mathematical functions, however, LFs may map a headword onto more collocates. In order for LFs to be seen as mathematical functions, the authors allow the values to denote sets of lexical items, instead of single lexical items (Kahane and Polguère, 2001); for instance,

$$Magn(role) = \{central, important, major\}.$$

The concept of collocation received the following formal definition, adapted from Mel'čuk (2003).

> (16) Let AB be a bipartite language expression, where A and B are lexical items of the language L, and let 'S' be the meaning of AB, 'A' the meaning of A, and 'B' the meaning of B. The expression AB is a *collocation* iff the following three conditions hold:
> (i) 'S' ⊃ 'A' (the meaning of S contains the meaning of A);
> (ii) A is selected by the speaker in a regular and non-restricted way[7];

---

[7] A linguistic operation is said to be performed in a *regular way* if it conforms to the lexicon and to the general rules of the grammar (general rules refer to rules involving classes of lexemes, as opposed to individual lexemes). It is performed in a *non-restricted way* if it can use any item of the lexicon and any grammar rule, without mentioning other lexical items (Mel'čuk, 2003).

(iii) B is not selected in a regular and non-restricted way, but depending on A and the meaning 'S' to express.

Thus, in the MTT approach it is considered that the meaning of the collocation preserves the meaning of one of its constituents (i.e., A), which is selected by the speaker in an unconstrained way, but not necessarily the meaning of the other (i.e., B), whose selection is contingent on the first.

Mel'čuk (2003) discusses the example of the collocation *café noir* (lit., *coffee black*, "coffee without milk"). The word *café* is selected without any restriction, while the word *noir* is selected in an irregular way (since *noir* is the only possible choice in expressing the required meaning in combination with *café*, and it has to be specified by a rule), and in a restricted way (*noir* means "without milk" only in combination with the specific lexeme *coffee*, and not with other lexemes like *tea* or *chocolate*). It can be noted that, unlike in many other approaches, in MTT the collocation is understood as an asymmetrical relation, since the collocate is dependent on the base, but not the opposite.

The MTT approach had a big impact on the NLP work devoted to collocations. A number of studies explored the use of lexical functions as a semantic formalism in applications like machine translation and natural language generation (Heylen et al., 1994; Heid and Raab, 1989; Wanner, 1997). A formalization of lexical functions that is computationally tractable was proposed in Kahane and Polguère (2001). At the same time, in a couple of electronic dictionaries,[8] collocations are encoded using a simplified and more formalised description in terms of LFs, which is based on the description used in ECD dictionary (Mel'čuk et al., 1984, 1988, 1992, 1999). Also, an ambitious lexicographic project led to the creation of a large collocational database by enriching the entries of an entire bilingual dictionary with LF information (Fontenelle, 1997a,b). The resources built could enable the development of LF-based NLP applications at a large scale, a goal that is actively pursued in current research (Mille and Wanner, 2008; Ramos et al., 2008).

2.4.4 Semantics and Metaphoricity

In order to capture fine-grained distinctions of collocational meaning, Fontenelle (2001) proposed to enhance the LF-based collocation description with concepts from the Frame Semantics theory (Fillmore, 1982; Baker et al., 1998). In this approach, the link between the items in a collocation is expressed as the relation between the central word evoking a *frame* (i.e., a conceptual structure modelling a situation) and the *frame elements*. For instance, the link between *teacher*, *fail*, and *student* can be deciphered by recognising the semantic frame evoked by *fail*,

---

[8] For example, Dico and LAF (Polguère, 2000), Papillon (Boitet et al., 2002; Sérasset, 2004), (Mangeot, 2006), DAFLES (Selva et al., 2002).

namely, the examination frame, and by associating *teacher* and *student* with the frame elements *Examiner* and *Examinee*.

The phenomenon of collocation has also been addressed in the literature in connection with studies on *semantic prosody* (Sinclair, 1991; Louw, 1993; Stubbs, 1995; Hoey, 1997), which noted the tendency of co-occurring words to share either a positive, or a negative connotation. Semantic prosody is defined as the "consistent aura of meaning with which a form is imbued by its collocates" (Louw, 1993, 157). As Sinclair (1991) remarks:

> Many uses of words and phrases show a tendency to occur in a certain semantic environment. For example, the verb *happen* is associated with unpleasant things–accidents and the like (Sinclair, 1991, 112).

A few researchers also indicate that collocations may sometimes constitute metaphors. For instance, Fontenelle (1997a) remarks that associations like *clouds of arrows, storm of applause, wave of protests* are clearly metaphorical. A similar remark is made by Gross (1996), who observes that collocations have a semantic component that is non-compositional, and suggests that this fact might be due to a metaphorical relation: "on pourrait parler de métaphore [we could talk about metaphor]" (Gross, 1996, 21).

2.4.5 Lexis-Grammar Interface

From a syntactic perspective, the collocation phenomenon has been studied in relation to *colligation* or *grammatical patterning*, i.e., the typical syntactic environment in which a word usually occurs.[9] According to Hargreaves (2000),

> knowledge of a collocation, if it is to be used appropriately, necessarily involves knowledge of the patterns or colligations in which that collocation can occur acceptably (Hargreaves, 2000, 214).

In direct relation to this approach, the collocation was considered by more recent studies on lexis-grammar interface as a typical linguistic phenomenon occurring at the intersection between lexicon and grammar (Sinclair, 1991; Renouf and Sinclair, 1991; Hunston et al., 1997; Hoey, 1997; Hunston and Francis, 1998; Hoey, 2000). These studies consider that grammar and lexicon are interrelated to such a degree that no clear distinction can be drawn between the two. According to Francis (1993),

> It is impossible to look at one independently of the other (...) The interdependence of syntax and lexis is such that they are ultimately inseparable (Francis, 1993, 147).[10]

---

[9] Firth (1968, 183) describes the concept of colligation as "the interrelation of grammatical categories in syntactical structure".

[10] Sinclair's position on the syntax-lexicon continuum and the place of collocations is even more radical: "The decoupling of lexis and syntax leads to the creation of a rubbish dump that

But long before the lexis-grammar approaches, and before the advent of the computer era which boosted the corpus-based linguistic studies, the French linguist Maurice Gross conducted in the 1970s an impressive work of lexicon-grammar resource compilation. This work was empirically based and aimed at describing the syntax of French nouns, verbs and adverbs in the formalism of transformational grammar (Gross, 1984). The lexicon-grammar model of lexical description is nowadays largely used as the basis of computational work, thanks to the implementation provided by the INTEX system (Silberztein, 1993).

Summing up, collocation is a language phenomenon that has captured the attention of researchers in multiple subfields of linguistics. It has been studied from different angles, which were all concerned with the same issue: word associations giving rise to idiosyncratic semantic implications. In contextualism, collocating words *define* each other; from the point of view of text cohesion, they contribute to the *semantic unity* of the text; and in Meaning-Text Theory, the collocate word *expresses* a given meaning in combination with (and depending on) the base word. Collocations have also been taken into account in a number of other semantic theories, while in syntactic theories they are currently considered as elements that are found at the intersection between lexicon and grammar.

2.5 Linguistic Descriptions

Although collocations have attracted the attention of linguists for a long time and now have a recognized linguistic and lexicographic status (McKeown and Radev, 2000, 507), they still lack a systematic characterization. In this section, we provide a review of the various semantic and morpho-syntactic properties of collocations that have been considered so far in theoretical and practical studies.

2.5.1 Semantic Compositionality

The characterization of collocations is often made in semantic terms, on the basis of the *semantic compositionality criterion*, i.e., by checking whether the overall meaning of the collocation is obtained through the composition of the meanings of individual words. This is because the particular importance of collocations arises from their arbitrariness and unpredictability (see Section 2.3), properties which indicate that the process of lexical selection is not a semantically regular one. As in the case of other phraseological units, "the non-compositionality of a string must be considered when assessing its holism" (Moon, 1998, 8).

---

is called 'idiom', 'phraseology', 'collocation', and the like. (...) The evidence now becoming available casts grave doubts on the wisdom of postulating separate domains of lexis and syntax" (Sinclair, 1991, 104).

In the current literature, collocations are seen as expressions that "fall somewhere along a continuum between free word combinations and idioms" (McKeown and Radev, 2000, 509). Thus, it is generally considered that collocations populate the grey area between one extreme which is represented by entirely compositional combinations, and the other extreme of completely opaque combinations. The boundaries separating the three main groups—regular combinations, collocations and idioms—are rather fuzzy, therefore no clear distinction can be drawn between them (Moon, 1998; Wehrli, 2000; McKeown and Radev, 2000).[11]

It is therefore unsurprising that different descriptions of collocations make contradicting observations with respect to compositionality. On the one hand, Cruse (1986, 40) states that collocations are "fully transparent" and that "each lexical constituent is also a semantic constituent"; similarly, Sag et al. (2002, 7) describe them as "syntactically and semantically compositional, but statistically idiosyncratic". On the other hand, Choueka (1988) considers that the meaning of a collocation "cannot be derived directly from the meaning or connotation of its components", while Manning and Schütze (1999) describe collocations using the three criteria below, of which the first two are traditionally associated with idioms.[12]

(17)   a. *non-compositionality*: "the meaning of a collocation is not a straightforward composition of the meaning of its parts";

   b. *non-modifiability*: "many collocations cannot be freely modified with additional lexical material or through grammatical transformations";

   c. *non-substitutability*: "we cannot substitute near-synonyms for the components of a collocation" (Manning and Schütze, 1999, 172–173).

In the same vein, van der Wouden (1997, 5) considers collocation as a general phenomenon of "idiosyncratic restriction on the combinability of lexical items", which encompasses the class of idioms:

I will use the term collocation as the most general term to refer to all types of fixed combinations of lexical items; in this view, idioms are a special subclass of collocations (van der Wouden, 1997, 9).

The same view according to which collocations include idioms as a particular case is found in other accounts in the literature (Moon, 1998; Venkatapathy and Joshi, 2005). However, contrary to this view, collocations are usually distinguished from idioms, whose meaning is considered much more opaque. Manning and Schütze (1999, 151) themselves observe that not all collocations are completely non-compositional, but there are also some "milder forms of non-compositionality",

---

[11] Nevertheless, some studies have attempted to grade the compositionality of phraseological units, e.g., McCarthy et al. (2003), Baldwin et al. (2003), Venkatapathy and Joshi (2005), and Piao et al. (2006). A larger number of works focused, more generally, on distinguishing between compositional and non-compositional units: see, among many others, Bannard (2005), Fazly and Stevenson (2007), McCarthy et al. (2007), Cook et al. (2008), Diab and Bhutada (2009).

[12] Only the criterion of non-substitutability (17c) is commonly associated with collocations.

in which the meaning of the overall expression is nearly the composition of the parts. However, they indicate that "there is always an element of meaning added to the combination" (Manning and Schütze, 1999, 184), arguing, for instance, that the meaning of a collocation like *white wine* contains an added element of connotation with respect to the connotation of *wine* and *white* together.

Most researchers agree that collocations are fairly transparent and their meaning is deducible from the meaning of the parts. While collocations represent indeed idioms of encoding, their meaning is nonetheless easy to decode: "Idiomaticity applies to encoding for collocations, but not to decoding" (Fillmore et al., 1988). More precisely, collocations are easily interpretable on the basis of the individual words, but are difficult to generate because the collocate is unpredictable.

Unlike in idioms, "the individual words in a collocation can contribute to the overall semantics of the compound" (McKeown and Radev, 2000, 507). However, the contribution of the individual words to the overall meaning of the collocation is uneven. While the meaning of the semantic head is preserved (e.g., the meaning of *wine* in the collocation *white wine*), that of the other word (*white*) does not participate in a straightforward way to the meaning of the collocation.

In fact, Hausmann (1979, 1985) describes collocations as "polar" combinations, in which the item whose meaning is preserved is called *base*, and the other, which is selected by the base, is called *collocate*. In a collocation, the collocate is lexically selected by the base (Hausmann, 1985). The base can be interpreted outside the context of the collocation (i.e., the base is *autosemantic*), whereas the interpretation of the collocate is contingent upon the specific collocation (i.e., the collocate is *synsemantic*) (Hausmann, 2004). A similar distinction is drawn in the MTT framework (Section 2.4.3), where collocations are considered as semi-idiomatic. As Polguère (2000) states,

> (18)   The notion of COLLOCATION refers to semi-idiomatic expressions L1+L2 such that one of the components, the COLLOCATE, is chosen to express a given meaning, in a specific syntactic role, contingent upon the choice of the other component, called the BASE of the collocation (Polguère, 2000, 518).

Summing up, the semantic accounts of collocations in terms of compositionality generally regard collocations as combinations that are rather transparent and fairly easy to decode. Unlike in the case of idioms, whose meaning is rather opaque, the individual words of a collocation contribute to the overall meaning. Their contribution is, however, uneven, as the meaning of the base is preserved in the meaning of the collocation, while that of the collocate contributes in non-straightforward way to the latter.

2.5.2 Morpho-Syntactic Characterisation

As stated at the beginning of this section, the linguistic literature does not provide a precise morpho-syntactic characterization of collocations; however, the practical NLP work often relies on particular assumptions about the possible surface realization of collocations. Thus, many collocation extraction methods consider only certain lexical categories when selecting the items of candidate pairs (i.e., open-class syntactic categories such as N, A, V, and Adv), while excluding other categories (the closed-class categories, e.g., P, D, Conj).[13] In addition, they only retain certain types of combinations as valid; typically, the patterns that are considered collocationally relevant are N-A, N-N, N-V, V-N, V-Adv, A-Adv (Hausmann, 1989; Heid, 1994).[14] In general, there is a marked divergence among existing methods with respect to the categories and combinations allowed, their choice being made in a rather arbitrary way.

One of the few theoretical definitions that focuses on morpho-syntactic aspects is definition (9), provided by Hausmann (1989, 1010) (Section 2.2.2). In addition to clearly specifying the POS for participating words, this definition alludes to the underlying syntactic structure of the collocation (e.g., subject-verb or verb-object). Unlike Hausmann, however, many researchers consider that collocations can be found in virtually any syntactic configuration. For instance, Fontenelle (1992) considers that:

(19) The term collocation refers to the idiosyncratic syntagmatic combination of lexical items and is independent of word class or syntactic structure (Fontenelle, 1992, 222).

Lexicographic evidence confirmed that, in fact, collocations may appear in a large spectrum of configurations. Thus, the BBI collocation dictionary (Benson et al., 1986a) provides a very comprehensive list of *grammatical collocations*, along with the classical *lexical collocations*. Arguing against the a priori exclusion of function words from collocation patterns, van der Wouden states that "lexical elements of almost any class may show collocational effect" (van der Wouden, 2001, 17).[15]

Some attempts have been made to characterize collocations from the point of view of the grammatical operations they can undergo, e.g., adjectival or adverbial modification, extraposition, pronominalization etc. For instance, Cruse (1986, 41) identified a subclass of collocations which is closer to idioms, and which he calls *bound collocations* (an example he provides is *foot the bill*). Unlike idioms, bound collocations are semantically transparent and modifiable (for instance, the noun modification is allowed: *foot the electricity bill*). But, like idioms, they resist certain operations, like separation or pronominalization (*I am expected not only to foot, but also to add up, all the bills; *I hope you don't expect me to foot it*). Generally speaking, syntactic restrictions and semantic opacity go hand in hand (Gross, 1996).

---

[13] The following abbreviations are used for part-of-speech categories: A – adjective, Adv – adverb, Conj – conjunction, D – determiner, Inter – interjection, N – noun, P – preposition, V – verb.

[14] These combinations correspond to the so-called lexical collocations according to Benson et al.'s description of collocations (1986a). Benson et al. divide the collocations in two broad classes, one allowing exclusively open-class words (*lexical collocations*) and one involving function words as well (*grammatical collocations*).

[15] On the same line, Kjellmer (1990, 172) notes that functional categories such as articles and prepositions are collocational in nature.

Providing a characterization of collocations in terms of syntactic behaviour seems very difficult, since most of them are rather syntactically permissive, even if the grammatical operations they allow vary from case to case. Indeed, Heid (1994) points out that:

> syntactic properties do not seem to have much discriminatory power, as far as colloca-
> tions and idioms, their borderline and the borderline with 'normal constructions' are con-
> cerned (Heid, 1994, 234).

Similarly, van der Wouden (1997, 19) states that it is impossible to formulate constraints on all collocations in syntactic terms. Collocational restrictions differ from selectional restrictions, as they "typically deal with restrictions between heads and complements at the *individual* level, whereas in cases of syntactic and semantic restriction *any member* of a syntactic or semantic class or category will do to satisfy the restrictions" (van der Wouden, 1997, 26). Also, whereas heads normally select arguments, in collocation—e.g., of verb-object type—the direction of subcategori-sation seems reversed (van der Wouden, 1997, 27).

As van der Wouden (1997, 43–44) remarks, collocations have an unclear lin-guistic status and they do not fit in current linguistic theories; certain subclasses are better understood, e.g., the phrasal verbs and the light verbs. Nonetheless, the collocational effects are ubiquitous and they must be taken into account in NLP applications.

2.6 What *Collocation* Means in This Book

As explained in the previous sections, the concept of collocation is differently under-stood and defined in the related literature. Since no commonly-accepted definition exists, we need to state which understanding we adopted in our work. In this section, we attempt to describe this as precisely as possible, while refraining from providing yet another definition.

First, we make a distinction between contextual and syntactic collocation, the first corresponding to the initial broader understanding adopted in contextualism, and the second to the more restricted, linguistically-motivated understanding (see Section 2.2). We adopt the restricted view throughout this work. As suggested in the recent literature, we use the term *collocation* to denote the linguistically-motivated concept, and the term *co-occurrence* for the broader, purely statistical understanding.

Second, we adhere to the five core features of collocations identified in Section 2.3. Collocations denote lexical combinations that are: (a) prefabricated, (b) arbitrary, (c) unpredictable, (d) recurrent, and (e) unrestricted in length.

The first three features motivate our work of collocation extraction from corpora, aimed, ultimately, at providing lexicographic support for their inclusion in dictio-naries. Insofar as the forth feature is concerned, we assume that even a single occur-rence of a pair in the source corpus justifies its selection as a collocation candidate.

This decision is mainly motivated by the problem of data sparseness in corpora.[16] Finally, the last feature occupies a prominent place in our work. Binary collocations are only one facet of the phenomenon we aim to model. Our work deals specifically with the identification of complex collocations, in which binary collocations are recursively embedded.

Third, we narrow the collocation acceptation according to the description proposed by Meaning-Text Theory in terms of syntagmatic lexical functions (Section 2.4.3). One of the two items of a collocation pair (potentially involved in longer collocations through recursive embedding) is *autosemantic*, i.e., semantically autonomous, and the other *synsemantic*, i.e., dependent on the first. While this choice does not really have an impact on the extraction methodology proposed, it proved useful in the further processing of identified collocations, in particular, in their automatic translation (Section 5.3). Also, collocations are distinguished in our work from idioms, whose meaning is difficult to decode, as well as from compounds, which have a lexical status and are rather limited in terms of syntactic behaviour. Again, this distinction has no bearing on the extraction methodology proper, but is taken into account in its evaluation.

From a syntactic point of view, the main constraint applied to the items of a candidate pair is to be linked by a syntactic relation. In principle, any generic head-dependent relation and any configuration are allowed. Still, a selection of collocationally relevant syntactic patterns is possible (Section 5.2). The existing implementations of our approach apply a pattern-based filter on the candidate data.

2.7 Summary

This chapter focused on theoretical aspects related to collocation. Proceeding chronologically, we surveyed the most salient linguistic and statistically motivated approaches to collocation from the multitude of collocation definitions in the literature. We noted that, from a linguistic point of view, collocations were most often characterized by taking semantic compositionality and morpho-syntactic information into account. Despite the heterogeneity of definitions and great divergence of opinion, it was still possible to identify some key recurrent features that appear to be unanimously accepted by different authors. These features were taken to define the "core" of the concept of collocation. Later, imposing several restrictions consistent with the lexical functions approach contributed to further refinement of our understanding.

---

[16] Usually, a frequency threshold is applied in related work to ensure the reliability of statistical association measures, as will be seen in Chapter 3. Instead, we consider that the initial selection of collocation candidates must be exhaustive, independent of the statistical computation, and that specific restrictions may be applied later depending on the subsequent processing.

In our discussion of how collocations have been conceptualized by other authors, we discussed the different perspectives taken on collocation phenomenon. We first mentioned the *lexicographic* and *pedagogical* perspectives which regard collocations as pre-constructed blocks learned as whole units. We then presented the *contextualist* view, in which the collocability of words refers to their combinatorial profile which is taken to be critical for defining their meaning. We also reviewed several *lexical-semantic* perspectives, in which collocations are accounted for by lexical functions or semantic frames.

Collocation is generally regarded as one of the most important elements contributing to *text cohesion*. Some studies of collocation are concerned with syntactic issues such as the syntactic context in which the collocations typically occur (*colligation*), or the role of collocations at the intersection of lexis and grammar (*lexis-grammar interface*). Other studies are more concerned with semantic matters such as the possible *metaphoric* nature of collocations or the shared positive or negative connotations among the collocation's items (*semantic prosody*). In the next chapter, we will see to what extent these theoretical considerations are reflected in practical work on automatically identifying collocations in text corpora.

Chapter 3
Survey of Extraction Methods

3.1 Introduction

As it emerged from the survey of definitions provided in the previous chapter, the term *collocation* is associated with a dichotomous acceptation. On the one side, collocation is seen as a purely statistical phenomenon of word co-occurrence, as in the description put forth by the British contextualist J.R. Firth and then adopted by his disciples, M.A.K. Halliday, M. Hoey, and J. Sinclair. On the other side, a restricted acceptation was later systematically adopted—for instance, by A.P. Cowie, P. Howarth, F.J. Hausmann, and I. Mel'čuk—which is grounded principally on linguistic considerations: collocation is no longer exclusively seen as a habitual association of words, but, most importantly, as a syntactically-bound combination.

In order to set these distinct understandings apart, the current literature tends to use the term *co-occurrence* in the first case, and to reserve the term *collocation* for the linguistically-motivated concept. Such a distinction is, however, harder to identify at a practical level, since the techniques employed for collocation extraction from corpora were subject to the availability of appropriate text analysis tools. Yet, it is still possible to observe a gradual evolution from the statistical understanding towards the linguistic one, as increasingly sophisticated tools became available.

3.2 Extraction Techniques

Before embarking into a survey of previous collocation extraction work (in order to reveal the level of linguistic processing performed in each case), we need to introduce the technical background of existing collocation extraction methodology. We begin with a discussion of the extent to which the theoretical characterisations of collocations, as discussed in Chapter 2, are followed in practice.

3.2.1 Collocation Features Modelled

Among the basic features of collocations mentioned in Section 2.3, *recurrence* is the one that is the easiest to model in practice. In the early NLP work dealing

V. Seretan, *Syntax-Based Collocation Extraction*, Text, Speech and Language Technology 44, DOI 10.1007/978-94-007-0134-2_3,
© Springer Science+Business Media B.V. 2011

with their automatic identification in corpora, collocations have been assimilated to frequent sequences of words and have been extracted using *n*-gram methods (where the term *n-gram* is understood as a sequence of adjacent words). *N*-gram methods also model another core feature of collocations, the *unrestricted length*, since they do not impose a specific length constraint on collocation candidates. For instance, the sequences extracted by Choueka et al. (1983) are up to 6 words long, and the "rigid collocations" identified by Smadja (1993) have an undetermined length.

Later, collocation was primarily seen as a phenomenon of lexical affinity or mutual attraction that can be captured by identifying statistically significant word associations[1] in large corpora (see Section 2.2). A wide range of statistical methods have been used to this end, that were either specifically designed for NLP, or adapted from related fields. Since such methods aim to quantify the degree of dependence or association between words, they are often called *association measures* (hereafter, AMs).

It could arguably be stated that the collocation feature that AMs try to model is their unity or holism, i.e., the fact that collocations constitute *prefabricated units* available to speakers in blocks. However, AMs achieve this goal only to a limited extent. Since they are usually limited to pairs of words, the extraction performed on their basis concern almost exclusively binary collocations. Therefore, unlike *n*-gram methods, AMs are not really suited for modelling the unrestricted length feature, as they sometimes fail to detect complete collocations; on the other hand, they have the advantage of allowing a certain degree of flexibility for the candidates proposed.

To a certain extent, it can also be said that *arbitrariness* is another feature of collocations that is modelled by methods based on AMs, since these try to pinpoint specific, typical, or idiosyncratic word associations, as opposed to merely recurrent combinations that are more likely to be regular.

It is less clear, instead, whether AMs succeed to model the last core feature of collocations, the *unpredictability*, which states that the affinity between collocation components is unpredictable from the syntactic and semantic rules of the language, and therefore the synonymous alternatives are blocked.[2] A few specific extraction techniques have been developed that model this feature by testing synonymous alternatives and checking if a word systematically selects as collocate a specific item from a synonymy set, while excluding others (Pearce, 2001a,b). Such techniques rely on the base-collocate distinction for the items in a collocation pair (Section 2.2), whereas existing AMs do not take into account the asymmetric role played by the components of a collocation.

As for the morpho-syntactic descriptions of collocations provided by some theoretical studies, these are unfortunately very limited and do not seem to have a

---

[1] In other words, pairs of words that are dependent on each other and co-occur more often than expected by chance.

[2] An AM that is considered to model the unpredictability feature is the log-likelihood ratio (Dunning, 1993) (presented in Section 3.2.4.2), since it is supposed to quantify how "surprising" a collocation candidate is.

sufficient discriminatory power. This might be the reason why these descriptions have not really been taken into account by practical work on collocation identification. In particular, techniques based on semantic criteria that have been successfully used to detect semantically opaque expressions (Lin, 1999; Fazly, 2007) are not applicable to collocations, which are rather compositional.

The work devoted to collocation extraction was hindered, in particular, by the difficulty to model features like holism, arbitrariness, and unpredictability, which can only be given an intuitive description, but not a formal one which could be easy to put in practice. Under the present circumstances, in which both a precise characterization of collocations and the appropriate means for implementing most of the identified features are lacking, it seems reasonable that the bulk of existing extraction work focuses almost exclusively on statistical aspects, more objective and easier to implement.

An impressive number of AMs have been proposed for collocation extraction over the last decades.[3] This work testifies to the continuous efforts put into the design of AMs that are appropriate for collocation extraction, and, at the same time, suggests that the quest for finding a completely satisfactory AM has not yet ended.

3.2.2 General Extraction Architecture

Generally speaking, a collocation extraction procedure (such as the one used in most of the work reviewed in Section 3.4) consists of two main steps:

– Step 1: candidate identification using specific criteria;
– Step 2: candidate ranking with a given AM.

The candidate ranking step relies on frequency[4] information about word occurrence and co-occurrence in a corpus (i.e., marginal and joint frequencies), as well as about the total number of co-occurrences observed in the source corpus. This information can be organised, for each word pair, in a 2×2 contingency table (as will be explained in Section 3.2.3). Based on the numbers listed in the contingency table, AMs compute a numerical value that represents the association score of a pair.

In the candidate identification step, extraction procedures may either consider word forms and the surface word order found in texts, or may rely on linguistic analysis tools such as lemmatizers, POS taggers, and parsers in order to cope with morphological and syntactic variability. It is often felt that it is necessary to perform a linguistic preprocessing for languages with a richer morphology and a freer word order, in order to conflate the instances belonging to the same pair type. The cumulative frequencies obtained for pair types are considered as more reliable for

---

[3] For instance, the inventory of Pecina (2005), still incomplete, lists more than 80 measures.

[4] In line with the related literature, we use the word *frequency* to denote occurrence counts in a corpus, rather than relative ratios (percentage of occurrences relative to the corpus size).

the score computation than the lower frequencies of disparate variants (this issue is further discussed in Section 3.3).

The output of an extraction procedure is called a *significance list* and consists of the list of candidates accompanied by their association score; when a score threshold is applied, then it only consists of a subset of this list. The association score assigned to candidates by the specific AM chosen induces an order on these candidates, which is taken into account in displaying the extraction results. The candidates that received higher scores reflecting a higher association strength are found at the top of the significance list and are considered more likely to constitute collocations. Conversely, the candidates with a lower score found at lower positions are, in principle, less likely to be collocational.

Most of the time, extraction procedures do not make a binary, but a fuzzy decision, since they do not draw a clear-cut distinction between collocations and non-collocations. Instead, they propose a continuous ordering, as implied by the numerical score. The fuzzy nature of the output is compatible with the theoretical views postulating a continuum between collocations and regular combinations (see Section 2.5). The numerical score is interpreted depending on the AM used. Typically, to each AM is associated a critical value against which the collocation score has to be compared, so that one can state, with a given level of confidence, whether or not a word association is statistically significant, i.e., it is likely to constitute a collocation.

Usually, the output list is truncated, so that only the top part of the significance list is eventually retained, all the candidates actually having much higher scores than the critical value associated with the AM. Therefore, all the pairs proposed are statistically significant. Nonetheless, errors are inherent to the statistical tests on which AMs are based. The output list may still contain erroneous candidates, or may miss interesting ones.

The extraction output is normally considered as a raw result that will undergo a necessary process of manual validation before its use, e.g., its inclusion in a lexicon. Deciding upon the collocational status of a candidate is a notoriously difficult task; it is, ultimately, the desired usage of the output that determines the validation criteria and the acceptable level of extraction precision. For instance, for lexicographic purposes it was indicated that even a precision of 40% would be acceptable (Smadja, 1993, 167).

3.2.3 Contingency Tables

In statistics, *contingency tables* are used to display sample values (i.e., values observed in a sample drawn from a population) in relation to two or more random variables that may be contingent (or dependent) on each other.

The process of candidate identification in a corpus which takes place in the first extraction step (see Section 3.2.2) can be seen as a sampling process, in which a subset of pairs is collected from an infinitely large set of pairs in the population, the language. In order to detect an affinity (or dependency) between the component items of a candidate pair, two discrete random variables (X and Y) can be introduced, each associated with one position in the pair: X with the first position, and Y with the second.

For a particular candidate (u, v), where u and v denote lexical items[5], the values displayed in the contingency table are u and $\neg u$ for variable X, and v and $\neg v$ for variable Y ($\neg u$ means any lexical item except u, and $\neg v$ any lexical item except v). The contingency table for the pair (u, v) might therefore look similar to Table 3.1, which also shows the typical notations for the marginal and joint frequencies.

Table 3.1 Contingency table for the candidate pair (u, v). X, Y = random variables associated with each position in the pair; a = joint frequency; R_1, C_1 = marginal frequencies for u, resp. v; N = sample size

	$Y = v$	$Y = \neg v$	
$X = u$	a	b	$R_1 = a + b$
$X = \neg u$	c	d	$R_2 = c + d$
	$C_1 = a + c$	$C_2 = b + d$	$N = a + b + c + d$

Thus, a represents the number of items in the sample—i.e., in the candidate data—that have u in the first position and v in the second; b represents the number of items that have u in the first position and $\neg v$ in the second, and so on. In other words, a is the frequency of the candidate pair in the source corpus, and is called *co-occurrence frequency* or *joint frequency*.[6] The sum $R_1 = a + b$ is the frequency of all pairs with u in the first position, also written as $(u, *)$ or $(u, \bullet)$; similarly, $C_1 = a + c$ is the frequency of all pairs with v in the second position, written as $(*, v)$ or $(\bullet, v)$. These sums are referred to as the *marginal frequencies*. The quantity $N = a + b + c + d$ represents the total number of candidate pairs identified in the corpus, or the *sample size*. The tuple (a, R_1, C_1, N) formed by the joint frequency, the marginal frequencies, and the sample size is called the *frequency signature* of a candidate pair (Evert, 2004b, 36). Note that the number d of $(\neg u, \neg v)$ pairs is less obvious to compute in practice, because one can normally search for occurrences of a specific string in a corpus, not for non-occurrences. It can, however, be easily obtained as shown in Equation (3.1).[7]

$$d = N - (a + b) - (a + c) + a = N - R_1 - C_1 + a \qquad (3.1)$$

As will be explained in Section 3.2.2, the numbers in the contingency table typically refer to pair types, as u and v denote lemmas rather than word forms; in the

---

[5] More precisely, in our work u and v denote lemmas of lexical items. Refer to Section 3.3.2 for a discussion on using full word forms vs. lemmas.

[6] We might also refer to this number simply as to frequency of the pair, or f.

[7] The frequency of the pairs $(\neg u, \neg v)$ is equal to the total number of pairs from which we subtract the number of pairs containing u in the first position and that of pairs containing v in the second position, but to which we add up the number of pairs (u, v), because these were subtracted twice.

absence of lemmatization, however, they can denote word forms. The computation of contingency values follows, in this case, the same principles.

For certain configurations of the contingency table—for instance, for skewed tables in which a is very small and d is very large—AMs fail to make reliable dependency predictions, especially if they assume that the lexical data is normally distributed.[8] In this case, their mathematical predictions might not be borne out for word cooccurrences (Evert, 2004b, 110). In order to cope with this problem (and, at the same time, to reduce the complexity of the extraction procedure), a commonly adopted solution is to apply a frequency threshold on the candidate pairs; for instance, only pairs with $a \geq 30$, $a \geq 10$, or $a \geq 5$ are considered as collocation candidates.

This practice leads, however, to the loss of a high proportion of interesting pairs, since the combinations that occur only once or twice in the corpus (*hapax-legomena* and *dis-legomena*) constitute the main body of pairs in a corpus. A better solution to this problem would be to use AMs that do not rely on the assumption of normal distribution (see Section 3.2.4). As recent theoretical studies have shown (Evert, 2004b, 133), a frequency threshold of 5 is, however, sufficient for ensuring a reliable statistical analysis. Therefore, we consider that the application of higher thresholds is not necessary.[9]

3.2.4 Association Measures

An *association measure (AM)* can be defined as "a formula that computes an association score from the frequency information in a pair type's contingency table" (Evert, 2004b, 75). This section introduces the AMs standardly used for collocation extraction.

3.2.4.1 Hypothesis Testing

AMs are very often based on statistical hypothesis tests (but not only, as will be seen in the description of AMs provided later in this section). Given a population and a random sample drawn from that population, a *statistical hypothesis test* (also, *statistical test*) is a technique of inferential statistics used to test if a hypothesis about the population is supported by evidence data, i.e., by the data observed, or the data in the sample.

Hypothesis testing consists in contrasting the hypothesis that is put forward by the statistical test (called *alternative hypothesis*, H_1) against the default hypothesis

---

[8] That is, they assume that the frequency curve of words in a corpus is bell-shaped: the frequency of most words is close to the mean frequency, and there are relatively few words whose frequency is much lower or much higher than the mean.

[9] Our choice, as stated in Section 2.6, is not to apply a threshold on the candidate data at all, but let specific AMs to make an appropriate decision later.

(called *null hypothesis*, H_0) that is believed to be true by default and that serves as a basis for the argument. In testing word association, the alternative hypothesis is that the items u and v of a candidate pair are dependent on each other; the null (default) hypothesis is that there is no such dependence between the two items:

- H_0 (null hypothesis): u and v are independent;
- H_1 (alternative hypothesis): u and v are mutually dependent.

The result of a test is given in terms of the null hypothesis, H_0: either H_0 is rejected in favor of H_1 (therefore, it can be concluded that H_1 may be true), or H_0 is not rejected, which means that there was not enough evidence in favor of H_1 (i.e., it is impossible to conclude from the observed data that H_1 may be true). In our case, if the null hypothesis of independence is rejected, then the two items may be dependent on each other and the candidate pair (u, v) may constitute a collocation. If it is not rejected, it means that there was not enough evidence supporting the alternative hypothesis of mutual dependence; therefore, it cannot be said that (u, v) forms a collocation.

One cannot be entirely sure about the outcome of a statistical test, but can only reject the null hypothesis with a certain degree of confidence (which is typically set at 95 or 99%). The value obtained by the test is compared against a threshold value (called *critical value*) in order to decide if the null hypothesis can be rejected. This threshold depends on the test type[10] and on the desired degree of confidence. The degree of confidence is more usually expressed in terms of *significance level*, or α-*level*, which represents the probability of the test wrongly rejecting the null hypothesis.

The errors that can be made by a hypothesis test are classified as:

- *Type I errors*: wrongly rejecting the null hypothesis, when it is in fact true;
- *Type II errors*: not rejecting the null hypothesis, when it is in fact false.

Type I errors affect the *precision* of the collocation extraction procedure: the candidate tested is wrongly considered to be a collocation, i.e., it is a *false positive*. Type II errors affect its *recall*: the candidate tested is not considered as a collocation when it should, i.e., it is a *false negative*. Using a smaller α-level ensures that the test produces fewer type I errors, but has instead the disadvantage of introducing more type II errors; the opposite holds when increasing the α-level. Therefore, selecting an appropriate α-level means finding a compromise between type I errors and type II errors, i.e., striking the right balance between precision and recall.

A test can be either *one-sided (one-tailed)* or *two-sided (two-tailed)*. For a *one-sided* test, it is known beforehand that the score obtained will be much higher

---

[10] One-sided or two-sided (see below). For two-sided tests, a threshold corresponds to twice as lower confidence with respect to one-sided tests.

than that expected under the null hypothesis, or that it will be much lower. On the contrary, for a *two-sided* test both alternatives are possible and the test does not specify the nature of the difference. As far as collocation extraction is concerned, this means that one-tailed tests distinguish between positive and negative associations, whereas two-tailed tests do not[11]:

– A *positive association* occurs when the score is sufficiently high to reject the null hypothesis: the items in a candidate pair co-occur more often than expected by chance, if they were independent.
– A *negative association* occurs when the score is sufficiently low to reject this hypothesis: the items co-occur less often than if they were independent.[12]

Finally, statistical tests can be either *parametric* or *non-parametric*:

– *Parametric tests* (e.g., t-score, z-score, LLR) involve numerical data and often make assumptions about the underlying population; most usually, they assume that the data is normally or binomially[13] distributed.
– *Non-parametric tests* (e.g., χ^2) involve ordinal data and are more effective than parametric tests when certain assumptions about the population are not satisfied (Oakes, 1998, 11).

3.2.4.2 Description of Standard AMs

This section introduces the typical association measures used for collocation extraction, namely, the t-score, the z-score, the chi-square test (χ^2), the log-likelihood ratio, and mutual information. These measures have been presented in more or less detail in a number of other publications (Kilgarriff, 1996; Oakes, 1998; Manning and Schütze, 1999; Evert, 2004b; Villada Moirón, 2005). For the purpose of our literature survey and for the benefit of the non-expert reader, we will provide here a self-contained, explicit description in rather intuitive terms.

In relation to contingency tables (presented in Section 3.2.3), we will first introduce some more notation, as shown in Tables 3.2 and 3.3 and in Equation (3.2).

Thus, for a cell (i, j) of the contingency table, with $1 \leq i, j \leq 2$, O_{ij} represents the *observed frequency value* of the corresponding pair in a sample (as introduced in Section 3.2.3). Each E_{ij} represents the *expected frequency value* under the null

---

[11] Among the tests described in this section, t-score and z-score are one-sided, while χ^2 (chi-square) and LLR are two-sided.

[12] van der Wouden (2001, 31) uses the term *negative collocation* to denote "the relationship of a lexical item has with items that appear with less than random probability in its (textual) context".

[13] In binomially distributed lexical data, it is supposed that the occurrence of a word can be compared to the outcome of a Bernoulli trial, like in a coin-tossing experiment.

Table 3.2 Contingency table for the candidate pair (u, v): observed values

	$Y = v$	$Y = \neg v$	
$X = u$	$O_{11} = a$	$O_{12} = b$	$R_1 = a + b$
$X = \neg u$	$O_{21} = c$	$O_{22} = d$	$R_2 = c + d$
	$C_1 = a + c$	$C_2 = b + d$	N

Table 3.3 Contingency table for the candidate pair (u, v): expected values under the null hypothesis

	$Y = v$	$Y = \neg v$
$X = u$	$E_{11} = \dfrac{(a + b)(a + c)}{N}$	$E_{12} = \dfrac{(a + b)(b + d)}{N}$
$X = \neg u$	$E_{21} = \dfrac{(c + d)(a + c)}{N}$	$E_{22} = \dfrac{(c + d)(b + d)}{N}$

hypothesis and is calculated as in Equation (3.2) below, where each R_i is a row marginal ($R_1 = a + b$, $R_2 = c + d$) and each C_j is a column marginal ($C_1 = a + c$, $C_2 = b + d$).

$$E_{ij} = \frac{R_i C_j}{N} \tag{3.2}$$

Indeed, if the two items u and v of the candidate pair were independent of each other, their expected co-occurrence in a sample of N pairs would be the product of:

- the probability of seing u as the first item in a pair,
- the probability of seing v as the second items in a pair,
- the sample size, N.

Since the individual probabilities are estimated on the basis of the actual frequencies of u and v in the sample, we obtain the expressions of the expected frequencies from Equation (3.2). Below we illustrate this computation for the cell $(1, 1)$:

$$E_{11} = N \times P(u, *) \times P(*, v) = N \times \frac{R_1}{N} \times \frac{C_1}{N} = \frac{R_1 C_1}{N} \tag{3.3}$$

The values in the other cells are computed in a similar way, on the basis of $P(u, *)$, $P(\neg u, *)$, $P(*, v)$, and $P(*, \neg v)$.

The t-score. The t-score AM—used, for instance, by Church et al. (1991), Breidt (1993), Krenn (2000b), Krenn and Evert (2001)—applies the Student's t test in the task of collocation discovery. The t test is a one-sided parametric test which assumes that the sample is drawn from a normally-distributed population. It compares the mean of the sample, $\bar{x}$ (i.e., the observed mean), with the mean of the population, μ (i.e., the mean estimated by assuming the null hypothesis). A high difference indicates that the sample was not drawn from a population in which the null hypothesis holds. Thus, in the case of lexical data, a high t value suggests that the sample was not drawn from a population in which the two lexical items are independent, and therefore indicates a strong positive association (Pedersen, 1996, 194).

The difference is expressed relative to the standard error of the means, $\sqrt{\dfrac{s^2}{N}}$ (s^2 is the sample variance). The t-test uses the following formula:

$$t = \frac{\bar{x} - \mu}{\sqrt{\dfrac{s^2}{N}}} \tag{3.4}$$

In order to estimate $\bar{x}$, μ and s^2, it is usually assumed that observing the pair (u, v) in the sample is equivalent to a Bernoulli trial (i.e., like in a coin-tossing experiment). Under this assumption, the sample mean, the sample variance and the population mean can be estimated from the sample on the basis of $P(u, v)$, the probability of observing the pair (u, v), as in Equations (3.5), (3.6), and (3.7) below (Manning and Schütze, 1999, 154).[14]

$$\bar{x} = P(u, v) = \frac{O_{11}}{N} \tag{3.5}$$

$$s^2 = P(u, v)(1 - P(u, v)) \approx P(u, v) = \frac{O_{11}}{N} \tag{3.6}$$

$$\mu = P(u, v) = P(u, *)P(*, v) = \frac{R_1 C_1}{N^2} \tag{3.7}$$

The t-score formula then becomes:

$$t = \frac{\dfrac{O_{11}}{N} - \dfrac{R_1 C_1}{N^2}}{\sqrt{\dfrac{O_{11}}{N^2}}} = \frac{O_{11} - \dfrac{R_1 C_1}{N}}{\sqrt{O_{11}}} = \frac{O_{11} - E_{11}}{\sqrt{O_{11}}}$$

$$= \frac{a - \dfrac{(a+b)(a+c)}{N}}{\sqrt{a}} = \frac{aN - (a+b)(a+c)}{N\sqrt{a}} \tag{3.8}$$

---

[14] Evert (2004b, 77, 83) questions the applicability of the t-score to co-occurrence data, as the normal distribution required by the t test is incompatible with the binomial distribution assumption made when estimating, in particular, the sample variance.

The z-score. The z-score is one of the first AMs used to identify collocations (Berry-Rogghe, 1973; Lafon, 1984; Smadja, 1993). Like the t-score, it is a one-sided parametric test which assumes that the data is normally distributed. It computes the difference between an observed value x and the mean of the population μ, expressed relative to population standard deviation σ, as in Equation (3.9):

$$z = \frac{x - \mu}{\sigma} \tag{3.9}$$

Smadja (1993) uses this standard z-score formula for detecting collocations that are significantly frequent, by considering x = the frequency of a word, μ = the average frequency of its collocates, and σ = the standard deviation of the frequency of its collocates.

But, in general, the z-score AM is used to measure the significance of the difference between the observed and expected frequencies for a candidate pair, as in Equation (3.10) below:

$$z\text{-}score = \frac{O_{11} - E_{11}}{\sqrt{E_{11}}} = \frac{a - \frac{(a+b)(a+c)}{N}}{\sqrt{\frac{(a+b)(a+c)}{N}}} = \frac{aN - (a+b)(a+c)}{\sqrt{N}\sqrt{(a+b)(a+c)}} \tag{3.10}$$

Berry-Rogghe (1973) essentially uses this formula, with a small modification in the denominator (which is multiplied by the probability of the collocate v occurring in a span around u).

The chi-square test (χ^2). This test is relatively less used for collocation extraction than other AMs; it has been used, for instance, by Krenn (2000b) and Evert and Krenn (2001).

It is a two-sided non-parametric hypothesis test, which does not assume a particular distribution for the data. It compares the observed with the expected frequencies (under the null hypothesis) in each cell of the contingency table, as in Equation (3.11) shown below. If the overall difference is large, then the null hypothesis of independence is rejected.

$$\chi^2 = \sum_{i,j} \frac{(O_{ij} - E_{ij})^2}{E_{ij}} = \frac{N(ad - bc)^2}{(a+b)(a+c)(b+d)(c+d)} \tag{3.11}$$

The derivation of the explicit formula from the left-hand side expression is shown in Appendix C.

Log-likelihood ratio. LLR (Dunning, 1993) is a two-sided parametric test that has largely been used in relation with collocation extraction (Daille, 1994; Lin, 1999; Orliac and Dillinger, 2003; Lü and Zhou, 2004). As its name suggests, LLR computes the association score for a candidate pair (u, v) by, basically, contrasting two likelihoods and considering the logarithm of the result:

- the likelihood of observing the counts in the contingency table under the null hypothesis of independence;
- the likelihood of observing these counts under the alternative hypothesis of dependence.[15]

Under the null hypothesis H_0, the probability p of observing the second item in the pair (v) is independent of the first item (u) being observed. Therefore, p can be estimated solely on the basis of the frequency of v in the corpus:

$$p = P(*, v) = \frac{C_1}{N} = \frac{a+c}{N} \tag{3.12}$$

On the contrary, under the alternative hypothesis H_1, the probability of observing v is dependent on whether or not u is observed; it is denoted by p_1 in the first case and p_2 in the second. When u is observed, p_1 is $P(v|u)$; when u is not observed, p_2 is $P(v|\neg u)$. Using corpus frequencies, p_1 and p_2 are computed as follows:

$$p_1 = \frac{P(u, v)}{P(u, *)} = \frac{\frac{a}{N}}{\frac{a+b}{N}} = \frac{a}{a+b} \tag{3.13}$$

$$p_2 = \frac{P(\neg u, v)}{P(\neg u, *)} = \frac{\frac{c}{N}}{\frac{c+d}{N}} = \frac{c}{c+d} \tag{3.14}$$

Assuming a binomial distribution $B(k; n, x) = \binom{n}{k} x^k (1-x)^{n-k}$, the probability of observing the values in the contingency table is computed using the following probabilities:

- under H_0:

  (1) probability of observing v when u is present: $P_{H_0}(v|u) = B(a; a+b, p)$;
  (2) probability of observing v when u is not present: $P_{H_0}(v|\neg u) = B(c; c + d, p)$;

---

[15] We follow Manning and Schütze (1999) in this presentation of LLR. But for the sake of accuracy, we must mention that Dunning (1993) does not refer to the second likelihood as the alternative hypothesis, but as the maximum likelihood reached when the independence constraint is relaxed. However, as it can be seen in Dunning (1993, 67), this maximum is in fact reached for exactly the same probability values p_1 and p_2 that are computed under the alternative hypothesis (see below).

– under H_1:

(1) probability of observing v when u is present: $P_{H_1}(v|u) = B(a; a+b, p_1)$;
(2) probability of observing v when u is not present: $P_{H_1}(v|\neg u) = B(c; c + d, p_2)$.

The LLR test considers $L(H_0) = P_{H_0}(v|u)P_{H_0}(v|\neg u)$ the overall likelihood of observing the contingency values under H_0, $L(H_1) = P_{H_1}(v|u)P_{H_1}(v|\neg u)$ the overall likelihood under H_1, and λ their ratio.

Then, the LLR score is defined and computed as in Equation (3.15).[16] The computation steps for obtaining the explicit LLR formula are shown in Appendix C.

$$
\begin{aligned}
LLR = -2\log \lambda &= -2\log \frac{L(H_0)}{L(H_1)} \\
&= 2(a\log a + b\log b + c\log c + d\log d \\
&\quad -(a+b)\log(a+b) - (a+c)\log(a+c) \\
&\quad -(b+d)\log(b+d) - (c+d)\log(c+d) \\
&\quad +(a+b+c+d)\log(a+b+c+d))
\end{aligned}
\tag{3.15}
$$

As Evert (2004b, 89) remarks, the LLR formula is equivalent to the following formula for the *average-MI* association measure: $2\sum_{i,j} O_{ij} \log \frac{O_{ij}}{E_{ij}}$.

Pointwise Mutual Information. Abbreviated as PMI or sometimes simply as MI, this measure introduced to NLP by Church and Hanks (1990) is perhaps the most popular one in collocation extraction; it has been used, among many others, by Calzolari and Bindi (1990), Breidt (1993), Daille (1994) and Lin (1998).

Unlike the AMs presented above, it is not a hypothesis test, but a measure related to information theory concepts. For two events in a series of events (like, in our case, the occurrence of two specific words in a corpus), MI quantifies the amount of information, in information-theoretic terms, an event (in our case, the occurrence of a word) conveys about the other.

If $I(h; i)$ is the information provided about the event h by the occurrence of event i, defined as $I(h; i) = \log_2 \frac{P(h|i)}{P(h)}$, then this information is equal to the information provided about i by the occurrence of h, i.e., $I(i; h) = \log_2 \frac{P(i|h)}{P(i)}$, hence the name *mutual information*. MI is computed according to the formula in Equation (3.16), where $P(h, i)$ represents the joint probability of h and i (i.e., the probability of observing h and i together).

$$
MI = \log_2 \frac{P(h, i)}{P(h)P(i)}
\tag{3.16}
$$

---

[16] Given λ, the quantity $-2\log \lambda$ is asymptotically χ^2-distributed (Dunning, 1993, 68).

For lexical co-occurrence, MI is computed as in Equation (3.17) below, using the following probabilities:

- $P(u, v)$ – the probability of observing u and v together: $P(u, v) = \dfrac{a}{N}$;
- $P(u, *)$ – the individual probability of item u: $P(u, *) = \dfrac{R_1}{N} = \dfrac{a+b}{N}$;
- $P(*, v)$ – the individual probability of item v: $P(*, v) = \dfrac{C_1}{N} = \dfrac{a+c}{N}$.

$$MI = \log_2 \frac{P(u, v)}{P(u, *)P(*, v)} = \log_2 \frac{\dfrac{a}{N}}{\dfrac{a+b}{N}\dfrac{a+c}{N}} = \log_2 \frac{aN}{(a+b)(a+c)}$$

(3.17)

3.2.5 Criteria for the Application of Association Measures

The collocation extraction practice has seen various AMs being applied in different settings, without clearly defined criteria for using one particular AM rather than another. However, there exist theoretical reasons that make some AMs more appropriate for collocation extraction than others, in a given setting.

Thus, the applicability of certain tests, like the *t* test and *z-score*, to the discovery of significant word associations has often been contested in the literature,[17] since these tests make the assumption that language data is normally distributed, and this assumption is not borne out by evidence. In a normal (bell-shaped) distribution, most data is grouped around the mean and there are only a few extreme values that are either much lower or much higher than the mean,[18] whereas the lexical data has a skewed, Zipfian distribution, with a small proportion of high values (i.e., frequent events) and a majority of low values (i.e., rare events).

The AMs which are based on the assumption of normal distribution work well for frequent events, but are less reliable for rare events, which actually constitute the main body of textual data (Dunning, 1993). The use of t-score and z-score is therefore not recommended for low-frequency candidates. In addition, the z-score is not recommended for small samples (small N values), for which the t-score is instead better suited (Oakes, 1998, 12). Also, *MI* is unreliable for low-frequency pairs, whose significance is overestimated, in particular if they occur exactly once. In fact, Church and Hanks (1990) suggest using a frequency threshold of 5 ($f \geq 5$). On large, frequency-filtered data, MI was shown to lead to competitive results (Pecina, 2010).

---

[17] For instance, in Dunning (1993, 61), Kilgarriff (1996, 35), or Evert (2004b, 83).

[18] In normally distributed data, about two thirds of all values fall within one standard deviation away from the mean.

The *chi-square* (χ^2) test overcomes the normal distribution problem, as it makes no assumptions about the data. It is less sensitive to low frequencies, but still overemphasizes rare events. Other disadvantages of χ^2 are that it overemphasizes common events as well (Kilgarriff, 1996, 35). Like the z-score, χ^2 is inaccurate when the sample size is very small (Manning and Schütze, 1999, 161).[19]

Contrary to the measures mentioned above, *LLR* is argued to be appropriate to both rare and common phenomena, and to both large and small text samples (Dunning, 1993, 62). As a matter of fact, LLR is generally considered as the most appropriate measure for collocation extraction (Daille, 1994; Evert, 2004b; Orliac, 2006), even though conflicting reports exist.[20] Still, it has been pointed out that low values of expected frequencies in the contingency table (less than 1) may affect the reliability of LLR (Pedersen, 1996, 191). In addition, some researchers, amongst whom Stubbs (2002, 73), argue against the assumption of random (e.g., binomial) distribution that some tests, including LLR, make: a text cannot be compared to the outcome of a Bernoulli trial, as in a coin-tossing experiment. Note, however, that the random assumption is generally considered more plausible than the normality assumption.

Selecting a specific AM as the best measure for ranking collocation candidates is a difficult process, because one has to take into account the particular setting in which the extraction experiment takes place, like—as shown before—the sample size and the observed and expected frequencies in the contingency table. Moreover, as argued by Evert and Krenn (2005, 452), the type of collocations to extract, the domain of the source corpora, the amount of low-frequency data excluded by the frequency threshold, and the linguistic preprocessing also play a role in the practical relevance of an AM.

The comparative evaluation of AMs is a topic largely dealt with in the literature (Daille, 1994; Pedersen, 1996; Barnbrook, 1996; Krenn, 2000b; Krenn and Evert, 2001; Schone and Jurafsky, 2001; Pearce, 2002; Thanopoulos et al., 2002; Evert, 2004b; Pecina, 2010). But, as a matter of fact, the particular results of the evaluation experiments carried out can hardly be generalized or transferred to different extraction settings. Consequently, there is no single all-purpose measure that can be proposed. The focus of recent research shifted from comparing the individual merits of standardly used AMs, to discovering alternative, less widely used AMs that may provide optimal results in a given setting,[21] and to using machine learning techniques to find the optimal combination of AMs to apply in a specific extraction task (Pecina, 2008a, 2010).

---

[19] More precisely, when N is smaller than 20, or it is between 20 and 50 and the expected frequencies are 5 or less (Manning and Schütze, 1999, 161).

[20] For instance, in a particular extraction setting involving PP-V data in German, LLR was found to perform worse than the t-score on lower positions in the significance list (Krenn, 2000b; Evert and Krenn, 2001; Krenn and Evert, 2001). Also, in the comprehensive AM comparison provided by Pecina (2010), LLR showed an average performance, lower than that of MI but higher than that of the t-score.

[21] For instance, the Dice coefficient emerged as a more competitive measure from experiments involving A-N data in German (Evert, 2008b).

Surprisingly, the raw *co-occurrence frequency* was found in many settings to produce results that are as reliable as those obtained by sophisticated AMs; see, for instance, Daille (1994, 154), Krenn and Evert (2001), or Villada Moirón (2005). The question if AMs are better suited to model word collocability than the frequency measure remains open. The very utility of statistical tests for collocation discovery is actually questioned by Stubbs (2002), who shows that in large corpora (e.g., 200 million words) the expected frequencies are so low that virtually any pair occurs more often than expected by chance; thus, citing a level of significance is pointless.

Manning and Schütze (1999, 155–156) found, indeed, that most pairs extracted from a 14-million word corpus occurred significantly more often than chance. They further pointed out that, while the level of significance is practically never looked at, what matters is the ranking obtained. Stubbs (2002, 75) adopts a rather skeptical point of view, suggesting that "whatever quantitative findings or statistics are produced by the computer, they must be interpreted by the human analyst". Nonetheless, AMs are nowadays widely used in extraction systems and produce sufficiently accurate results that are used as raw material in lexicography (Kilgarriff et al., 2004; Charest et al., 2007; Kilgarriff et al., 2010).

3.3 Linguistic Preprocessing

According to the general architecture of collocation extraction systems described in Section 3.2.2, the first extraction step consists of the identification of collocation candidates in text. This step is usually based on a linguistic preprocessing of the source corpus. Regardless of the subsequent statistical computation dealing with candidate ranking and the identification method itself (from *n*-gram methods to window-based or more sophisticated methods), the linguistic analysis of the source text is often seen as an inescapable requirement for obtaining competitive extraction results.

The level of analysis performed by an extraction system depends on (i) the kind of targeted results (i.e., semantically-motivated co-occurrences or syntactically-bound pairs, according to the particular understanding adopted for the concept of collocation); (ii) the ranking method applied in the second extraction step (since specific AMs may require a larger candidate set or higher frequencies, which can be obtained by clustering the instances of a pair through lemmatization and syntactic analysis); and (iii) the language involved, which might pose particular problems especially insofar as the presence of long-range dependencies is concerned. In most of the cases, this analysis includes at least sentence boundary detection and tokenization. Lemmatization, POS tagging and a syntactic analysis are also often necessary, for reasons that are explained below.

3.3.1 Lemmatization

In general, collocation extraction systems deal with lemmas rather than with full word forms (inflected words). Unless there are specific reasons to extract collocations involving inflected words—or practical reasons like the absence of appropriate tools—extraction systems typically rely on lemmatization in order to abstract away from morphological variants and to recognize a lexical item in all its inflected forms. Therefore, the extraction results generally consist of collocation types encompassing a relatively large number of morphologically distinct tokens.

The usefulness of lemmatization was put forth, for instance, by Heid (1994, 250): "it seems useful to have an option in statistical programs to calculate the measures for lemmas rather than word forms". Also, Stubbs (2002), who performed a detailed lexicographic analysis on the collocates of several English words, remarked that lemmatization helps detect strong associations more easily. Thus, in Stubbs (2002, 82–83) he discusses the example of the word *resemblance*, whose collocates in a corpus, and, in particular, the verb *bear*, are scattered through different forms. Put together, these forms make up a high proportion of the total number of collocates. Example 1 displays, using the author's notation, the total number of collocates and the ratio of each form.

(1) resemblance 1, 085 <bears 18%, bear 11%, bore 11%, bearing 4%> 44%

Also, as indicated by Evert (2004b, 35), the grouping of all inflected variants under the same lemma leads to more significant statistical results. Clustering word forms is particularly important for languages with a rich morphology, because otherwise, the low frequencies recorded in the contingency table could prevent the applicability of many AMs (as discussed in Section 3.2.5).

However, as noted, for instance, by Calzolari and Bindi (1990, 57), lemmatization has the inconvenience that the specific information on inflection is, at least in principle, lost; this information might be required for the subsequent treatment of results in other NLP applications.[22] Another remark made by Calzolari and Bindi (1990, 57), and also by Stubbs (2002, 28, 69), is that different word forms of the same lemma may have different collocates, as well as different frequencies of occurrence.[23]

3.3.2 POS Tagging

The preprocessing of source corpora based on part-of-speech analysis brings considerable improvements to the identification of collocation candidates. *POS (part-of-speech) tagging* is therefore performed in most of the extraction work, often in relation with a more detailed analysis at the syntactic level.

Firstly, POS tagging is very useful to better pinpoint candidates in the source text, thanks to the lexical disambiguation it provides. Church and Hanks (1990) showed, for instance, that POS tags help distinguish phrasal verbs involving the preposition *to* (e.g., *allude to*) from verbs followed by the infinitive marker (e.g.,

---

[22] Refer to Table 5.3 in Section 5.1 for an example of collocation in which considering word forms instead of lemmas would have been preferable.

[23] Stubbs (2002, 30), for instance, gives the example of *heated argument* vs. *hot argument*.

tend to). The authors note that "we see there is considerable leverage to be gained by preprocessing the corpus and manipulating the inventory of tokens" (Church and Hanks, 1990, 25).

Secondly, POS tagging is largely used to filter out the combinations that are considered from the start as "noisy" or uninteresting, e.g., the combinations made up exclusively of function words (D-P, Conj-D, etc). As a matter of fact, most extraction systems only retain certain types of POS combinations, like N-V, V-N, N-N, A-N, Adv-V, Adv-A, or V-P.[24] The candidate pairs that do not correspond to these predefined patterns are ruled out.

The literature reports systematically on drastic improvements obtained in the extraction precision when a POS filter is applied, based on simple syntactic patterns like the ones mentioned above (Church and Hanks, 1990; Breidt, 1993; Smadja, 1993; Daille, 1994; Justeson and Katz, 1995) (see also Section 3.4). However, a strong POS filter works to the detriment of extraction recall. Some authors argue against the a priori exclusion of non-content words (van der Wouden, 2001) and against the relatively arbitrary exclusion of most POS combinations (Dias, 2003).

According to theoretical stipulations, the collocation phenomenon appears to involve any category of words and any syntactic structure. As Fontenelle (1992, 222) states, "the term *collocation* refers to the idiosyncratic syntagmatic combination of lexical items and is independent of word class or syntactic structure". Also, according to van der Wouden (1997, 13), "for almost every category it seems, in principle, to be possible to participate in collocations"; "syntactically, (almost) everything is possible in collocation" (van der Wouden, 1997, 14). Nonetheless, he notes that:

> there are constraints in terms of syntactic structures or on the combination of syntactic categories. For example, I cannot think of many collocations of noun plus adverb, numeral plus adverb, verb plus determiner, etc. Probably, some notion of constituency or projection is needed to establish the necessary relationship between the collocants (van der Wouden, 1997, 14).

While these arguments are directed against the a priori exclusion of many combination patterns from the very start, providing an abstraction of collocations at POS level by means of tagging remains an incontestably important concern. As Firth (1968, 181) states, "grammatical generalizations of word classes and the setting up of categories for the statement of meaning in terms of syntactical relations is clearly indispensable".

With respect to the distinction drawn in Section 2.2.3 between semantically and syntactically motivated combinations (co-occurrences vs. collocations), a preprocessing based on lemmatisation and POS tagging is sufficient for detecting instances of the first type. However, the detection of collocations in the restricted linguistic sense requires a finer analysis of the text, that goes beyond the use of simple syntactic patterns as suggested by POS combinations. As Heid (1994) states, "computational tools which would just look for combinations of adjacent lexemes would not

---

[24] The POS labels have been introduced in Section 2.5.2.

retrieve all combinations which fall under the syntactic definitions". Such a detailed analysis is provided by parsing.

3.3.3 Shallow and Deep Parsing

Shallow parsing (or *chunking*) is performed more often than deep parsing in the pre-processing stage of extraction procedures, since the former is more widely available. Whereas (full) deep parsing aims to build a complete syntactic structure for a sentence and to identify predicate-argument relations, chunking only provides partial and relatively simple structures for contiguous intra-clausal constituents, like AdvP, AP, NP, PP, or verbal complexes.

The identification of collocation candidates from chunked text is considered as more reliable than the identification based on POS-tagged text, thanks to the presence of a (constituent-internal) syntactic link between the items in a pair, on the one hand, and to the POS-disambiguation performed, on the other hand.[25] Chunking also makes the extraction more tractable with respect to the window method, which relies exclusively on POS information and considers all the combinatorial possibilities in a collocation span (usually consisting of 5 content words). Yet, a major drawback of the extraction based on chunking is that the numerous syntactic relations holding between words in disconnected chunks, as well as the predicate-argument relations, are missed.

However, some shallow parsers aim at recovering such relations, or at least part of them. Thus, Basili et al. (1994) present an extraction approach that copes with this problem by relying on a "not so shallow" syntactic analysis. This analysis retrieves long-distance dependencies by means of so-called *skip rules* defined in a "discontinuous grammar" framework. The authors find that "adding more syntactic knowledge to the recipe significantly improves the recall and precision of detected collocations, regardless of any statistical computation" (Basili et al., 1994, 447).

Dependency parsing, which captures the relations between a head word and the dependent words and thus provides a bridge between shallow and deep parsing, has also been used to identify collocation candidates (Lin, 1998, 1999; Charest et al., 2007; Pecina, 2010). The main advantage of this kind of preprocessing is that there is no a priori limitation for the distance between two items in a candidate pair, as in the case of POS-tagging or shallow-parsing preprocessing.

More recently, *deep parsing*—either symbolic or stochastic—has also been used to preprocess the source corpus, but in a much fewer number of works with respect to shallow parsing, undoubtedly because of its much more reduced availability (Blaheta and Johnson, 2001; Pearce, 2001a; Schulte im Walde, 2003; Lü and Zhou, 2004; Villada Moirón, 2005). Deep parsing makes it possible for collocation extraction systems to deal with the syntactic transformations that some candidate pairs

---

[25] Lexical ambiguity pervades language. For English, it has been estimated that it affects about 40% of the tokens in a text (Hajič, 2000).

often undergo—especially the ones involving a verb (passivization, relativization, interrogation, apposition, etc). As in the case of dependency parsing, the linear distance between the two candidate items is irrelevant; the criterion used to identify a candidate pair is the syntactic proximity, instead of the linear proximity of items in text.

There are multiple advantages of relying on syntactically analysed text for collocation extraction. The use of a syntax-based criterion for selecting collocation candidates should translate, first, into a higher extraction precision and recall, and second, into an improved tractability of the candidate ranking step, as many erroneous candidates are ruled out from the start. Also, by detecting those pair instances that are subject to complex syntactic operations, syntax-based methods help compute more accurate frequency information for candidates, which in turn should help AMs propose a more accurate ranking for candidates. Moreover, AMs become more reliable when different syntactic variants of pairs are clustered thanks to the syntactic analysis, in the same way in which morphological variants are clustered through lemmatization. Another possible advantage of syntactically preprocessing the source corpora is that AMs can also benefit from the tuning to the syntactic configuration. In fact, the performance of AMs seems to be dependent on the syntactic type of candidate data (Evert and Krenn, 2001).

The possible inconveniences of adopting a syntax-based extraction approach instead of a syntactically-uninformed one are the dependence on the language or on a specific linguistic theory, and, more importantly, the limited availability of adequate tools (i.e., efficient parsers allowing for the accurate, robust and fast preprocessing of a whole source corpus). In addition, it is necessary to specify a priori the set of relevant syntactic configurations and to ensure that it has a satisfactory coverage, tasks which can be difficult in practice.

3.3.4 Beyond Parsing

As it has been pointed out in the related literature, in certain cases, even a detailed syntactic analysis might be insufficient for retrieving some collocation instances. The following example from van der Wouden (2001, 33) supports the author's claim that automatic search procedures will never find all instances of some combinations.

(2)   As to *collecting*, we're not interested in coins, books, ... Our sole concern is *stamps* (van der Wouden, 2001, 33).

In fact, no existing extraction technique would succeed in retrieving the verb-object link between *collecting* and *stamps*.

Similarly, Stone and Doran (1996, 92) discuss the example of the collocation *narrow escape*, in which one of the items (*escape*) does not even occur in the text, but could be identified as an external discourse entity:

(3)   Whew! [after burrowing and swimming out of Alcatraz, amid nearby shots and searchlights] That was *narrow*! (Stone and Doran, 1996, 92)

The authors suggest that collocations should also be seen as holding between "objects in an evolving model of discourse", not only between overt words. They explain that collocations introduce entities that are available for later reference (Stone and Doran, 1996, 92). In fact, it is not unusual that an item of a candidate pair occurs in a different sentence, and is replaced in the current sentence by a referring expression—usually a pronoun, as in Example 4 below (Stone and Doran, 1996, 92). Anaphora resolution techniques should therefore be used to link the pronoun *it* and its collocational antecedent, *escape*.

(4) Their *escape* had been lucky; Bill found *it* uncomfortably *narrow*.

Complementing parsing with discourse-level techniques is expected to benefit collocation extraction, in particular by promoting those candidate pairs in the significance list in which the collocate often happens to be pronominalized.

Another situation in which parsing alone does not suffice for retrieving candidate instances is when the items involved undergo a grammatical category change. Pairs like those shown in (5a) or in (5b) could, in principle, be considered as equivalent collocations, and therefore should count as instances of the same collocation type. But in order to achieve this more abstract grouping, parsing should be complemented by techniques such as stemming, paraphrasing, or syntactic transformation rules, as in the account proposed by Jacquemin et al. (1997) (see Section 3.4.3).

(5) a. to *make* a *decision, decision making*

     b. *strong argument, strength* of *argument*, to *argue strongly*, to *strengthen* an *argument*

3.4 Survey of the State of the Art

In this section, we present a survey of the existing collocation extraction work, organised by language—as will be seen, different languages are dealt with by slightly different methodologies, depending on their morpho-syntactic peculiarities. We aim at a rather inclusive review, therefore we take in considerations the various reports that exist on using extraction techniques based on statistical inference (see Section 3.2), even if the targeted linguistic phenomenon is more specific, more general, or labelled with a term other than collocation. For instance, we also include in this review related work on terminology extraction or on the acquisition of other types of multi-word expressions (e.g., compounds, verb-particle constructions, support-verb constructions). We do not discuss, however, work on deriving collocations cross-linguistically by exploiting parallel corpora via word alignment—e.g., (Kupiec, 1993; Wu, 1994; Smadja et al., 1996; Kitamura and Matsumoto, 1996; Melamed, 1997; Villada Moirón and Tiedemann, 2006; de Caseli et al., 2010)—or work focused on specific aspects, like the extraction of collocations made up of more than two words. We will refer to them in the dedicated sections in Chapter 5.

3.4.1 English

It goes without saying that the bulk of existing extraction work deals with the English language. The earlier methods developed are generally based on *n*-gram techniques, and are therefore capable of extracting sequences of adjacent words only; moreover, the AM used is the plain co-occurrence frequency (Choueka, 1988; Kjellmer, 1994; Justeson and Katz, 1995). The last method cited also applies a POS filter on candidates in the preprocessing stage. Similarly, the method of Church and Hanks (1989, 1990) also extracts adjacent pairs that are likely to constitute phrasal verbs by POS-tagging the source text, but then it applies MI for candidate ranking.

The Xtract collocation extraction system of Smadja (1993) detects "rigid" noun phrases (e.g., *stock market, foreign exchange, New York Stock Exchange, The Dow Jones average of 30 industrials*), phrasal templates (e.g., *common stocks rose *NUMBER* to *NUMBER**)[26], and, notably, flexible combinations involving a verb, called predicative collocations (e.g., *index (...) rose, stock (...) jumped, use (...) widely*). The system combines the z-score AM with several heuristics such as the systematic occurrence of two lexical items at a similar distance in text. A parser is later used to validate the results, and is shown to lead to a substantial increase in the extraction precision, from 40 to 80%. The evaluation of Xtract involved 4,000 randomly selected results, and was performed by a professional lexicographer.

In the Termight terminology extraction system developed by Dagan and Church (1994), technical terms—more precisely, NPs—are identified by means of regular expressions defining syntactic patterns over POS tags. The candidates are grouped under the same head noun and are sorted according to their frequency; a concordancer then displays the context of terms, as well as the context of their candidate translations found in a parallel corpus on the basis of word alignment.

Shallow parsing was first used by Church et al. (1989) for detecting verb-object collocations, which were then ranked using MI and t-score AMs. Also, in the Sketch Engine (Kilgarriff et al., 2004) collocation candidates are identified based on shallow parsing implemented as pattern matching over POS tags. The AM used is an adaptation of MI that gives more weight to the co-occurrence frequency. As is the case for these methods, several other methods are able to detect flexible pairs, as they rely on shallow, dependency, or deep parsing. For example, Grefenstette and Teufel (1995) extract V-N pairs by using a robust dependency parser, with the specific goal of identifying nominalisation constructions. Lin (1998, 1999) also uses a dependency parser for identifying candidate pairs of several types. For ranking them, the author uses a version of MI that incorporates information on the frequency of the syntactic relation (Lin, 1998) and the LLR measure (Lin, 1999).

Collocation extraction has also been performed from corpora analysed with a statistical parser—for instance, by Pearce (2001a), who studies restrictions on synonym substitution, and Blaheta and Johnson (2001), who extract verb-particle

---

[26] The term *phrasal template* denotes sequences of words with empty slots standing for POS tags (Smadja, 1993, 149).

constructions with a log-linear model they propose as an AM. A symbolic parser is instead used in the preprocessing stage by Goldman et al. (2001) (in an early version of our extractor), and later by Orliac and Dillinger (2003), Wu and Zhou (2003) and Lü and Zhou (2004). All these methods use LLR for ranking, except for the method of Wu and Zhou (2003) which uses *weighted MI*, a version of MI that compensates for the tendency of MI to overestimate rare pairs.

As Pearce (2002, 1530) states, at least as far as the English language is concerned, "with recent significant increases in parsing efficiency and accuracy, there is no reason why explicit parse information should not be used". Nonetheless, some of the recent work on collocation extraction still limits the preprocessing to POS tagging. For instance, Zaiu Inkpen and Hirst (2002) extract collocations from a POS-tagged corpus, the BNC.[27] They apply a POS filter for removing closed-class words, then use the BSP package[28] to extract adjacent pairs from the remaining tokens and to rank these pairs with several AMs. Also, Dias (2003), who argues against the use of predetermined syntactic patterns, bases his extraction on POS-tag sequences within a text window. The relative simplicity of English language in terms of both morphology and syntax facilitates the use of more basic techniques, like the application of AMs directly on plain text or on POS-tagged text inside a small collocational span. In other languages, however, a more advanced linguistic preprocessing is required in order to obtain acceptable results.

3.4.2 German

German is the second most investigated language from the point of view of collocability, thanks to the early work of Breidt (1993) and, more recently, to the work of Krenn and Evert that was centered on evaluation (Krenn, 2000b; Krenn and Evert, 2001; Evert and Krenn, 2001; Evert, 2004b; Evert and Krenn, 2005).

Before syntactic tools for German became available, Breidt (1993) extracted V-N pairs (such as *[in] Betracht kommen*, "to be considered", or *[zur] Ruhe kommen*, "get some peace") using the window method. The author evaluated the performance of MI and t-score AMs in a variety of settings: different corpora and window sizes, presence/absence of lemmatization, of POS tagging, and of (simulated) parsing. She argues that extraction from German text is more difficult than from English text because of the much richer inflection of verbs, the variable word order, and the positional ambiguity of arguments. She shows that even distinguishing subjects from objects is very difficult without parsing. She found that in order to exclude unrelated

---

[27] British National Corpus (BNC) is a 100 million word collection of samples of twentieth century British English which has been automatically POS tagged (URL: http://www.natcorp.ox.ac.uk/corpus/, accessed June, 2010).

[28] The Bigram Statistic Package (BSP) identifies bigrams in corpora and implements several AMs: MI, Dice coefficient, χ^2, LLR, and Fisher's exact test. Since it has been extended to handle n-grams, it has been renamed to NSP (Banerjee and Pedersen, 2003).

nouns, a smaller window of size 3 is preferable, although at the expense of recall. Increasing the corpus size leads to considerable improvement of recall, but causes a slight decrease in precision. Parsing (simulated by eliminating the pairs in which the noun is not the object of the co-occurring verb) was argued to lead to a much higher precision of results. The lemmatization alone did not help, because it promoted new erroneous candidates. The conclusion of the study was that a good level of precision can only be obtained for German with parsing: "Very high precision rates, which are an indispensable requirement for lexical acquisition, can only realistically be envisaged for German with parsed corpora" (Breidt, 1993, 82).

In fact, more recent work makes use of chunking for extracting particular types of collocations such as P-N-V, and is mostly concerned with the comparative evaluation of AMs (Krenn, 2000a,b; Krenn and Evert, 2001; Evert and Krenn, 2001; Evert, 2004b). For example, Krenn (2000a,b) describes an extraction experiment concerning adjacent and non-adjacent, full and base form P-N-V (PP-V)[29] candidates, aimed at distinguishing collocational from non-collocational combinations. Since POS information and partial parsing is employed, the set of candidates identified is argued to contain less noise than if retrieved without syntactic information (Krenn, 2000a). The experiment compares several AMs—MI, the Dice coefficient, LLR, and the relative entropy—with two newly-proposed identification models: (a) the *phrase entropy* of P-N pairs, as a low entropy is considered an an indicator of collocability, and (b) the *lexical keys model*, based on lists of typical support verbs. Evaluation based on manually classified data containing more than 30, 000 candidates showed that the quality of results depends on the frequency threshold applied, on whether lemmatization is used or not, and on the type of collocations extracted (the author distinguishes between figurative expressions and support-verb constructions). The study found that P-N entropy outperforms AMs on higher frequency, full form data, i.e., unlemmatized data on which a frequency threshold of 5 or 10 is applied. However, its advantage is less pronounced when base forms and lower frequency data are included ($f \geq 3$). Also, the combination of entropy with the lexical keys model proved very helpful in identifying support-verb constructions, but proved less helpful in identifying figurative expressions.

Like in a subsequent comparative evaluation experiment (Krenn and Evert, 2001), the PP-V candidates can be grammatically incorrect, since the PP and V items are only required to occur within the same sentence and no parsing is performed to ensure that there is indeed a grammatical relation holding between the two. The reported n-best precision, computed using the same gold standard of manually extracted PP-V collocations, showed that more accurate results are obtained for higher frequency data: thus, the precision is 40% for $f \geq 3$ and higher than 50% for $f \geq 5$. It has also been found that the t-score is the best AM for identifying PP-V collocations, and that no AM performs significantly better than the simple

---

[29] These patterns describe expressions that are similar to those retrieved by Breidt (1993), e.g., *zur Verfügung stellen* (lit., *at the availability put*, "make available"), *am Herzen liegen* (lit., *at the heart lie*, "have at hearth").

co-occurrence frequency.[30] The experiment involved full form data, but the authors reported that similar differences could be observed among the compared AMs on base form data.

Evert and Krenn (2001) performed a similar evaluation experiment in which, in addition to PP-V collocations, they extracted adjacent A-N pairs using a POS tagger. The authors found that LLR is the best AM for identifying A-N collocations, while χ^2 and MI perform worst, as in the case of PP-V data. Evaluation has also been performed separately on different frequency strata, i.e., for high and low frequencies. On high frequency PP-V data, LLR outperformed the t-score on the top 10% of the significance list, but then t-score outperformed LLR on the remaining part. Another finding of the study was that, contrary to previous claims in the literature, MI did not perform better on high frequency data than on low-frequency data: its relative performance with respect to other AMs did not improve with a higher frequency, as one could have expected (see Section 3.2.5). As for low-frequency data, all AMs had similar performance on PP-V data, while on A-N data LLR emerged as the best AM. The study also showed that on these data the raw co-coccurrence frequency was significantly worse than all AMs.

Also, Evert and Kermes (2002, 2003) focused on the evaluation of linguistic preprocessing—as opposed to the evaluation of AMs—since this stage is considered to have a crucial influence on the final results obtained. The authors evaluated the grammaticality of A-N pairs extracted using three different methods: (a) identification of adjacent A-N with a POS-tagger, (b) identification of an A followed by an N within a window of 10 words, and (c) identification based on chunking. Evaluation against A-N pairs extracted from the same corpus (i.e., the Negra treebank containing syntactic annotations) showed that the highest recall is obtained with chunking, but the precision of the chunk-based method remains similar to that of the adjacency method.[31]

In addition to the work centered on evaluation, collocation extraction work has also been performed, for instance, by Zinsmeister and Heid (2002, 2004), who compared the collocational behaviour of compound nouns with that of their base noun, and showed that this is correlated with semantic transparency. Also, Zinsmeister and Heid (2003) focused on detecting A-N-V triples and classifying them into idiomatic combinations, combinations of collocations, mixed triples[32] and regular combinations by means of machine learning techniques. In addition, Schulte im Walde (2003) built a collocation database for a variety of syntactic types, that contained subcategorization details for nouns and verbs. All these methods use LLR for candidate ranking and are based on the full stochastic parsing of the source texts.

---

[30] In particular, LLR performs significantly worse than frequency, although better than other AMs (Krenn and Evert, 2001).

[31] This result is not surprising, given the rigidity of the syntactic type considered.

[32] An example of each is: *[das] letzte Wort haben* – "have the last word" (idiomatic combination), *klare Absage erteilen* – "clearly reject" (combination of collocations), *rote Zahlen schreiben* – "be in the red" (mixed triple). Mixed triples associate a collocational with a regular combination.

This analysis is argued to be indispensable for identifying verbal collocations (in particular, the constructions with split particles), and to lead to a higher precision and recall with respect to partial analyses.

Yet, chunked text has been used in several other works, e.g., for identifying A-V collocations in predicative constructions (Kermes and Heid, 2003), or for identifying morpho-syntactic preferences in collocations: thus, Evert et al. (2004) deal with number and case of nouns in A-N collocations, while Ritz (2006) focuses on number, case, determination, modification for nouns, and on negation and subtype—main, auxiliary, modal—for verbs in V-N collocations. This work is continued, for instance, by Heid and Weller (2008) and Weller and Heid (2010).

Also, Wermter and Hahn (2004) used a POS tagger and a shallow parser in order to extract collocational and idiomatic PP-V combinations by applying the limited modifiability criterion: the pairs which are frequent and in which the adjectival modifiers of the noun in the PP constituent show a lower dispersion are promoted in the significance list.[33] This method was found to perform significantly better than the co-occurrence frequency both in this particular experiment involving high-frequency PP-V pairs ($f > 10$), and in a different extraction experiment concerning high-frequency terms in English ($f > 8$) (Wermter and Hahn, 2006).

3.4.3 French

Outstanding work on lexicon-grammar carried out before computerized tools even became available (Gross, 1984) makes French one of the most studied languages in terms of distributional and transformational potential of words. Automatic extraction of collocations was first performed by Lafon (1984), and later, to a certain extent, in the framework of terminology extraction systems which deal specifically with NPs, but which apply the same extraction methodology in order to discover significant word combinations.

Thus, Lafon (1984) extracts significant co-occurrences of words from plain text by considering (directed and undirected) pairs in a collocational span and by using the z-score as an AM. The preprocessing step consists solely of detecting sentence boundaries and ruling out the functional words. The author notes that verbs rarely occur among the results, probably as a consequence of the high dispersion among different forms (Lafon, 1984, 193). Apart from the lack of lemmatization, the lack of a syntactic analysis was identified as one of the main source of problems encountered in extraction. The author concludes that any interpretation of results should be preceded by the examination of results through concordancing (Lafon, 1984, 201).

The LEXTER terminology extractor (Bourigault, 1992a,b) detects NPs by using surface analysis and making the assumption that the grammatical form of terminological units is relatively predictable. First, the frontiers of maximal-length NPs are

---

[33] More precisely, the method promotes the pairs in which the adjectival modifier has a high relative frequency.

detected based on POS information; elements like inflected verbs, pronouns, conjunctions, and prepositions (other than *de* and *à*) are considered as frontier markers.
Second, these maximal NPs (e.g., *disque dur de la station de travail*) are further
split into smaller units, like N-A (*disque dur*) and N-P-N (*station de travail*), using
shallow parsing. Up to 800 different structures are identified by the shallow parser
module (Bourigault, 1992b, 979). The author states that given the high quality of
results already obtained by relying on a surface analysis, a complete syntactic analysis is unnecessary for extracting this kind of units.

Similarly, the ACABIT system (Daille, 1994) extracts compound nouns defined
by specific patterns, e.g., N-A, N-N, N-*à*-N, N-*de*-N, N-P-D-N, by relying on
lemmatization, POS tagging and on shallow parsing with finite state automata over
POS tags. For ranking the candidate terms, the system applies a series of AMs; their
performance is tested against a domain-specific terminology dictionary and against a
gold standard manually created from the source corpus with the help of three human
experts. The evaluation study was performed on 2,200 N-*de*-(D-)N candidates (e.g.,
circuits de commande), of which 1,200 were eventually classified as compounds,
which means that a precision of 54.5% was attained. The study highlighted LLR as
the best performing AM, and several other AMs were retained as appropriate.[34] The
raw frequency of pairs was also found as a good indicator of termhood, but it has
the disadvantage of not being able to identify rare terms (Daille, 1994, 172–173). In
fact, a high number of terms were found between low-frequency pairs, with $f = 2$
(Daille, 1994, 154). LLR was eventually preferred for its good behaviour on all corpus sizes and also for promoting less frequent candidates (Daille, 1994, 173). The
author argues that by using finite state automata for extracting candidates in different
morpho-syntactic contexts without a priori limiting the distance between two words,
a better performance is achieved than by using the sliding window technique. The
author's claim is that the linguistic knowledge drastically improves the quality of
stochastic systems (Daille, 1994, 192).

Despite the fact that in these extraction systems the targeted phenomenon is quite
specific (i.e., NPs), as pointed out in Jacquemin et al. (1997), the candidates are still
subject to numerous linguistic variations, from both a morphological and syntactic
point of view. Therefore, Jacquemin et al. (1997) takes derivational morphology
information into account and defines transformational rules over syntactic patterns,
in order to achieve a broader extraction coverage. The derivational morphology
accounts for correspondences like between *modernisateur* and *modernisation*. Syntactic transformations (such as *fruits tropicaux – fruits et agrumes topicaux, stabil-
isation de prix – stabiliser leurs prix*) are inferred from a corpus by first looking at
collocations within a window of 10 words,[35] then by applying a syntactic filter based
on shallow parsing. The transformation rules are defined as regular expressions over

---

[34] The retained AMs are FAG – Fager and MacGowan coefficient, cubic MI, LLR, and frequency
(Daille, 1994, 137).

[35] The authors argue that a collocational span of 5 words as commonly used for English is insufficient for French, since French has "longer" syntactic structures (Jacquemin et al., 1997, 27).

POS tags, and are proposed on the basis of both linguistic and empirical considerations. Nonetheless, certain linguistic phenomena (such as sentential complements for nouns and long distance dependencies) cannot be accounted for by this approach, and the authors suggest that these phenomena might require a deeper syntactic analyzer (Jacquemin et al., 1997, 28).[36]

Collocation extraction proper—as opposed to term extraction—has been performed in Goldman et al. (2001) in an early version of our extractor. Candidate data involving a wide range of syntactic configurations are first identified in French texts using deep parsing, then they are ranked using LLR. Long distance dependencies can be retrieved even if subject to complex grammatical transformations. For example, some instances of verb-object collocations were detected in which the constituent items were separated by as many as 30 intervening words (Goldman et al., 2001, 62).

Also, Tutin (2004) extracts collocations using the local grammar formalism and the INTEX system (Silberztein, 1993). Furthermore, Archer (2006) detects collocations consisting of a verb and an adverb expressing the meaning of intensity for inclusion in the Papillon lexical database (e.g., *changer radicalement*, "to change radically"). The candidate pairs, which are identified from syntactically-analysed text, are ranked with the weighted MI measure introduced by Wu and Zhou (2003). Then, they are filtered on the basis of their conceptual similarity to an existing list of intensifying adverbs. A few other works exist for French, e.g., Ferret (2003), Ferret and Zock (2006),[37] that are not really concerned with collocations, but with co-occurrences (or collocations in the broader statistical sense, according to the distinction drawn in Section 2.2.3).

More recently, collocation extraction based on a dependency parser has been performed in the framework of the Antidote RX system (Charest et al., 2007). Like the parser used in Goldman et al. (2001), this parser is capable of a deep analysis, which recovers pairs in a syntactic relation even if they undergo syntactic transformations. LLR is used as an AM to score the candidate pairs, which are then manually validated and displayed in a concordancer.

3.4.4 Other Languages

Collocation extraction work has also been performed for a number of other languages, including the ones mentioned below. In most cases, the extraction is based

---

[36] The evaluation of extraction results showed that the discovery of term variants lead to a drastic improvement of recall over text simplification techniques based on stemming; in particular, the recall triples to reach 75.2%.

[37] This work (Ferret, 2003; Ferret and Zock, 2006) is focussed on topic segmentation, and relies on the extraction of co-occurrences involving A, N and V lemmas within a window of length 20. The AM used to rank co-occurrences is MI.

on the reuse of existing techniques for English or on improved versions of these techniques. The preprocessing stage is usually limited to POS tagging.

Italian. Calzolari and Bindi (1990) used the sliding window method on plain (unprocessed) text in order to identify candidates and MI for ranking.[38] Later, Basili et al. (1994) made use of parsing information, as discussed in Section 3.3.3.

Japanese. Ikehara et al. (1995) applied an improved *n*-gram method in order to extract interrupted and non-interrupted collocations.

Korean. Kim et al. (1999) relied on POS tagging and proposed an AM that takes into account the relative positions of words; they argue that an Xtract-like technique (Smadja, 1993) is inappropriate for Korean, due to the freer word order.

Chinese. Wu and Zhou (2003) and Lü and Zhou (2004) extracted Chinese collocations by using the same parse-based techniques they used for English collocations (see Section 3.4.1). Also, Lu et al. (2004) employed a method similar to Xtract (Smadja, 1993), while Huang et al. (2005) used POS information and regular expression patterns borrowed from the Sketch Engine (Kilgarriff et al., 2004). The authors pointed out that an adaptation of these patterns for Chinese is necessary in order to cope with syntactic differences and the richer POS tagset.

Dutch. Villada Moirón (2005) retrieves P-N-P and PP-V candidates (such as *in het kader van*, "in the framework of" and *in pand houden*, "keep in custody") by using POS filtering and, partly, parsing. Then she applies several AMs for ranking the candidates. In particular, she applies the log-linear model defined in Blaheta and Johnson (2001), but this is found to perform worse than traditional AMs such as LLR or χ^2 (Villada Moirón, 2005, 106).[39] Chunking was also previously considered for PP-V identification as an alternative to parsing, but it proved impractical for Dutch because of the syntactic flexibility and the relatively free word order (Villada Moirón, 2005, 162).

Czech. The work of Pecina (2005, 2008a, 2010), focused on the comparative evaluation and on the combination of AMs, made use of syntactically annotated text from a dependency treebank for Czech. In addition to dependency bigrams, surface bigrams were also extracted as adjacent, POS-filtered word pairs.

Romanian. Todiraşcu et al. (2008) used the window method on POS-tagged text and applied a series of filters on candidate data—for instance, a filter based on the distance between words, as in Smadja (1993); a LLR score filter; and a pattern matching filter that takes into account contextual information (like the presence of a second complement, or of a specific PP).

Other languages have also been tackled, some of which in the context of the multilingual development of the Sketch Engine (Kilgarriff et al., 2004).

---

[38] A standard window size of 5 words has been considered.

[39] It was also found that LLR performed best on P-N-P data (Villada Moirón, 2005, 84), and second best on PP-V data (Villada Moirón, 2005, 118) after the *salience* AM (Villada Moirón, 2005, 60).

3.5 Summary

Over the past several decades, collocation extraction has been a very active research area that has seen impressive development with respect to both the techniques used to rank candidate pairs according to their collocational strength and to the techniques of text preprocessing used to identify candidate pairs in corpora.

Collocation extraction experiments have been performed in a large number of languages, with English and German being by far the most thoroughly investigated. After presenting the foundations of the candidate ranking methodology and the most popular association measures (AMs), in this chapter we provided a review of the existing extraction work focused, in particular, on the level of linguistic analysis performed in the preprocessing stage by each extraction system. Regardless of the AMs used to rank candidates and the methods used to identify them—which may range from simple methods considering adjacent words to more complex techniques developed to recover long-range dependencies—extraction procedures are typically preceded by a preprocessing step in which linguistic analysis of the text supports identification of collocation candidates using lemmatization, POS tagging, chunking or, more rarely, parsing. Sometimes, however, candidates are selected directly from plain text, with a combinatorial procedure applied to a limited context (i.e., the sliding window method). While this basic procedure performs reasonably well for English, the strategy of widening the collocational window has proven inefficient for languages such as for German or Korean which exhibit richer morphology and a freer word order. For these languages at least, many of the studies reviewed pointed out that linguistic analysis is necessary to obtain acceptable results.

Rudimentary extraction techniques are still widely used nowadays, even for those languages for which syntactic tools are available. We believe these methods are inadequate and therefore argued that detailed linguistic analysis beyond morphological analysis or shallow techniques based on pattern matching over POS categories is necessary to obtain highly reliable extraction results. We shall show in Chapter 4, that dramatic advances in syntactic parsing now permit the shift to more reliable syntax-based approaches to collocation extraction.

Chapter 4
Syntax-Based Extraction

4.1 Introduction

As seen in the previous chapter, the past decades have witnessed intense activity in the area of collocation extraction, with a high number of languages being investigated. Most often, the extraction work has been based on statistical techniques such as hypothesis testing (see Section 3.2.4). A wide range of word association measures have been proposed, among which the log-likelihood ratio measure (LLR) (Dunning, 1993), selected by numerous researchers as one of the most useful thanks to its particular suitability to low-frequency data.

Typically, the existing collocation extraction systems rely on the linguistic preprocessing of source corpora in order to better identify the candidates whose association strength is then quantified by association measures. However, the analysis performed is most of the time limited in scope—e.g., POS tagging or shallow parsing based on pattern matching over POS categories. Many researchers have pointed out that successful collocation extraction requires a more detailed analysis, since collocations are often syntactically flexible. As shown in Example 1 below, some collocation instances can cross the boundaries of phrases and even those of clauses.[1]

(1) a. *play – role*
         It is true, we must combat the menace of alcoholism in young people, and this text successfully highlights the *role* that families, teachers, producers and retailers must *play* in this area.

     b. *article – state*
         The first *article* of the EC-Vietnam Cooperation Agreement which we signed with the government of Vietnam in 1995 *states* that respect for human rights and democratic principles is the basis for our cooperation.

     c. *important – issue*
         The *issue* of new technologies and their application in education naturally generates considerable interest and is extremely *important*.

---

[1] All the examples provided in this book are sentences actually occurring in our corpora.

Many researchers—e.g., Smadja (1993), Pearce (2002), Krenn (2000a), and Evert (2004b)—have pointed out that ideally, collocation extraction should rely on the syntactic analysis of source corpora in order to properly identify candidate pairs, since recent developments in the field of parsing now enable the analysis of large bodies of text:

> Ideally, in order to identify lexical relations in a corpus one would need to first parse it to verify that the words are used in a single phrase structure (Smadja, 1993, 151)

> with recent significant increases in parsing efficiency and accuracy, there is no reason why explicit parse information should not be used (Pearce, 2002, 1530)

> the latter two approaches [window method and POS information] are still state-of-the-art even though the advantage of employing more detailed linguistic information for collocation identification is nowadays largely agreed upon (Krenn, 2000a, 210)

> Ideally, a full syntactic analysis of the source corpus would allow us to extract the cooccurrence directly from parse trees (Evert, 2004b, 31).

As a matter of fact, recent extraction work shows a growing interest in the deep parsing of source corpora prior to the statistical computation. As could be seen from the general review from Section 3.4, a number of systems are based on parsers or on syntactically-annotated text (Lin, 1998, 1999; Pearce, 2001a; Blaheta and Johnson, 2001; Zinsmeister and Heid, 2003; Schulte im Walde, 2003; Orliac and Dillinger, 2003; Wu and Zhou, 2003; Lü and Zhou, 2004; Villada Moirón, 2005). A closer look at this work reveals, however, that the aim of fully-fledged syntax-based extraction is still far from being reached.

Lin (1998, 1999): Lin's system based on dependency parsing for English (1998; 1999) has several shortcomings. In order to reduce the number of parsing errors, only sentences containing less than 25 words are processed, and only the complete analyses are considered for extraction (Lin, 1998, 58). Parsing errors appear to cause such a serious problem, that the author has to (semi-automatically) correct them before collecting collocation candidates from the output structures. The author reports that 9.7% of the output pairs checked in a small evaluation experiment involved parsing errors (Lin, 1999, 320). This error rate is rather high, given that the pairs evaluated were taken from the top-scored results.

Wu and Zhou (2003), Lü and Zhou (2004): A similar error rate (7.85%) was reported for the top collocations extracted with the system of Wu and Zhou (2003) and Lü and Zhou (2004) based on the NLPWin parser. In fact, 157 out of 2,000 randomly selected items from the top ranked results were erroneous candidates (Lü and Zhou, 2004). Another limitation of this system is that it only takes into account three syntactic types, namely, V-O, N-A, and V-Adv, which are considered as the most important.

Villada Moirón (2005): The problem of parsing precision is also faced by the extraction system of Villada Moirón (2005). The numerous PP-attachment errors made by the Alpino parser forced the author to consider an alternative, chunk-based approach for the detection of P-N-P constructions in Dutch, and an ad-hoc method for the identification of PP-V constructions. This method consists of combining each verb and each PP in a sentence; the parser only contributes with information on phrase boundaries (Villada Moirón, 2005, 97). As in the case of Lin (1998; 1999), sentences longer than 20 words are excluded, because they are problematic for the parser.[2]

Orliac and Dillinger (2003): The parser used by Orliac and Dillinger (2003) also suffers from several limitations. Although it succeeds in identifying predicate-argument relations from passive and gerundive constructions, it is unable to handle other constructions, like relative clauses. In an experiment that evaluated the extraction coverage, relative constructions have been found responsible for nearly half of the candidate pairs missed by this collocation extraction system.

Other syntax-based systems: The main shortcoming of the extraction methods based on statistical parsing—e.g., Pearce (2001a) and Blaheta and Johnson (2001) for English, or Zinsmeister and Heid (2003) and Schulte im Walde (2003) for German—is arguably that they are difficult to apply on new corpora which are different from the ones used for training the parsers.

Given the limitations mentioned above, it is apparent that the existing extraction methodology based on parsing is not yet fully developed, and its major shortcomings are related to parsing robustness, precision, and coverage. In our opinion, the requirements that must be met by an ideal collocation extraction system based on (full) deep syntactic parsing are the following:

R1: Being able to process robustly and at acceptable speed large bodies of textual data, regardless of the domain or the characteristics of the input text (e.g., sentence length);

R2: Being able to handle the typical syntactic constructions that challenge the candidate identification process by introducing long-distance dependencies (e.g., passive, relative, interrogative and cleft constructions, but also coordinations, subordinations, parenthesized clauses, enumerations and appositions)[3];

R3: Allowing generality in what concerns the syntactic type of combinations extracted (i.e., allowing the extraction of a wide range of types, instead of being tailored to one or a few specific types);

R4: Recovering candidate pairs from partial analyses, when a complete parse tree cannot be built for a sentence;

R5: Producing better extraction results than syntax-free methods.

Among the systems reviewed above, that of Lin (1998, 1999) and Villada Moirón (2005) do not satisfy the requirement R1, concerning robustness. Regarding R2, the system of Villada Moirón (2005) uses a parser that licenses many of the syntactic constructions cited, but the extraction does not exploit the complete parser's output. It is not clear to what extent this requirement is satisfied by the statistical parsers,

---

[2] The author notes that newer versions of the parser are able to process these sentences as well.

[3] See the examples provided later, in Section 4.2.

whether they can deal or not with long-distance dependencies. As discussed above, the system of Orliac and Dillinger (2003) only satisfies R2 in part. As for R3, all extractors, except those of Lin (1998) and Schulte im Walde (2003), are limited to a maximum of three syntactic types. The system of Lin (1998) does not comply with R4, because it only extracts candidates from complete parses, and ignores the potential candidates in the partial structures. Finally, many authors reported precision problems caused by the low accuracy of parsers, which questions the fulfillment of R5 (Lin, 1998, 1999; Villada Moirón, 2005).

In the remainder of this chapter, we present the specific design choices made in our collocation extraction system, which aims to fulfill the above-stated requirements. The system relies on the syntactic parser Fips, introduced in the next section.

4.2 The Fips Multilingual Parser

Fips (Wehrli, 1997, 2004, 2007) is a deep symbolic parser developed in the past decade at the Language Technology Laboratory of the University of Geneva. It currently supports the following languages: English, French, Spanish, Italian, German, and Greek. A number of other languages are under development, including Romanian, Romansch, Russian, and Japanese.

This parser is based on an adaptation of generative grammar concepts inspired by the Minimalist Program (Chomsky, 1995), the Simpler Syntax model (Culicover and Jackendoff, 2005), and LFG – Lexical Functional Grammar (Bresnan, 2001). Each syntactic constituent is represented as a simplified X-bar structure of the form $[_{XP} \text{ L X R}]$ with no intermediate level(s), where X denotes a lexical category, like N (noun), A (adjective), D (determiner), V (verb), Adv (adverb), etc. L and R stand for (possibly empty) lists of left and right subconstituents, respectively. The lexical level contains detailed morpho-syntactic and semantic information available from the manually-built lexica: selectional properties, subcategorization information, and syntactico-semantic features that are likely to influence the syntactic analysis. Thus, the parser relies on a strong lexicalist grammar framework.

Written in Component Pascal, Fips adopts an object-oriented implementation design that enables the coupling of language-specific processing modules to a generic module. The generic module is responsible for the parser's main operations: *Project* (assignment of constituent structures to lexical entries), *Merge* (combination of adjacent constituents), and *Move* (creation of chains by linking the surface position of "moved" constituents to their "original", canonical position). This module also defines the basic data types and the features applying to all the supported languages.

The parsing algorithm proceeds in a left-to-right and bottom-up fashion, by applying at each step one of the operations enumerated above. The application of the *Merge* operation, in which a left or right subconstituent is attached to the current structure, is constrained by language-specific licensing rules such as the agreement rules. Moreover, the attachment can only be made to a node that is active, i.e., a node that accepts subconstituents. The alternatives are pursued in parallel, and several pruning heuristics are employed for limiting the search space.

Given an input sentence, the parser provides both the phrase structure representation and the interpretation of constituents in terms of arguments, stored as a predicate-argument table that is similar to LFG's f-structure. It also provides an interpretation for clitics, *wh*-elements, and relative pronouns, and creates chains linking extraposed elements to empty constituents in canonical positions. The parser is able to handle a wide range of constructions, like the ones listed in Example 2 below (Fips successfully captured the syntactic relation between the words in italics in each example):

(2)   a.   *passivization*
           I see that *amendments* to the report by Mr Méndez de Vigo and Mr Leinen have been *tabled* on this subject.

      b.   *relativization*
           The communication devotes no attention to the *impact* the newly announced policy measures will *have* on the candidate countries.

      c.   *interrogation*
           What *impact* do you expect this to *have* on reducing our deficit and our level of imports?

      d.   *cleft constructions*
           It is a very pressing *issue* that Mr Sacrédeus is *addressing*.[4]

      e.   *enumeration*
           It is to be welcomed that the Culture 2000 programme has allocated one third of its budget to *cultural*, archaeological, underwater and architectural *heritage* and to museums, libraries and archives, thereby strengthening national action.

      f.   *coordinated clauses*
           The *problem* is therefore, clearly a deeply rooted one and cannot be *solved* without concerted action by all parties.

      g.   *interposition of subordinate clauses*
           The *situation* in the regions where there have been outbreaks of foot-and-mouth disease is *critical*.[5]

      h.   *interposition of parenthesized clauses*
           Could it be on account of the regulatory *role* which this tax (which applies to international financial transactions) could *play* in relation to currencies (. . .)

      i.   *apposition*
           I should like to emphasise that the broad economic policy *guidelines*, the aims of our economic policy, do not *apply* to the euro zone alone but to the entire single European market (. . .)

(3)   This too is an issue the Convention must address.

---

[4] Note that a relative reading is also possible for this example.

[5] The subordinate clause in this example is the relative introduced by *where*.

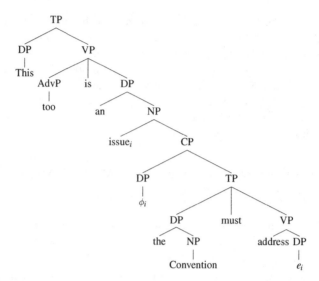

Fig. 4.1 Parse tree built by Fips for the sentence *This too is an issue the Convention must address*

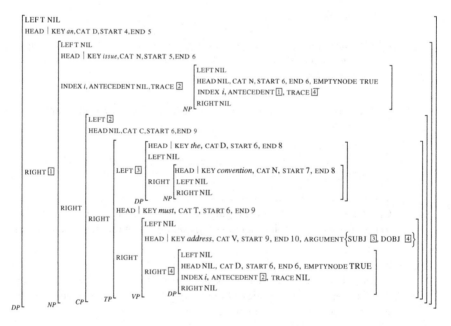

Fig. 4.2 Attribute-value matrix representation of the parser output obtained for the sentence fragment *an issue the Convention must address* from Example 3 (partial information)

Figure 4.1 illustrates the parse tree built by Fips for the sentence in Example 3, which involves a relative construction. The relative pronoun—in this case, the zero-pronoun ϕ—is linked via co-indexation (see index i) to the antecedent *issue* and to its trace denoted by the empty constituent e found in the canonical position of direct object, next to the verb *address*. A simplified representation of the parser output, corresponding to the substructure associated to the sentence fragment *an issue the Convention must address*, is shown in Figure 4.2.

Fips can robustly process large text corpora at a reasonable speed (approximately 150 tokens/s). Its precision is currently being measured in the framework of two parsing evaluation campaigns for French, namely, *EASy – Evaluation des Analyseurs SYntaxiques*[6] and *PASSAGE – Produire des Annotations Syntaxiques à Grande Echelle*.[7] For the time being, no definitive evaluation results have been made available.

4.3 Extraction Method

In this section, we introduce our syntax-based method for extracting binary collocations from text corpora. We detail the two main extraction steps that the extraction method applies, according to the general architecture of extraction systems presented in Section 3.2.2.

4.3.1 Candidate Identification

Binary collocation candidates are identified from the parse structures built by Fips as the analysis of the text goes on. In most of the similar works based on parsing, the identification is done after parsing has been completed, either by re-interpreting the textual representation of the parser's output—as in Villada Moirón (2005)—or by reading the syntactic annotations of the source corpus—as in Blaheta and Johnson (2001) and Pearce (2001a). In our method, the internal representation of syntactic structures built by the parser was used directly. The benefit for the identification process is twofold: the parse information is readily available, and it contains all the rich and complex details provided for the current analysis.

The linguistic preprocessing step is therefore not entirely separated, in our system, from the candidate identification step. The two steps alternate, as candidates are identified as soon as a sentence has been analysed by Fips. However, from an architectural point of view, the parsing and the extraction system are actually separated, and the parser Fips permits the plug-in of customized modules—such as the candidate identification module, in our case—for post-processing the analyses obtained for a sentence.

---

[6] URL: `http://www.elda.org/easy/`, accessed June, 2010.

[7] URL: `http://atoll.inria.fr/passage/`, accessed June, 2010.

Each structure returned by Fips—be it a complete analysis for a sentence, or one of the partial analyses built for subconstituents when a complete analysis is not possible—is checked for potential collocation candidates by recursively examining the head of the current phrase and its left and right subconstituents (details on the typical syntactic structure built by Fips have been provided in Section 4.2).

A collocation candidate consists of a directed pair[8] of lexical items that are syntactically related. Therefore, the main criterion for selecting a pair as a candidate is the presence of a syntactic link between the two items. In addition, in order to qualify as a valid candidate, the pair in cause must satisfy some more specific constraints.

Morphological constraints on the component items. The head lexeme X of the currently checked structure must satisfy specific constraints, depending on its category:

- noun: the lexeme must be a common noun not representing a title (e.g., *Mr.* or *General*); proper nouns are excluded.
- verb: the lexeme must be an ordinary verb; auxiliary and modal verbs are excluded (e.g., in English, *has, must*).

Syntactic constraints on candidate pairs To form a valid candidate, the head lexeme of the current structure can combine with any element of its left or right constituents, provided that the combination involves a specific syntactic relation. For instance, a noun can combine with an adjective that is the head of (one of) its left constituent(s) since they are in a head-modifier relation. Similarly, a noun can combine with an adjective dominated by a right constituent, as in Example 4 below (the right constituent of the noun is an FP, i.e., a functional phrase, or small clause). If the adjective is participial, has a passive sense, and the matrix verb is transitive, then a verb-object relation is hypothesised between the verb (*to prepare*) and the noun (*exams*).

(4) $[_{DP}$ exams$_i$ $[_{FP}$ $[_{DP}$ $e_i]$ $[_{AP}$ prepared$]]]$
     prepare – exam (verb-object)

The collocation identification procedure relies on the normalized form of the sentence as provided by Fips, in which words are assigned their base form and are considered in the canonical order (e.g., with subjects preceding verbs, and objects following them). Therefore, it can easily account for variation caused by inflection and inversion.

The candidates of type subject-verb, verb-object, and verb-preposition-noun are easily identified from the predicate-argument tables built by Fips, even if they involve long-distance dependencies. Thus, the verb-object pair *address – issue* will be identified in a straightforward way from the sentence shown in Example 3 in which the noun *issue* is extraposed, since the argument table for the verb *address* contains *issue* in the direct object position. All the computation needed

---

[8] Prepositions are also included along with noun lexemes for readability reasons.

Table 4.1 Some of the syntactic configurations accepted by our extraction system

Type	POS combination	Syntactic relation	Example
A-N	Adjective-noun	Head-modifier	*Wide range*
N-A	Noun-adjective	Head-modifier	*Work concerned*
N-N	Noun-noun	Head-modifier	*Food chain*
N-P-N	Noun-preposition-noun	Head-modifier	*Fight against terrorism*
S-V	Noun-verb	Subject-verb	*Rule apply*
V-O	Verb-noun	Verb-object	*Strike balance*
V-P-N	Verb-preposition-noun	Verb-preposition-noun	*Bring to justice*
V-adv	Verb-adverb	Head-modifier	*Desperately need*
V-P	Verb-preposition	Verb-particle	*Point out*
A-adv	Adjective-adverb	Head-modifier	*Highly controversial*
A-P	Adjective-preposition		*Concerned about*

for recovering the verb-object link (i.e., recognizing the presence of a relative construction, building its normalized form with the empty constituent e in the object position, linking e to the relative zero-pronoun ϕ and further to the antecedent *issue*, and, finally, adding *issue* to the argument table of *address*) is done by the parser beforehand.

Table 4.1 shows some of the most representative syntactic configurations currently used by our extraction system.[9] A couple of extraction examples have already been provided at the beginning of this chapter (Examples 1 and 2). They illustrate the potential of our parse-based system to detect collocation candidates even from particularly complex sentences.

Table 4.2 Examples of collocation candidates involving complex lexical items

Item 1	Complex 1	Item 2	Complex 2	Type
Ban	−	Animal testing	+	V-O
Be	−	Integral part	+	V-O
Budget surplus	+	(Of) full employment	+	N-P-N
Draw	−	Peace plan	+	V-O
Elected representative	+	(Of) people	−	N-P-N
Electronic equipment	+	(From) mobile phone	+	N-P-N
Give	−	Green light	+	V-O
Integral part	+	(Of) social life	+	N-P-N
Key point	+	Be	−	S-V
Local	−	Public transport	+	A-N
Maintain	−	Close contact	+	V-O
Promote	−	Equal opportunities	+	V-O
Protect	−	Intellectual property	+	V-O
Provide	−	added value	+	V-O
Second	−	World war	+	A-N
Strengthen	−	Rule of law	+	V-O

---

[9] Far from being exhaustive, this list is continuously evolving since many new combinations emerge as collocationally relevant as more data is processed (see also the considerations in Section 3.3.2 on the syntactic configuration of collocations).

It is also worth noting that each item in a candidate pair can in turn be a complex lexical item (e.g., a compound or a collocation). If present in the lexicon and successfully recognized by the parser, it will be considered as a unit that can participate in other collocation candidates as a single item. Several examples of long candidates identified in an English corpus are displayed in Table 4.2.

4.3.2 Candidate Ranking

For each candidate pair identified from the syntactic structures built by Fips, the extraction system stores both syntactic information and information related to its occurrence in the corpus, which enables the link back to the source documents. The following information is specified for a candidate pair:

- key1, key2: the base word form of the two lexical items;
- lex1, lex2: the number identifying the two lexical items in the parser's lexicon[10];
- type: a numerical code representing the syntactic type of the pair;
- cat1, cat2: the grammatical category of the two items;
- prep_key: the preposition, if the syntactic type contains a preposition;
- poslex1, poslex2: the linear position of the two items in the input sentence;
- source: the name of the source file;
- charlex1, charlex2: the position of the two items in the source file;
- lexicalized: a boolean value indicating if the identified pair forms a collocation that is already present in the parser's lexicon.

As indicated in Section 3.2.2 (which introduced the general architecture of an extraction system), the selected candidates are ranked with an association measure that assigns to each candidate a score reflecting its collocational strength. But before applying this measure, the candidate data is partitioned into syntactically homogeneous classes, according to the field type. This strategy is argued to have a positive impact on the ranking proposed by association measures (AMs), as their performance is sensitive to the syntactic type (Evert and Krenn, 2001).

A number of measures have been implemented in the framework of our extraction system (Seretan, 2008). Among these, we retained the log-likelihood ratio measure (LLR) (Dunning, 1993) as the default AM for our extraction experiments, this choice being both theoretically and empirically motivated.[11] However, the method described is not tailored to a specific AM.

---

[10] Thanks to parsing, the readings of a lexical item are syntactically disambiguated. It might therefore happen that two pairs that are identical in form (the key fields are the same) actually contain different lexical items.

[11] Section 3.2.5 discusses in detail the issue of choosing an appropriate AM.

Unlike most of the existing extractors, our system does not impose a frequency threshold on candidate pairs, therefore no items are a priori excluded from the initial pair sets. This decision is motivated, first, by the high number of infrequent pairs that might constitute collocations; second, by the good performance of LLR on low-frequency data; and third, by the increased tractability of our method thanks to the elimination of erroneous candidates from the very start (many extractors prune the initial set of candidates only to cope with the problem of computational complexity).

As in the case of frequency, the system sets no threshold for the LLR score, all the initial pairs being returned regardless of how high a score they obtained.[12] When LLR is not applicable to a candidate pair (this situation occurs when a value in its contingency table is 0), the pair receives by convention a minimal score (0). Also, the candidate pairs that are already present in the parser's lexicon[13] are marked as "lexicalized" and are not ranked; instead, they receive a conventional maximum score by default. In the case, the frequencies of the individual lexemes are, however, taken into account in the score computation, because they contribute to the frequency signature of other candidates (i.e., to the corpus frequencies listed in their contingency table, as explained in Section 3.2.3).

4.4 Evaluation

In this section, we present the evaluation experiments performed in order to assess the performance of the syntax-based collocation extraction method described in Section 4.3. We first provide an overview of the current state of collocation evaluation methodology, and discuss some of the main issues relevant to this topic (Section 4.4.1). Then, we introduce the evaluation method we chose (Section 4.4.2), and present the two evaluation experiments carried out (Sections 4.4.3 and 4.4.5). The differences between these experiments lie in the source corpora used for extraction, in the languages dealt with, in the level of the significance list that was investigated, and in the classification used to annotate the extraction results.

4.4.1 On Collocation Extraction Evaluation

Currently, there is no established methodology for evaluating collocation extraction systems, although some steps have recently been taken in this direction through proposals made by Krenn (2000b), Evert and Krenn (2005) and through the creation of repositories of evaluation resources (Grégoire et al., 2008).

---

[12] The selection of higher-scored pairs can be made a posteriori, according to the desired degree of confidence (see Section 3.2.4).

[13] As noted in the previous section, the system can recognise those pairs of lexemes that make up known collocations, i.e., collocations that are stored in the parser's lexicon.

Thanks to these efforts, it is now common practice for authors to assess the quality of extraction results by using measures such as precision, recall, F-measure, mean average precision, or uninterpolated average precision, borrowed from the related field of information retrieval (Krenn, 2000b; Krenn and Evert, 2001; Villada Moirón, 2005; Pecina, 2008a; Ramisch et al., 2008; Kilgarriff et al., 2010; Weller and Heid, 2010). In earlier literature, evaluation experiments were only sporadically reported. Quality measurement reports were often replaced by general statements accompanied by examples selected among the top results in the significance list, or they were based on evaluations of small amounts of data only. Exceptionally, large-scale evaluation experiments can be found in Smadja (1993), Daille (1994), and Krenn (2000b) (see the review in Section 3.4).

An evaluation experiment typically consists of the following steps:

1. The test data is selected among the results, according to a particular data design strategy.
2. Each item in the test set is classified as either positive or negative (in two-way classification tasks), or it is assigned one among several finer-grained categories (in multi-way classification tasks).[14] The classification is either manual, when it is performed by human annotators, or automatic, when gold standard resources exist that can be used as reference data.
3. The performance is computed according to the selected measures (typically, precision and recall). In task-based evaluation, the performance is computed as the impact of integrating collocation extraction results in another application, e.g., in a machine translation application.
4. Usually, performance results are interpreted in relation to a given reference. They are often contrasted against the performance of state-of-the-art systems, of previous versions of the same system, or against a baseline. In this step, statistical tests are used to check if the difference observed is significant, i.e., it is not due to chance.

A number of decisions intervene in these steps, each alternative having its own advantages and disadvantages. Below, we describe some of the most important choices that can be made in an evaluation experiment focused on collocations.

Data design strategy. Usually, the data that will be tested are selected among the top *n* results of a system, where *n* is of the order of several hundreds (Evert and Krenn, 2001; Pearce, 2002) or thousands (Krenn, 2000b).[15] This strategy corresponds to the typical usage scenario, in which users inspect the significance list item by item in order to identify lexicographically interesting results. Moreover, different frequency or score thresholds may be applied to select the test data. For instance,

---

[14] For example, in Smadja (1993), the lexicographers classified each item as N (not a good collocation), Y (good collocation), and YY (good collocation, but of lesser quality than a Y collocation).

[15] The precision computed on the top *n* results is referred to as the *n-best precision* (Evert, 2004a).

Evert and Krenn (2001) adopted a data design strategy based on frequency strata, and tested both high frequency and low frequency results. Such strategies that take into account low-frequency data are highly desirable, since, according to Zipf's law, lexical data is characterised by a high sparsity. Random sampling—used, for instance, by Smadja (1993)—has been shown to be a particularly useful strategy, because it reduces the amount of manual annotation work required (Evert and Krenn, 2005).

Nature of tested items. An important decision is whether to evaluate the identified types or tokens. As extraction systems conflate the different occurrences of a pair type when computing the joint frequencies, it seems reasonable to test types rather than tokens. This alternative has the important advantage of reducing the redundancy of the data to be tested. However, it also has drawbacks. The association between types and tokens may sometimes be wrong (for instance, in case of linguistic preprocessing errors). Annotators may only be able to look at a small number of tokens; therefore, the final classification of types on the basis of a limited number of tokens might be erroneous. Moreover, a type-based classification fails to account for more subtle distinctions, like between a literal and non-literal usage; for this purpose, a token-based classification is preferable (Cook et al., 2008; Diab and Bhutada, 2009; Fritzinger et al., 2010).

Type of classification. The manual classification of the items in the test set is time-consuming and requires multiple annotators and clear guidelines to be reliable. Moreover, it has been suggested that the judgements should be provided by experts with thorough linguistic training, rather than by non-specialists (Krenn et al., 2004; Krenn, 2008).[16] A further problem is the difficulty in interpreting the value that chance-corrected inter-annotator agreement statistics—such as κ (Cohen, 1960)—provide. While it is undoubtedly important to ensure a certain degree of agreement, it is unclear what the minimally acceptable κ value should be. Artstein and Poesio (2008) suggest that the κ threshold for ensuring annotations of reliable quality is 0.8; they acknowledge, however, that no single cutoff point is appropriate for all purposes. For the task of collocation extraction, an alternative to Cohen's κ was proposed in Krenn et al. (2004). It is based on a distinction between true and chance agreement, whereas κ assumes that the agreement is only due to chance.

The automatic classification can be seen as a more convenient alternative to manual classification. The test items are classified according to their presence in reference resources, which include: machine-readable dictionaries and terminological databases (Pearce, 2002; Daille, 1994), thesauri and lexical databases (Thanopoulos et al., 2002; Wermter and Hahn, 2006; Ramisch et al., 2008), available testbeds[17] (Pecina, 2008b). The major drawback of this solution is the low coverage of such resources, as pointed out by Daille (1994) and Justeson and

---

[16] The inter-annotator agreement achieved by non-specialised students is lower (Krenn, 2008).

[17] A number of testbeds have been released after the Shared Task for Multiword Expressions (Grégoire et al., 2008).

Katz (1995).[18] An additional problem, as explained by Evert and Krenn (2005), is the bias introduced towards a given extraction method if the resource in cause has itself been compiled using corpus-based methods. As a matter of fact, most evaluation experiments rely on judgements provided by annotators, who are, in the best case, trained linguists (Krenn et al., 2004; Pecina, 2010) or lexicographers (Smadja, 1993; Evert, 2008b; Kilgarriff et al., 2010).

4.4.2 Evaluation Method

The evaluation experiments described in this chapter compare the performance of the syntax-based collocation extraction method (introduced in Section 4.3) against a baseline represented by the sliding window method (presented later in this section). While the first method relies on syntactic information provided by the parser Fips (Wehrli, 2007), the sliding window method can be described as syntax-free. It only takes into account the linear proximity of words in text (as opposed to structural proximity), and ignores the syntactic relations in a sentence.

From a theoretical point of view, our syntax-based method is expected to perform much better (as argued in Section 3.3.3). Nonetheless, this claim must be empirically tested in an actual extraction setting, because the parsing errors may lead to more extraction noise than the one that is inherently produced by the window method. In fact, as shown in the review of syntax-based extractors (Section 4.1), the parsing errors sometimes pose a serious problem, forcing authors to perform additional pre-processing to correct the systematic mistakes (Lin, 1998, 1999), or even to discard the structural information produced by the parser and only keep information on phrase boundaries (Villada Moirón, 2005).

It is also worth mentioning that the results of the window method tend to be more accurate at the top of the significance list. This is a consequence of using AMs that promote pairs with higher frequencies. The erroneous pairs tend to appear on lower positions because of their lower co-occurrence frequency. As more and more data is processed, the n-best precision of the window method increases. If the precision reached were comparable to that of syntax-based methods and the user were only interested in the top results of an extraction system (which is rather implausible), then there would be no need for parsing. The inclusion of additional data also compensates for the long-distance pairs that are missed by the window method; thus, using a parser to capture such pairs might not be considered a necessity.[19] (Again,

---

[18] For instance, Daille (1994, 145) reported that only 300 out of the 2,200 terms tested (13.6%) were found in a reference list containing about 6,000 terms from the same domain as the source corpus, namely, that of satellite telecommunications. A similar coverage (13.4%) is reported in Justeson and Katz (1995): only 13 of the identified 97 terms are found in a dictionary containing more than 20,000 terms of the same domain. We can speculate that when the domain is not the same, the intersection is virtually insignificant.

[19] See Section 4.6 for a discussion on the effect that ignoring such long-distance pairs has on the extraction results.

this argument only holds if there is no interest in the corpus-based study of syntactic variability of collocations, but evidence from recent research work—e.g., Evert et al. (2004), Ritz (2006), Heid and Weller (2008), Weller and Heid (2010)—shows the contrary).

In both extraction methods, the same association measure—namely, log-likelihood ratio (Section 3.2.4.2)—is used in the candidate ranking step. Therefore, only the candidate identification step is different. This strategy allows us to better quantify the effect of the syntactic filtering step on the final results. In accordance with Evert and Kermes (2003), we consider that collocation extraction methods should not only be evaluated at the end of the extraction process, but separately after each extraction step. More precisely, (a) after the candidate identification step, in order to evaluate the quality of proposed candidates with a specific criterion (e.g., the grammatical well-formedness); and (b) after the candidate ranking step, in order to evaluate the quality of the extraction output in terms of collocability—and, indirectly, the efficiency of the AM used. Since the two methods use the same AM in the second extraction step, we can still compare their final results directly, and we will be able to assess the impact of the candidate identification step on the outcome.

In both experiments, we follow a data design strategy based on stratified sampling. Several fixed-size samples are drawn from the output of each method at various levels in the corresponding significance lists. Each item in the test sets is manually classified by taking into account the judgements provided by at least two judges; these are trained linguists, native or near-native[20] speakers of the language considered. The items tested represent pair types rather than pair tokens. In each experiment, a multi-way classification is performed, using a different set of categories. The items that are identically annotated by the majority of judges are associated with the dominant label (henceforth, *mark*), and are added to the reference set. The items for which no consensus is reached are discarded. The inter-annotator agreement is computed using Cohen's κ statistic (1960) when the evaluation involves two annotators, and Fleiss' κ (1981) statistic when it involves more than two annotators.

The performance of the two methods is reported by taking into account the precision obtained relative to the corresponding reference sets. The precision is computed as the percentage of true positives in the agreed-upon part of the test sets; a true positive is a pair from the reference set that was marked as a collocation. Uniterpolated average precision (Manning and Schütze, 1999) is also reported for the first experiment (the test data in the second experiments contains too few true positives to allow for a meaningful comparison). Recall, although essential in measuring the performance of extraction methods, was only assessed in a small scale experiment, mainly because of the lack of appropriate resources.

Since it is rather difficult to judge the output pairs isolated from their context—especially if they do not incorporate syntactic information, as it is the case for the window method—the annotators used a concordance tool, part of our collocation

---

[20] As explained in Chapter 2, the collocation phenomenon is more acutely perceived by near-native than by native speakers.

extraction system (Seretan et al., 2004; Seretan, 2009).[21] This tool displays the context (in the source file) of each instance of a pair type. The annotators usually referred to the first instance displayed by the tool, but, in case of doubt, they could also consult other instances. The policy adopted for judging a pair type, in case of uncertainty, was to make a decision on the basis of the majority of tokens. The grammatical information associated to a pair (i.e., the syntactic relation or POS categories involved) was required to be correct; otherwise, the pair was classified as erroneous.[22] In our opinion, referring back to the original contexts is a necessary condition for a sound evaluation of extraction results, since, as Evert and Kermes (2003) point out, a pair may seem a true positive when looked at in isolation, while in reality it may be erroneous with respect to the corpus (this is the case, for instance, of the pair *human organization* from Example 2 in Chapter 1).

The baseline considered in our experiments is the sliding window method. It was implemented as follows.

Step 1: Lemmatization. First, the source corpora are POS-tagged and lemmatized. To this end, we used the parser Fips, as in the case of our parse-based method.[23] As a consequence, the POS ambiguity is practically eliminated, since only the POS tags that are compatible with the sentence context are kept among those possible for a token.[24]

Step 2: POS-filter of lexemes. Function words and auxiliary verbs are ruled out, so that only the content words are retained (nouns, adjectives, verbs, and adverbs). Punctuation marks are retained in this step, for the purpose that is explained below (Step 3).

Step 3: Generation of candidate pairs. Candidate pairs are subsequently identified as directed combinations inside a 5 content-word window (i.e., by allowing a maximum of 4 content words in-between). In order to avoid combinations that cross sentence or clause boundaries, no punctuation marks are allowed between the two items of a pair.

---

[21] In Pecina (2010), for instance, the judges decided upon the status of a pair without referring to context.

[22] We used this strict policy because one of our objectives was to measure the quality of the candidate identification step. Yet, the correctness of grammatical information may have less relevance in practice: the mere presence of the component words in a collocation may be sufficient for lexicographers to spot it and consider it for inclusion in a lexicon. In fact, Kilgarriff et al. (2010) categorise such wrongly analysed pairs as true positives.

[23] This choice can be seen as biasing the candidate identification process, since parsing errors are reflected in the POS tags assigned. We argue, however, that the assignment of tags in case of ambiguity is more precise if done with Fips than without parsing information, and that, on the contrary, our choice makes the two methods more comparable: rather than introducing errors with another POS tagger, we would retrieve the same errors, and could more easily highlight the differences between the two extraction approaches.

[24] According to a study by Hajič (2000) cited in Section 3.3.3, about 40% of the tokens in an English text are POS-ambiguous.

Step 4: POS-filter of candidate pairs. Among all of the possible POS combinations, only those that suggest a syntactic relation have been retained, namely, N-A, A-N, N-N, N-V, and V-N, which are typically taken into account in the existing extraction systems.[25] Table 4.3 displays the corresponding syntactic configurations in our parse-based extraction method. In order to enable the comparison between the two methods, we restricted the output of our method accordingly.

Step 5: Candidate ranking. Finally, as in our method, the log-likelihood ratio (LLR) score has been computed for all the combinations obtained, after partitioning them into homogeneous sets defined by the POS pattern (no frequency threshold was applied). The aim of this partitioning is to apply LLR on syntactically homogeneous data, but since no syntactic information is available, the POS pattern was taken into account.

It is important to note that the window method implemented as described above represents a rather strong baseline against which we compare our method based on parsing. A number of choices have been made that are likely to alleviate the candidate identification process and, in particular, to increase the precision of the window method: POS disambiguation based on parsing information, elimination of pairs with interposed punctuation marks, and selection of only those pairs that suggest a grammatical relationship.

Table 4.3 POS combinations used by the window method and the corresponding syntactic configurations in the parse-based method

Window method	Parse-based method
Adjective-noun (A-N)	Adjective-noun (A-N)
Noun-adjective (N-A)	Noun-adjective (N-A)
Noun-noun (N-N)	Noun-noun (N-N), noun-preposition-noun (N-P-N)
Noun-verb (N-V)	Subject-verb (S-V)
Verb-noun (V-N)	Verb-object (V-O), verb-preposition-noun (V-P-N)

4.4.3 Experiment 1: Monolingual Evaluation

The first evaluation experiment was performed on French data from the Hansard corpus of Canadian parliamentary proceedings. It investigated the top 500 pairs returned by each of the two methods compared, i.e., the parse-based method and the sliding window method. Each pair was annotated by three trained linguists with one of the following 3 categories: *erroneous pair*, *regular pair*, and *interesting pair* (introduced later in this section).

---

[25] For instance, combinations involving an adverb have not been considered, since ignored by most window-based extraction systems.

Table 4.4 Statistics on the source data used in Experiment 1

Statistic	Value
Size (MB)	8.02
Files	112
Words	1,209,050
Tokens (words and punctuation)	1,649,914
Sentences	70,342
Average file length (sentences)	628.1
Average sentence length (tokens)	23.46
Sentences with complete parses	50,458
Percentage sentences with complete parses	71.7
Parsing speed (tokens/s)	172.2

Source data. For this experiment, a number of 112 files were chosen from the Hansard corpus that cover one month of proceedings and total slightly more than 1.2 million words. Table 4.4 provides more details about this file collection, including information available after performing the syntactic analysis with Fips in the preprocessing stage of our method.

Collocation candidates were extracted from this collection using, first, our method based on deep parsing and, second, the sliding window method which does not make use on syntactic information (as explained in Section 4.4.2). Table 4.5 presents comparative statistics on the extraction results: total number of candidate pairs extracted by the each method, token-type ratio, percentage of pairs scored (i.e., pairs for which LLR is defined),[26] and syntactic distribution of pair tokens (see also the type correspondences displayed in Table 4.3).

As can be seen, despite the strong filter applied by the window method (Steps 2 and 3 in the description from Section 4.4.2), the number of candidate pairs it generates still considerably outweighs the one of syntactically filtered candidates. This huge number leads to increased computational complexity with respect to the parse-based method, particularly insofar as the score computation is concerned.

Table 4.5 Extraction statistics for Experiment 1

	Window method	Parse-based method
Pairs extracted	1,024,887	370,932
Token-type ratio	1.8	2.5
Pairs scored (%)	99.4	83.1
Adjective-noun pairs (%)	9.6	6.7
Noun-adjective pairs (%)	12.4	17.2
Noun-noun pairs (%)	32.6	21.5
Noun-verb pairs (%)	17.0	16.4
Verb-noun pairs (%)	28.4	38.2

---

[26] LLR is not defined for those pairs that contain a 0 value in their contingency table.

Table 4.6 Number of pair tokens in the test sets from Experiment 1

Method	TS1	TS2	TS3	TS4	TS5	TS6	TS7	TS8	TS9	TS10	All
Parsing	12,147	4,498	3,435	2,507	2,183	1,872	1,536	1,176	1,404	1,020	31,778
Window	17,241	5,586	4,696	3,009	3,195	2,872	2,739	2,297	1,767	1,920	45,322

Test data. This experiment compares the top 500 result items proposed by each method, where an item consists of a pair type (as opposed to a pair instance, or token). We split the 500 pairs into 10 test sets of 50 pairs each. Table 4.6 lists the total number of pair tokens in each test set.

The total number of pair types evaluated in this experiment is 1,000. Appendix D.1 displays the entire test data and Appendix D.1 displays, in addition, the annotations produced by the three judges for these data.

Annotation. In this first experiment, each pair tested was classified by annotators as either *erroneous*, *regular*, or *interesting* combination. The first two labels correspond to false positives, while the third denotes, by convention, a true positive. Each label is described below.

– Label 0: *erroneous pair* – a pair in which an item has a wrong POS category (e.g., *entreprendre petite*[27]), or in which the items are not syntactically related (e.g., *président de élection*, extracted from a context like *je voudrais donc saisir cette occasion pour féliciter le Président de son élection*);
– Label 1: *interesting pair* – a grammatically well-formed pair which is worth storing in the lexicon, since it constitutes (part of) a multi-word expression, be it compound, collocation, idiom, named entity, etc. (e.g., *prendre la parole*, *emploi à long terme*);
– Label 2: *regular pair* – a pair which is grammatically well-formed, but uninteresting from a lexicographic point of view, since it is completely regular and allows paradigmatic variation (e.g., *économie canadienne*).

As collocations are notoriously difficult to distinguish from other subtypes of multi-word expressions (McKeown and Radev, 2000) and there are no objective criteria that can be applied for this task (see Section 2.5), we first used this coarse-grained classification, which does not separate collocations from other multi-word expression (MWE) pairs. As in (Choueka, 1988) and (Evert, 2004b) (see definitions in Appendix B), we consider that the dominant feature of collocations is that they are unpredictable for non-native speakers and therefore have to be stored in a lexicon.

Reference data. The performance of the two methods in terms of grammatical and MWE precision is reported by taking into account the annotations produced by the human judges. As mentioned before, in this experiment a team of three

---

[27] This pair has been erroneously extracted from the phrase *petite entreprise* (see the error analysis in Section 4.5).

judges evaluated the output of each method. The team was different for each method. The reference sets included those items in each test set that received a consistent annotation from at least 2 annotators.[28] The reference label assigned to a pair (its mark) was the dominant label. The reference set built from the output of the parse-based method contains 496 items overall, while the one corresponding to the window method contains 488 items.

Table 4.7 displays the inter-annotator agreement for each of the 10 test sets considered. The first two rows show the raw agreement, computed as the percentage of pairs on which at least two annotators agreed; the next two lines show the raw agreement computed as the ratio of pairs on which all annotators agreed; and the last two rows report the Fleiss' κ values of chance-corrected agreement. *Fleiss' κ* (Fleiss, 1981) is a measure of chance-corrected inter-annotator agreement that applies to more than two raters. Its computation is, in principle, similar to that of Cohen's κ statistic (Cohen, 1960) (described in Section 4.4.5), which quantifies the agreement between two raters; the same scale is used to interpret the results. The overall Fleiss' κ, computed on the entire test data—when the 10 test sets are considered altogether—is 0.39 for the parse-based method and 0.50 for the window method. According to the interpretation scale, the agreement among the three annotators can be considered as *fair* in the first case and *moderate* in the second.

These agreement results are in line with those obtained by similar studies—for instance, Pecina (2010) reports a comparable Fleiss' κ value (0.49) for three annotators. The results show that despite the relatively rough classification used, there are still numerous cases of ambiguity, in which one category cannot be easily distinguished from another. For instance, the distinction between multiword expressions and regular combinations is particularly difficult to draw.

In fact, if we leave out the cases in which a pair was annotated by at least one judge as erroneous, we end up with 198 cases of ambiguous pairs in the output of the parse-based method. From these, 107 pairs were considered as MWE by the majority of judges, while the other judge considered them as regular; for the other 91, the opposite holds. In the output of the window method, there are 135 such pairs, divided into 86 of the first type (MWEs with tendency towards regularity) and 49 of the second type (regular combinations with MWE tendency).

Table 4.7 Agreement statistics for the test sets in Experiment 1: raw agreement and Fleiss' κ

	Method	TS1	TS2	TS3	TS4	TS5	TS6	TS7	TS8	TS9	TS10	Avg
Raw-majority (%)	Parsing	98	98	100	100	100	100	98	98	100	100	99.2
Raw-majority (%)	Window	100	96	100	98	100	96	96	98	96	96	97.6
Raw-unanimity (%)	Parsing	68	62	54	58	38	54	54	60	56	68	57.2
Raw-unanimity (%)	Window	58	58	64	56	56	66	50	54	58	36	55.6
Fleiss' κ	Parsing	0.42	0.39	0.27	0.35	0.18	0.37	0.37	0.42	0.40	0.56	0.37
Fleiss' κ	Window	0.34	0.44	0.51	0.50	0.53	0.62	0.45	0.49	0.54	0.33	0.47

---

[28] The same strategy is used, for instance, in Daille (1994).

We provide several examples of such ambiguous pairs below (more examples can be found by consulting the annotations in Appendix D.1).[29]

- MWEs with tendency towards regularity: *attention particulier, communauté international, consentement unanime, créer emploi, développement de ressource, dire mot, exploitation forestier, exprimer point de vue, faire travail, grand nombre, grave problème, lésion grave, membre de famille, même chose, personne handicapé, remettre à travail, ressource naturel, retirer troupe, seuil pauvreté, vie humain, vote libre*;
- regular combinations with MWE tendency: *an prochain, argent de contribuable, construction de pont, corriger situation, déposer rapport, dernier année, déve-loppement régional, fin de guerre, opposition officiel, présidente suppléant, processus de consultation, programme établi, proposer amendement, relation de travail, représentant élu, situation financier.*

4.4.4 Results of Experiment 1

Table 4.8 shows the evaluation results obtained in the experiment described in Section 4.4.3, for each of the 10 test sets considered; the same results are graphically presented in Appendix D.2. The performance is reported both in terms of grammaticality and MWE-hood. Grammatical precision and MWE precision are computed as shown in (4.1) and (4.2), respectively. The computation takes into account the mark[30] of the agreed-upon items in each test set: 0 = *erroneous pair*, 1 = *interesting pair*, and 2 = *regular pair* (see the description in Section 4.4.3). Appendix D.2 also displays the precision lines for the two methods on the entire test data.

$$Grammatical\ precision\ for\ TS_i = \frac{number\ of\ items\ in\ TS_i\ with\ mark \neq 0}{number\ of\ items\ in\ TS_i\ having\ a\ mark}$$

(4.1)

$$MWE\ precision\ for\ TS_i = \frac{number\ of\ items\ in\ TS_i\ with\ mark = 1}{number\ of\ items\ in\ TS_i\ having\ a\ mark}$$

(4.2)

Table 4.8 Evaluation results for Experiment 1: grammatical precision and MWE precision

Measure	Method	TS1	TS2	TS3	TS4	TS5	TS6	TS7	TS8	TS9	TS10	Avg
P (grammatical)	Window	92.0	84.0	82.0	72.0	72.0	78.0	62.0	80.0	74.0	68.0	76.4
	Parsing	100.0	95.9	100.0	98.0	100.0	98.0	100.0	100.0	100.0	98.0	99.0
P (MWE)	Window	76.0	68.8	70.0	53.1	56.0	43.8	50.0	57.1	50.0	43.8	56.9
	Parsing	73.5	73.5	74.0	74.0	54.0	68.0	53.1	63.3	62.0	64.0	65.9

---

[29] Note that the pairs contain lemmas rather than word forms.

[30] Recall from Section 4.4.2 that the mark represents the dominant label of an annotated pair.

Table 4.9 Evaluation results for Experiment 1: uninterpolated average precision for the top 500 results

Measure	Window method	Parse-based method
UAP (grammatical)	83.4	97.7
UAP (MWE)	67.3	70.7

In addition, on the total test data, the uninterpolated average precision, UAP (Manning and Schütze, 1999) is computed for each method. This measure has the advantage of reflecting, at the same time, the quality of the ranking proposed. UAP is the average of precision values computed at each point in the output list where a true positive is found. Among two methods that return the same number of true positives, the one that ranks the true positives on upper positions is better. The UAP values obtained in our experiment are shown in Table 4.9.

As the results show, the method based on parsing clearly outperforms the standardly used window method. On the 10 test sets extracted from the top of the significance lists, the parse-based method is on average 22.6% better in terms of grammaticality. Syntactic parsing leads to a drastic reduction in error rate, from 23.6% to only 1%. As hypothesized in Section 4.4.2, the very first results of the window method are also quite acceptable. On average, 86% of the pairs in the first 3 sets (i.e., the top 150 pairs) are grammatical. But on the remaining test sets, the average drops to 72.3%. As can be seen in the figures from Appendix D.2, the precision line of the window method shows a clear decay, whereas that of the parse-based method remains stable at an optimal level of 99–100%. The average precision of the parse-based method on the 10 test sets is 99%. The difference in the grammatical precision is statistically significant (at $\alpha = 0.001$).

As for the MWE precision, the parse-based method is on average by 9.1% better than the window method on the 10 test sets considered. This means that parsing contributes to the discovery of a higher number of MWEs (i.e., potential collocations). Surprisingly, the window method performs comparatively well on the first test sets considered, corresponding to the top 150 items in the significance list. With an average of 71.6% for the first 3 sets, the precision of the window method reaches a level comparable to that of the parse-based method (73.7%), and is even slightly higher on the first set. The difference between the two methods is not statistically significant on this part of the test data; only after the first 150 pairs it becomes significant (at $\alpha = 0.05$). On the remaining sets, the MWE precision of the window method decreases to an average of 50.5%, while the precision of the parse-based method decreases more slowly and achieves an average of 62.6%.

Overall (when the union of the 10 test sets is considered for each method), there are 278 pairs that were marked by annotators as MWE for the window method, and 327 for the parse-based method; similarly, 382 pairs are grammatical in the case of the window method, and 491 in that of the parse-based method. Therefore, parsing helped discover 1.18 times more MWEs than the window method, and retrieved 1.29 times more grammatical results.

The conclusion that can be drawn from Experiment 1 is that, in accordance with the theoretical expectations and despite the challenges posed by parsing large amounts of unrestricted text, a syntax-based approach to collocation extraction is indeed worth pursuing, as it leads to a substantial improvement in the quality of results. The difference with the window method widens particularly after the very first results. In our experiment performed on a corpus of about 1.2 million words, the difference was significant after the top 150 pairs in the significance list. It is also worth mentioning here that the method against which we compared the syntax-based method represents a strong baseline, since the standard window method was enhanced through a series of design choices that tend to boost its performance (as discussed in Section 4.4.2).

A closer examination of the pairs in the reference sets built by taking into account the annotations produced by the judges revealed that there are 38 pairs that were inconsistently annotated among the pairs tested for each method. For instance, in TS1 (shown in Appendix D.1), the following pairs received inconsistent marks: *gouvernement fédéral, président suppléant, vote libre*. The 38 cases include 14 pairs labeled as *interesting* in the reference set of the parse-based method, and as *regular* in that of the window method. Vice versa, 24 pairs were found in the opposite situation. This means that a slight advantage was given to the window method. If the cases of ambiguity were settled, an even higher difference in MWE precision might be observed in favour of the parse-based method. The inconsistencies were due to the fact that the teams of judges that annotated the output of the two methods were different. At the end of the annotation process, we did not check for inter-team inconsistencies, but only for intra-annotator inconsistencies—that is, the pairs labeled differently by the same annotator were solved by that annotator.

Nevertheless, we attempted to solve the 38 disagreements by assigning the overall dominant label to a pair, i.e., the most frequent among the 6 labels produced by the two teams of judges in total. Our attempt only succeeded in a minority of cases, namely, 6 of 38. Therefore, the impact on the reported results is very little. For the majority of cases, there was a perfect balance among the labels assigned: 3 judges chose the label *interesting pair* and the other 3 judges the label *regular pair*. A few examples of pairs in this situation are: *ministre chargé, payer impôt, réduire déficit, réduire dépense, région rural, répondre à question, solution à problème*.

This result confirms once again the difficulty in distinguishing MWEs from regular, fully-productive combinations. Yet, this is only a preliminary step in performing a more collocation extraction in-depth evaluation.

4.4.5 Experiment 2: Cross-Lingual Evaluation

In the second evaluation experiment, a finer-grained classification of the result pairs was provided, with respect to the first experiment. The classification was performed by teams of two judges (trained linguists), and considered the following 6 categories: *erroneous pair, regular pair, named entity, collocation, compound*, and *idiom*. In addition, the experiment investigated multiple levels of the significance lists. It was performed on a dataset in 4 languages—French, English, Spanish and Italian—taken from the Europarl parallel corpus (Koehn, 2005).

Table 4.10 Statistics on the source data used in Experiment 2

Statistic	English	French	Italian	Spanish
Size (MB)	21.4	23.7	22.9	22.7
Files	62	62	62	62
Words	3,698,502	3,895,820	3,829,767	3,531,796
Tokens (words and punctuation)	4,158,622	4,770,835	4,134,549	4,307,360
Sentences	161,802	162,671	160,906	172,121
Average file length (sentences)	2609.7	2623.7	2595.3	2776.1
Average sentence length (tokens)	25.7	29.3	25.7	25.0
Sentences with complete parses	92,778	94,100	67,276	87,859
Percentage sentences with complete parses	57.3	57.8	41.8	51.0
Parsing speed (tokens/s)	96.1	113.9	138.1	162.0

Source data. A number of 62 parallel files were chosen from the Europarl corpus, for each of the four languages that were supported by the parser at the time the experiment was carried out. These files correspond to the complete 2001 collection of parliamentary proceedings and total between 3.5 and 3.9 million words per language. More detailed statistics on this corpus are presented in Table 4.10. Table 4.11 presents the same comparative statistics on the extraction results as in Experiment 1: the number of candidate pairs (tokens) extracted by each method, the token-type ratio for pairs, the percentage of pairs scored, and the syntactic distribution of pair tokens. The correspondences between the syntactic configurations used in the first method and the POS combinations used in the second are specified in Table 4.3.

Table 4.11 Extraction statistics for Experiment 2

Statistic	Method	English	French	Italian	Spanish
Pairs extracted	Window	3,055,289	3,131,272	3,463,757	3,204,916
	Parsing	851,500	988,918	880,608	901,224
Token-type ratio	Window	2.1	2.2	2.5	2.4
	Parsing	2.6	3.0	2.6	2.9
Pairs scored (%)	Window	99.7	99.7	99.9	99.9
	Parsing	96.7	97.4	97.1	98.0
Adjective-noun pairs (%)	Window	15.0	10.9	11.5	11.3
	Parsing	21.7	6.7	11.8	10.1
Noun-adjective pairs (%)	Window	9.6	14.8	14.1	13.9
	Parsing	1.4	23.9	22.3	21.5
Noun-noun pairs (%)	Window	33.8	33.7	30.5	32.0
	Parsing	23.6	27.7	23.5	22.4
Noun-verb pairs (%)	Window	16.6	14.8	16.8	15.7
	Parsing	14.4	4.4	14.1	12.5
Verb-noun pairs (%)	Window	25.0	25.8	27.1	27.1
	Parsing	38.9	37.3	28.3	33.6

Table 4.12 Number of pair tokens in the test sets from Experiment 2

Language	Method	TS1	TS2	TS3	TS4	TS5	All
English	Parsing	16,215	1,030	226	185	88	17,744
	Window	27,960	770	224	270	81	29,305
French	Parsing	19,912	647	411	233	67	21,270
	Window	33,232	363	246	212	137	34,190
Italian	Parsing	28,935	702	362	80	91	30,170
	Window	46,884	480	371	171	139	48,045
Spanish	Parsing	25,638	866	348	265	102	27,219
	Window	31,462	353	430	194	121	32,560

Test data. For each of the 4 extraction languages, the performance of the two methods was evaluated on 5 different test sets. Each test set contains 50 contiguous items (pair types) situated at different levels in the significance lists: 0 (top), 1, 3, 5 and 10%. Table 4.12 displays the number of pair tokens in each test set. Overall, a number of 2000 pair types have been evaluated in this experiment. The full test data is listed in Appendix E.2, and the annotations produced by the judges are shown in Appendix E.1.

The levels chosen for creating the test sets are not as small as they might seem, because they refer to pair types rather than to pair tokens; the corpus processed is rather large; and no frequency threshold was applied to the candidate pairs. At a first sight, it might seem unfair to take into account relative positions rather than absolute positions in our data design strategy. We argue, however, that our comparison is meaningful since the test sets built as described above contain comparable frequency counts (as can be seen in Appendix E.2).

Annotation. Compared to Experiment 1, this evaluation experiment aims at a more precise measurement of the performance of the two methods in terms of their potential to retrieve collocations. It attempts to distinguish collocations from other multi-word expressions, therefore the general category of MWE (*interesting pair*) is further split into 4 more specific categories. Each item in the test set is associated by annotators with one of the following labels:

Label 0: *erroneous pair* – same interpretation as in Experiment 1, that is, POS error or syntactically unrelated words (e.g., the "A-N" pair *gross domestic* extracted from a sentence like *We have a budget surplus of nearly 5% of our* gross domestic *product*);

Label 1: *regular pair* – same interpretation as in Experiment 1, i.e., a pair that is grammatically correct, but uninteresting from a lexicographic point of view, since it is completely regular and allows paradigmatic variation (e.g., *next item*);

Label 2: *named entity* – a grammatically well-formed pair that constitutes (part of) a proper noun (e.g., *European Commission*);

Label 3: *collocation* – a grammatically well-formed pair that constitutes (part of) a collocation, in the acceptation we adopted in Section 2.6: the meaning of headword is preserved; the collocate typically combines with the headword, while paradigmatic variation is usually not allowed (e.g., *play role*);

Label 4: *compound* – a grammatically well-formed pair that constitutes (part of) a compound word, i.e., a combination that is inseparable and acts like a single lexeme; (e.g., *great deal*, part of *a great deal*);

Label 5: *idiom* – a grammatically well-formed pair that constitutes (part of) an expression whose meaning is opaque or figurative; the meaning of the headword is not preserved (e.g., *hit nail*, part of *to hit the nail on the head* which means "to be right about something").

Reference data. The 5 test sets extracted from the output of the two methods for each language were evaluated by 4 teams of two judges (one team per language). Intra-annotator disagreements, i.e., inconsistent annotations for the same annotator, were identified and solved. Only the items that were identically annotated by both members of a team were included in the reference set. Overall, 1,437 out of the 2,000 pairs that were evaluated satisfy this condition: 650 for the parse-based method, and 787 for the window method. Table 4.13 displays the agreement statistics for each test set. The first two rows show the raw agreement, defined as the percentage of pairs on which both annotators agreed. The last two rows display the value of the Cohen's κ statistic of chance-corrected inter-annotator agreement.[31]

The κ *statistic* (Cohen, 1960) is a measure of agreement that tries to factor out the agreement due to chance. It is computed according to the formula in Equation (4.3), where P_o is the observed proportion of agreement and P_e is the expected proportion of agreements due to chance. The denominator corresponds to the level of agreement achievable above chance $(1 - P_e)$, and the nominator to the level of agreement actually achieved above chance $(P_o - P_e)$.

$$\kappa = \frac{P_o - P_e}{1 - P_e} \tag{4.3}$$

Table 4.13 Agreement statistics for the test sets in Experiment 2: raw agreement and κ score

	Method	TS1	TS2	TS3	TS4	TS5	TS1	TS2	TS3	TS4	TS5
				English					Spanish		
Raw (%)	Parsing	86	66	48	70	62	56	64	52	56	50
	Window	88	90	86	80	82	66	84	74	80	72
κ	Parsing	0.80	0.40	0.23	0.51	0.44	0.38	0.45	0.28	0.34	0.21
	Window	0.83	0.82	0.72	0.61	0.67	0.54	0.54	0.41	0.54	0.49
				French					Italian		
Raw	Parsing	74	62	62	54	70	74	78	70	74	72
	Window	70	78	78	84	70	70	82	78	84	78
κ	Parsing	0.63	0.41	0.42	0.24	0.51	0.65	0.67	0.51	0.62	0.54
	Window	0.60	0.52	0.56	0.72	0.47	0.61	0.53	0.44	0.53	0.60

---

[31] The κ values are slightly divergent from those reported, on the same annotation data, in our previous publications (Seretan, 2008; Seretan and Wehrli, 2009). This is because we previously used a κ calculator that implemented a weighted version of Cohen's κ.

The chance agreement P_e is computed as follows. First, for each label l, the chance-agreement on that label is computed by assuming that the choices made by the two annotators are independent. If $trials$ represents the total number of items annotated, the chance-agreement on label l is:

$$P_{el} = \frac{total\ of\ labels\ l\ for\ judge\ A}{trials} \times \frac{total\ of\ labels\ l\ for\ judge\ B}{trials} \quad (4.4)$$

Then, P_e is considered as the sum of chance-expected agreements for all labels:

$$P_e = \sum_i P_{ei} \quad (4.5)$$

The κ values usually lie in the interval [0, 1], with κ values of 1 indicating a perfect inter-annotator agreement, and κ values of 0 indicating agreement equivalent to chance. The following conventional scale is used to interpret κ values (Landis and Koch, 1977):

- $0 \leq \kappa < 0.2$ - *slight* agreement;
- $0.2 \leq \kappa < 0.4$ - *fair* agreement;
- $0.4 \leq \kappa < 0.6$ - *moderate* agreement;
- $0.6 \leq \kappa < 0.8$ - *substantial* agreement;
- $0.8 \leq \kappa < 1$ - *almost perfect* agreement.

As far as our experiment is concerned, the rather mixed κ values obtained (Table 4.13) seem to highlight the difficulty of the classification task, particularly on the pairs with a lower frequency. From the 40 test sets, the agreement is *almost perfect* on 3 test sets, *substantial* on 10 sets, *moderate* on 21 sets, and *fair* on the remaining 6 sets. Given the small size of a test set (50 items) and the well-known shortcomings of the κ statistics, we chose not to discard any test set, even for lower values of κ. Lower κ values were found to originate in repeated disagreements of the same type (i.e., when two labels are systematically mixed up by the two annotators). The κ statistic drastically penalizes high values situated outside the main diagonal in the confusion matrix, even if most of the other cases are agreed upon. On the whole annotations set (when all test sets for both methods are considered together), the raw agreement is 71.9% and the κ value is 0.61, which indicates a *substantial* inter-annotator agreement overall.

4.4.6 Results of Experiment 2

Table 4.14 displays the comparative evaluation results obtained on the 5 test sets—corresponding to 5 different levels in the significance list—that were considered for each language. A graphical representation of these results is provided in Appendix E.2.

As in Experiment 1, the precision is computed relative to the corresponding reference set, i.e., the pairs in the test set that were identically annotated by both

Table 4.14 Evaluation results for Experiment 2: grammatical precision, MWE precision, and collocational precision

Measure	Method	TS1	TS2	TS3	TS4	TS5	TS1	TS2	TS3	TS4	TS5
		English					Spanish				
P (grammatical)	Parsing	97.7	97.0	100.0	88.6	71.0	100.0	96.9	92.3	92.9	84.0
	Window	86.4	35.6	32.6	25.0	36.6	72.7	9.5	13.5	15.0	27.8
P (MWE)	Parsing	67.4	75.8	66.7	31.4	25.8	71.4	40.6	46.2	35.7	16.0
	Window	47.7	15.6	7.0	12.5	4.9	54.5	7.1	10.8	12.5	16.7
P (collocation)	Parsing	41.9	69.7	58.3	31.4	16.1	39.3	31.3	42.3	32.1	16.0
	Window	31.8	11.1	7.0	10.0	4.9	36.4	7.1	10.8	12.5	16.7
		French					Italian				
P (grammatical)	Parsing	100.0	93.5	83.9	100.0	65.7	94.6	87.2	94.3	67.6	75.0
	Window	74.3	17.9	20.5	33.3	28.6	77.1	17.1	10.3	11.9	28.2
P (MWE)	Parsing	67.6	45.2	38.7	25.9	5.7	78.4	38.5	37.1	29.7	13.9
	Window	54.3	10.3	10.3	11.9	2.9	51.4	4.9	2.6	2.4	15.4
P (collocation)	Parsing	45.9	41.9	35.5	22.2	5.7	32.4	28.2	37.1	29.7	5.6
	Window	34.3	10.3	10.3	11.9	2.9	22.9	4.9	2.6	2.4	12.8

annotators in a team. In addition to the grammatical precision defined as in (4.1), we compute the MWE precision and the collocational precision on a test set TS_i as follows (recall that the annotation categories are: 0 = *erroneous pair*, 1 = *regular pair*, 2 = *named entity*, 3 = *collocation*, 4 = *compound*, and 5 = *idiom*):

$$MWE\ precision\ for\ TS_i = \frac{number\ of\ items\ in\ TS_i\ with\ mark \geq 2}{number\ of\ items\ in\ TS_i\ having\ a\ mark} \tag{4.6}$$

$$Collocational\ precision\ for\ TS_i = \frac{number\ of\ items\ in\ TS_i\ with\ mark = 3}{number\ of\ items\ in\ TS_i\ having\ a\ mark} \tag{4.7}$$

This means that we combine the last 4 annotation categories (*named entity, collocation, compound* and *idiom*) into a single category in order to report the MWE precision, as in Experiment 1.

The results obtained are in line with those of Experiment 1 conducted on French data. The method based on parsing performs better than the window method, for all the languages and all the parameters considered: grammatical, collocational and MWE precision. The benefit of using syntactic information for collocation extraction is therefore confirmed on a different, larger corpus[32] and for 4 different languages—English, French, Spanish, and Italian.

The parse-based method was found more precise at all the levels in the output list that were investigated, namely, 0, 1, 3, 5, and 10%. In terms of grammaticality, the precision line remains stable for the parse-based method on the first 4 levels (i.e.,

---

[32] This corpus is on average 3.1 times bigger than the corpus used in Experiment 1.

up to 5% of the significance list) at a value situated above 90% in most of the cases, and the average value on all languages for these levels is 92.9%. Then on the last level (10%), it shows a visible decay around the value of 70% (the average on all languages being 73.9%).

As for the window method, the good performance for the top level (0%) observed in Experiment 1 is confirmed in this experiment as well. An average grammatical precision of 77.6% is obtained on the first test set for all languages; the average for the parse-based method is 98.1%).[33] However, on the next four levels, the grammatical precision drops considerably, to only 22.7% on average. This means that 4 pairs out of 5 are actually extraction noise in the output of the window method. On the contrary, the average grammatical precision achieved with parsing on these levels is 86.9%. As can be seen from Table 4.15, on average we can report a difference of 20.5% on the first level investigated, and of 62.4% on the next four levels, in favour of the parse-based method.

A similar pattern is observed for the other two precision parameters, the MWE precision and the collocational precision (Table 4.15). On the first level, the performance of the window method approaches that of the parse-based method. However, for English and Italian, the difference is statistically significant. Then on the next levels, the performance of both methods decreases. While the average precision of the parse-based is above 30%, the window method performs very poorly, below 10%.

When the union of all test sets for all languages is considered, a total of 577 grammatical pairs are found among the 650 agreed upon for the parse-based method (that correspond to an overall precision of 88.8%), and only 261 among the 787 agreed upon for the window method (33.2%). Also, there are 281 pairs marked as MWE in the output of the first method (43.2% of the agreed pairs), and 135 in that of the second (17.2% of the agreed pairs). As for collocations, the parse-based methods discovers 214 of them (32.9% of the agreed pairs), and the window method only 101 (12.8%). All the differences observed are statistically significant.

Finally, a look at the disagreements observed in the annotation data (Table 4.16)[34] revealed that collocations are most often mixed up with regular

Table 4.15 Average precision values for the two methods (on all languages)

	Gram.			MWE			Colloc.		
	All	TS1	TS2-5	All	TS1	TS2-5	All	TS1	TS2-5
Parsing	88.8	98.1	86.9	43.2	71.2	35.8	32.9	39.9	31.4
Window	33.2	77.6	22.7	17.2	52.0	9.2	12.8	31.4	8.6
Parsing–window	55.6	20.5	64.2	26.1	19.2	26.6	20.1	8.5	22.8
Parsing/window	2.7	1.26	3.82	2.5	1.37	3.88	2.6	1.27	3.64

---

[33] The numbers in Experiment 1 were quite similar, i.e., 76.4% vs. 99.0% for the top 500 pairs.

[34] Disagreements involving erroneous pairs are not discussed here, since they are not linguistically relevant.

Table 4.16 Confusion matrix for the annotations in Experiment 2 (partial)

	Regular pair	Named entity	Collocation	Compound	Idiom
Regular pair	422	–	–	–	–
Named entity	6	26	–	–	–
Collocation	222	2	315	–	–
Compound	51	11	63	64	–
Idiom	7	0	11	5	11

combinations, followed by compounds and, to a lesser extent, by idioms. In fact, the largest fraction of the total disagreement cases represents pairs that are labeled as collocation by one annotator and as regular combinations by the other. These make up 39.4% of the 563 total disagreements for both methods (222/563). The confusion between collocations and compounds is responsible for another 11.2% of the total disagreements between annotators (63/563).

Several examples of such disagreements are presented below:

- disagreements between collocation and regular combination: *achieve turnover, affected area, animal product, definitive solution, frightening statistic, have initiative, honourable member, main priority, member of family, partnership agreement, present system, religion conscience, scientific assessment, support process* (English), *beneficiar de amnistía, explotación agrario, iniciativa concreto, objetivo cuantitativo, mostrar voluntad, practicar tortura, puesto de trabajo, región periférico* (Spanish), *argent public, associer à remerciement, changement climatique, commercialiser produit, facteur essentiel, flagrant lacune, niveau dans hiérarchie, organiser séminaire* (French), *caso particolare, combattere contraffazione, rinnovare appello, sicurezza alimentare* (Italian);
- disagreements between collocation and compound: *civil society, freight container, sea fleet* (English), *agente económico, entendimiento mutuo, estado miembro, interesado principal, potencia extranjero* (Spanish), *ampoule électrique, mode de vie, pays candidat, parlementaire européen, salaire minimum* (French), *diritto di uomo, peggiore ipotesi, processo decisionale* (Italian);
- disagreements between collocation and idiom: *cruel shortage, cut speaker, open door, remove breeding-ground* (English) *avoir lieu, page douloureux, revêtir importance* (French), *quadro completare, riprendere filo* (Italian);
- disagreement between collocation and named entity: *parti conservateur* (French), *emisfero sud* (Italian).

4.5 Qualitative Analysis

In this section, we extend the evaluation presented in Section 4.4 with a detailed qualitative analysis of the results obtained, in order to reveal the possible sources of errors, to compare the relative rankings proposed, and to measure recall at instance-level for the two methods compared. Our analysis will refer to data from both evaluation experiments performed.

4.5.1 Error Analysis

4.5.1.1 Experiment 1

Among the top 500 results returned by the parse-based method in Experiment 1 (Section 4.4.3), only 5 pairs were annotated as erroneous: *entreprendre petite* (rank 51), *faible revenir* (rank 84), *entreprendre moyenne* (rank 200), *ministre de ancien* (rank 257), and *président de élection* (rank 462). These false positives concern parsing errors caused exclusively by the syntactic ambiguity of source sentences. The analysis of their instances in the corpus showed that in 4 cases, the ambiguity is generated by the possibility to interpret a noun as the past participle of a verb (e.g., *entreprise*)[35], and an adjective as a noun (e.g., *faible*).[36] Thus, the A-N pairs *petite entreprise*, *moyenne entreprise*, *faible revenu* were analysed as V-O pairs in contexts like those shown in Example 5. The nouns (*entreprise, revenu*) were interpreted as past principles of the verbs (*entreprendre, revenir*), and the adjectives as their direct objects (*petite, moyenne*), or subjects (*faible*).

(5)   a. *entreprendre petite*
          En tant que patron de *petite entreprise* (. . .)

       b. *entreprendre moyenne*
          afin de réduire le déficit et favoriser le développement des petites et *moyennes entreprises*

       c. *faible revenir*
          les programmes de logements sociaux permettent d'améliorer les conditions de vie de familles à *faible revenu*

The sentence in Example 6 contains an instance of the incorrect pair *ministre de ancien*. Here, *anciens* was interpreted as the head of the noun phrase *Anciens combattants*, instead of adjectival modifier for the actual head, *combattants*.

(6)   *ministre de ancien*
      ministre de la Défense nationale et *ministre des Anciens* combattants

As for the last erroneous pair (*président de élection*), the source of ambiguity was the PP-attachment: in contexts like the one shown in Example 7, the phrase *de son élection* was interpreted by the parser as a right constituent attached to the noun *Président* instead of the verb (in this case, *féliciter*).

(7)   *président de élection*
      je voudrais donc saisir cette occasion pour féliciter le *Président* de son *élection*

Both alternatives are in fact possible and in the source contexts for this pair, the attachment to the noun was even more frequent that to the verb. Out of 25 pair

---

[35] *Entreprise* can be either a noun ("company") or the past of the verb *entreprendre* ("to undertake").

[36] *Faible* can be an adjective ("weak") or a noun ("weak person").

instances, 23 are found in contexts like in Example 8, and only 2 instances concern attachments to the verb. Therefore, we may consider that the pair *président de élection* is actually correct, but it was wrongly annotated by the judges because the first context shown to them was the one in 7 (see also the discussion on type-level vs. token-level evaluation in Section 4.4.1).

(8)   *président de élection*
      Le *président d'élection* (M. Hopkins) . . .

In addition to the pairs labelled as *erroneous*, the pairs labelled as *regular* are also considered as irrelevant extraction results. The number of pairs in this situation is 164. The most frequent of them are combinations of type N-A (48), N-P-N (48), and V-O (33). We noted that only 65 of these pairs were actually unanimously considered as regular by the three judges, mostly the N-P-N pairs (21) and V-O pairs (15). The others were divided into regular pairs with MWE tendency and MWE pairs with tendency towards regularity, as shown in Section 4.4.3.

In the output of the window method, as many as 106 of the total 500 pairs are erroneous. The distribution among combination types is the following: N-N – 75 pairs, N-A – 14 pairs, A-N – 10 pairs, N-V – 6 pairs, and V-N – 1 pair. The error rate for each combination type is as follows: N-N – 41.1%, N-V – 26.1%, A-N – 23%, N-A – 9%, V-N – 1%. The main cause of errors is the absence of a syntactic relation between the items of a pair. A detailed analysis of the erroneous pairs allowed us to classify them as follows.

1. Erroneous subparts of frequent longer expressions (32 pairs), e.g.:

   (9)   a. *arbitrage final*
             arbitrage des offres *finales*

         b. *susceptible mort*
             force *susceptible* de causer la *mort* ou des lésions corporelles graves

         c. *commune général, commune solliciteur*
             leader du gouvernement à la Chambre des *communes* et *solliciteur général* du Canada

         d. *défense combattant*
             ministre de la *Défense* nationale et ministre des Anciens *combattants*

         e. *président Canada*
             président du Conseil privé de la Reine pour le *Canada*

         f. *seconde mondial*
             Seconde Guerre *mondiale*

         g. *développement humain*
             Développement des ressources *humaines*

2. Erroneous associations with a very frequent domain-specific term, like, in our case, *Canada, gouvernement, ministre, pays* (46 pairs). For instance, associations with *Canada* include: *Canada Canada, Canada Canadien, Canada Chambre, Canada député, Canada gouvernement, Canada ministre, Canada Monsieur, Canada président, Canada programme, Canada question.*

3. Erroneous associations, not necessarily with a domain-specific term (19 pairs),
   e.g., *dollar ministre, député programme, emploi Chambre, question premier.*
4. Associations with wrong POS labels originating in tagging errors (6 pairs):

   (10)   a. *Monsieur présider* (N-V), correct: *Monsieur le Président* (N-N)

          b. *petite entreprendre* (N-V), correct: *petite entreprise* (A-N)

          c. *monsieur présider* (N-V), correct: *monsieur le Président* (N-N)[37]

          d. *faible revenir* (N-V), correct: *faible revenu* (A-N)

          e. *nouveau députer* (N-V), correct: *nouveau député* (A-N)

          f. *moyenne entreprendre* (N-V), correct: *moyenne entreprise* (A-N)

A second class of errors in the output of the window method are the false
positives represented by the *regular* pairs: their number is 104 (i.e., 63% less than in
the case of the parse-based method). Among the most frequent combination types,
we find N-N combinations (40), N-A combinations (34), and V-N combinations
(15). Only 48 regular pairs are common to both methods.

4.5.1.2 Experiment 2

The analysis of the erroneous pairs obtained with the parse-based method in Experiment 2 (Section 4.4.5) revealed various causes of errors, among which:

1. wrong assignment of POS labels for homographic words, caused by the ambiguity of the text: for example, the pair *sous de forme* identified in the context
   en tirent un avantage financier et sous d'autres formes has been considered as a
   N-P-N pair, the word *sous* being wrongly tagged as a noun (the plural form of
   sou, "coin") instead of preposition. Both readings are, strictly speaking, possible
   for this sentence.
2. wrong assignment of syntactic type[38]: for instance, the pair *succéder catastrophe*
   has been incorrectly interpreted by the parser as a V-O pair instead of S-V in the
   context *Mais peut-on voir se succéder les catastrophes qui ont frappé mon pays.*
3. absence of a syntactic link between the two pairs, when the parser fails, for
   instance, to recognize a complex lexical unit (these errors can be removed by
   adding such items in the parser's lexicon): e.g., the pair *fait inapproprié* extracted
   from *J'estime qu'il est tout à fait inapproprié que* ... is erroneous, since *fait* is
   part of the adverb *tout à fait.*

Among the sources of parsing errors specific to English data, we identified the
nominal compounds (for instance, in *gross domestic product*, the parser analyses
gross domestic as an A-N pair), and the confusion between gerunds and nouns (e.g.,
in *a barrage of fire targeting Arafat*, the pair *barrage of targeting* is identified as

---

[37] The parser distinguishes between *Monsieur* (title) and *monsieur* (common noun) and therefore
considers them as two different lexemes.

[38] Note that the window method cannot be subject to such errors as long as no syntactic type is
associated with the output pairs, but only POS labels.

N-P-N). As far as the Spanish and Italian outputs are concerned, the parsing errors are more numerous because of the more limited lexical and grammatical coverage of the Fips parser for these languages.

As for the window method, erroneous pairs are very numerous in the extraction output obtained in Experiment 2. The analysis of a number of randomly selected pairs suggests that the same conclusions drawn in Experiment 1 hold here as well.

4.5.2 Intersection and Rank Correlation

4.5.2.1 Experiment 1

A comparison of the output obtained by the two methods has been performed at pair-type level. In Table 4.17, the column *common* reports the number of pair types that were extracted both by the parse-based method and the window method in Experiment 1 (Section 4.4.3).

The intersection is computed for the top *n* pairs, with *n* ranging from 50 to 500 at intervals of 50. Thus, 30 pairs are common to the top 50 results of each method, then the percentage of common pairs decreases as we look further in the significance list: from 60% for top 50, it goes down to 56% for top 100 and 150, and only 46.2% overall (231 pairs are common in the top 500 results). These results refer to all of the pairs in the test sets, regardless of their annotation mark (*erroneous*, *regular*, or *interesting*).

When we consider only the pairs marked as *interesting*, i.e., the pairs that are likely to constitute MWEs, we obtain the results shown in the column *MWE pairs*: the number of common MWE pairs identified in the top 50 results is 22 (44%). Overall, 141 MWE pairs are common to the two methods in the top 500 results (28.2% of the annotated data).

Table 4.17 also reports the Spearman's ρ rank correlation coefficient on the common pairs returned by the two methods. This value, ranging from -1 to 1, indicates the degree of correlation between the rankings proposed. Given the set of common pairs ordered by each method according to the collocational strength

Table 4.17 Output comparison for the two methods in Experiment 1 (Section 4.4.3): intersection and Spearman's rank correlation coefficient for the top 500 results

	All pairs			MWE pairs		
Top	Common	Percentage	Spearman's ρ	Common	Percentage	Spearman's ρ
50	30	60.0	0.775	22	44.0	0.782
100	56	56.0	0.832	39	39.0	0.848
150	84	56.0	0.861	57	38.0	0.889
200	103	51.5	0.871	70	35.0	0.896
250	120	48.0	0.866	81	32.4	0.887
300	145	48.3	0.871	92	30.7	0.882
350	168	48.0	0.882	106	30.3	0.897
400	192	48.0	0.873	117	29.3	0.896
450	210	46.7	0.863	129	28.7	0.897
500	231	46.2	0.854	141	28.2	0.887

(so that higher-scored pairs are ranked first), the Spearman's ρ is computed as in Equation (4.8):

$$\rho = 1 - \frac{6 \sum_i (RW_i - RP_i)^2}{n(n^2 - 1)} \tag{4.8}$$

where RW_i and RP_i denote the ranks for the pair i proposed by the window method and the parse-based method, respectively, and n is the total number of common pairs. Values of ρ close to 1 indicate a high correlation of rankings, and values below 0 indicate a negative correlation. The rankings correlate significantly if the ρ value is higher than a critical value—in this case, 0.165 (Villada Moirón, 2005, 85).

The ρ values in Table 4.17 indicate a high correlation of the ranks proposed by the two methods for the top 500 pairs returned in Experiment 1. Thus, we can conclude that, as far as the top results are concerned, the difference between the two methods lies more in the content of the output lists, than in the relative order of the pairs identified.

4.5.2.2   Experiment 2

In Experiment 2 (Section 4.4.5), the number of pairs in the intersection of the two output lists—one corresponding to the window method, the other to the parse-based method—is very small (see Table 4.18).[39] The common pairs belong almost exclusively to the first test set, TS1 (i.e., to the top 50 results). As in the case of Experiment 1, the Spearman's coefficient indicates a high correlation of the ranks assigned to the common pairs by the two methods.

In a larger-scale comparison, we considered the complete output lists of the two methods and looked at the overall intersection and rank correlation. These parameters have also been computed on different sets of pairs satisfying the following criteria related to the rank, the log-likelihood score, and the corpus frequency of pairs:

– rank: lower than 1,000, 2,000, and 10,000;
– LLR score: higher than 1,000, 100, and 10;
– frequency: higher than 100, 10, and 3.

Table 4.18 Output comparison for the two methods in Experiment 2 (Section 4.4.5): intersection and Spearman's rank correlation coefficient for the pairs annotated for each language

	English	French	Italian	Spanish
Common (TS1 + TS2 + TS3 + TS4 + TS5)	24	20	22	31
Common (TS1)	23	20	22	31
Spearman's ρ	0.640	0.833	0.586	0.846

---

[39] This is mainly the consequence of the manner in which the test sets have been constructed, by considering non-adjacent sets at various levels in the output list (Section 4.4.5).

The results obtained are reported in Appendix F. We found that overall there is a significant correlation between the rankings of the pairs in the intersection (the Sperman's ρ is between 0.477 and 0.521 depending on the language, and 0.487 on average). The correlation is higher for the upper layers of the output lists, as given by the higher frequency or LLR score cutoffs. A relationship between ranks and correlation could not be established (i.e., the correlation function is non-monotone on ranks), a possible explanation being that the layers compared make up very different proportions in the whole output lists.

As for the common pairs, they make up a high percentage of the output returned by the parse-based method (75.59% for the English data, 73.48% for French, 79.58% for Italian, 80.81% for Spanish, and 77.36% on average), but constitutes only a small fraction of the much larger data retrieved by the window method (17.43% on average). For all of the languages considered, we can conclude—as in Experiment 1—that the relative order of output pairs is rather maintained from one method to another as far as the common pairs are concerned, and that the correlation is higher for the upper layers of the output lists.

4.5.3 Instance-Level Analysis

A more insightful comparison between the two extraction methods can be made by examining the totality of instances of the output pairs in the source corpus. We performed several case studies aimed at answering the following questions: How many instances of a pair type are retrieved from the source corpus by one method with respect to another? How many instances are identical, and, for those that are missed by one method, is there any particularity of the source text that explains why they were missed? How many instances are "true" and how many are "false" (in the sense that the source sentence is incorrectly associated with the pair in question)?[40] And, ultimately, is one method better than another in terms of recall, in a given setting?

4.5.3.1 Experiment 1

In the first case study, we considered the V-O pair *jouer rôle* from Experiment 1 (Section 4.4.3) and compared the instances identified by the parse-based method, on the one hand, with those identified by the window method, on the other hand. In the output of the window method, this pairs is ranked 39th, with 135 instances; in that of the method based on parsing, it is ranked 14th and has 190 instances.

A number of 131 instances are identical, meaning that almost all the corpus occurrences of this pair that have been detected by the window method have also been detected by the parse-based method; the 4 instances discovered exclusively by the window method are "true" instances that have been missed by the parser.

---

[40] For instance, Example 7 contains a false instance for the pair *président de élection*, while Example 8 contains a true instance.

The corpus-based analysis of these 135 instances confirmed that they are all "true" instances for which the average distance between the base *rôle* and the collocate *jouer* is very small (around one intervening word).

The parse-based method discovered 59 more instances. Among these, there are 43 cases of inversion that could not be detected by the window method, since this was designed for extracting directed pairs. The inversion was caused in the majority of cases by grammatical operations like relativization (37 instances), interrogation (4 instances) and passivization (2 instances). An example of each type is provided below.

(11) a. *relativization*
En outre, pourrait-il en profiter pour nous préciser le *rôle* que l'État, le gouvernement fédéral plus particulièrement, devrait *jouer* pour aider les familles?

   b. *interrogation*
quel *rôle* de premier plan pouvons-nous *jouer* pour voir à ce que ces résolutions soient respectées?

   c. *passivization*
Le *rôle joué* par le Canada et par M. Pearson dans cette crise (...)

As in the case of the window method, all the instances that were exclusively retrieved with the parse-based method are "true" instances. The conclusion we can draw from this case-study is that both extraction methods are precise (i.e., they both identify "true" instances), but the window method has a lower recall since it retrieves a lower number of instances. This happens mainly because of a design choice not allowing it to mix N-V and V-N surface pairs, since these POS combinations suggest different syntactic relations: S-V, in the first case, and V-O, in the second. As a consequence, the rank obtained with the window method is lower than that assigned by the parse-based method for some pairs. At a larger scale, this study suggests that the failure of the window method to detect all the instances of some pairs could lead it to artificially demote these pairs to lower positions in the significance list.

4.5.3.2 Experiment 2

Another pair whose instances were studied is the English S-V pair *vote take*, extracted from Experiment 2 (Section 4.4.5).[41] The window method finds 408 instances of it in the source corpus, while with the parse-based method only 325 instances are identified. A number of 325 instances are common to both methods, i.e., all the instances found by the parse-based method are also found by the window method. This suggests that the recall of the window method is, for this pair, at least as good as that of the parse-based method.

---

[41] This pair is actually part of the longer collocation *vote – take place* that should have been extracted if *take place* was included in the parser's lexicon (Chapter 5 presents a method for obtaining longer collocations by taking into account previously extracted pairs).

While the precision of the parse-based method is perfect (since all the instances identified are correct), as many as 81 out of the 83 occurrences that were found exclusively by the window method count as "false" instances:

– 10 instances are erroneous, for example:

> (12)   a. I merely wish to ask whether the written explanations of *vote* should not be *taken* first.
>
>   b. That means that, as often happens in these cases, the decision we take with our *vote* will not be *taken* into any account by the Council.

– 71 instances belong in reality to the V-O pair *take – vote*, for example:

> (13)   I propose that the sitting be suspended until the *votes* are *taken*.

The remaining 2 instances are "true" S-V instances that have not been identified by the parse-based method.

This second case study suggests that the "false" instances retrieved with the window method for some pairs are very numerous and they are difficult to distinguish from "true" instances as long as the syntactic context is ignored.

In an additional corpus-based investigation of instances of other output pairs, we discovered that there are several situations in which the window method behaves more robustly than our method committed to the syntactic parsing. It is, for instance, the case of pronominalization. Our method is not expected to recover a collocation with a noun when the latter is realized as an anaphoric pronoun (although this would be possible if an anaphora resolution module were coupled to our system). Instead, with the window method, the noun can be detected as long as it is found in the collocational span considered. For instance, in Example 14, the object of the verb *take* is the anaphoric pronoun *it* whose antecedent is the noun *vote*; therefore, the pair *take – vote* could be inferred as a V-O pair instance. The window method discovers the antecedent accidentally in the proximity of the verb *take* and succeeds in retrieving the pair instance from this sentence.

> (14)   No, we must take that 'no' *vote* seriously and *take* it on board in our reflections.

Another situation in which the absence of syntactic constraints actually helps extraction is when the text contains a noun phrase with a semantically "transparent" head, e.g., *un sou d'impôt, une partie d'impôt, un minimum d'impôt*. In such a phrase, the semantic head (i.e., the noun bearing the semantic content) does not coincide with the syntactic head (*sou, partie, minimum*), but with its right subconstituent (*impôt*). Collocational links establish between this subconstituent and external items, bypassing the syntactic head. This is why such a link cannot be retrieved in a straightforward manner and with strictly syntactic means. Additional computation and semantic information on nouns is required in order for the extraction procedure to work.[42, 43] On the contrary, these collocational links are easily identifiable with the window method, precisely because no syntactic constraint applies. Example 15 shows several instances of the V-O pair *payer impôt*, in which the object of the verb is an NP with a semantically-transparent head (underlined in text):

(15) a. sans qu'elles *paient* un <u>cent</u> d'*impôt*

   b. ne *payent* toujours pas un <u>sou</u> d'*impôt*

   c. les sociétés *paient* leur juste <u>part</u> d'*impôts*

   d. qui *paient* déjà la majeure <u>partie</u> des *impôts*

   e. *paient* un <u>minimum</u> d'*impôt*

   f. devra *payer* 200 $ d'*impôt* de plus

Although such instances are, strictly speaking, syntactically unrelated, they could be considered as true instances, since they are semantically correct. Other instances retrieved with the window method are even more difficult to infer syntactically, like the instance in Example 16 (which is, admittedly, at the limit of what can be considered as a true instance).

(16) *paye* exactement le même <u>montant</u> en *impôt*.

4.6 Discussion

The evaluation experiments carried out showed that by integrating a syntactic filter into a collocation extraction procedure, a considerable improvement is obtained over the standard sliding window method. This result is far from being obvious, since, first of all, the syntactic analysis of whole source corpora is a difficult endeavor that requires sufficiently fast and robust tools; and, secondly, because this particular implementation of the window method, which favours precision, represents a strong baseline for comparison.

The analysis of results provided in Section 4.5 pointed out several advantages and disadvantages of one method versus another, related, in the first place, to the pair instances detected in the corpus. Our case studies revealed that many of the instances identified with the window method are "false" instances; moreover, many instances that are found by the syntax-based method are instead missed by the window method. These (false or missed) instances falsify the frequency signature[44]

---

[42] Fontenelle (1999) discusses the problem of transparent nouns, by showing that they may involve a wide range of partitives and quantifiers, as in *shot <u>clouds</u> of arrows, melt a <u>bar</u> of chocolate, suffer from an <u>outbreak</u> of fever, a warm <u>round</u> of applause*. He proposes a lexical-function account for these nouns, in which the transparent nouns are considered as the value of the lexical function *Mult* (e.g., *Mult(arrow)=clowd*).

[43] In the current version of the system, the extraction method was adapted to perform this computation. In the lexicon of Fips, a specific flag is used for noun to signal that they are semantically transparent.

[44] This term was introduced in Section 3.2.3.

of the pairs concerned; as a consequence, these pairs are artificially promoted or demoted in the significance list, the quality of results being ultimately affected.

A more directly perceived inconvenience for associating false instances with a pair is that the corresponding source contexts are useless for lexicographic purposes, as well as for the interested NLP applications (i.e., whenever one tries to derive contextual information for an extracted collocation). Parsing helps to overcome this problem, as the wide majority of instances identified for a pair in text are correct instances.

Another shortcoming of the window method is that the results pairs are highly unreliable. Even if a POS combination suggests a syntactic link (e.g., N-V suggests an S-V relation), the pair may actually be erroneous, or may involve a syntactic type that is different from the one suggested; in contrast, the pairs returned by the parse-based method contain syntactic information assigned by the parser, which facilitates their interpretation and subsequent processing. The following example shows several pairs extracted by the window method in Experiment 1 (Section 4.4.3). Although they look correct in isolation, these are in reality wrong, as can be seen from the instances provided next to them.

(17)   a. *développement humain*
            Développement des ressources *humaines*

        b. *président Canada*
            président du Conseil privé de la Reine pour le *Canada*

        c. *gouvernement Canadien*
            le *gouvernement* du Canada invite tous les *Canadiens* à participer (. . .)

On the other hand, we found that one advantage of the window method over methods relying on syntax is that it can detect the collocate of a base word in the considered collocational span, even if this is not directly syntactically related to that word. Such situations include the pronominalization of the base word, as in Example 14, or its embedding in a larger NP whose syntactic head is a semantically-transparent noun, as in Example 15.

The main advantage attributed, in principle, to the window method is that it is fast, robust, and readily available for a new language, whereas syntax-based methods require high-performance, language-specific tools that are difficult to implement. The extraction experiments we performed in the framework of the comparative evaluation studies showed that, actually, the multilingual parser Fips is also fast and robust enough to process source corpora of several million words; that the syntactic filter applied to the candidate pairs leads to a drastic reduction of the candidate data that is later fed into the statistical inference procedure that computes the association strength, while, on the contrary, the much larger data produced by the window method slows down this procedure considerably. Moreover, the window method is not fully language-independent, because its performance relies on the accuracy of POS information that is in turn dependent on the word disambiguation depending on the syntactic context. Finally, it is also interesting to note that although Experiment 2 deals with more data than Experiment 1 (i.e., 3–4 times as much data), no improvement was obtained in the results of the window method.

As an alternative to the window method, we could compare our method against methods based on shallow parsing, since these are expected to produce more accurate results than the syntax-free approach.[45] While the precision of these methods could certainly compete with that of parse-based methods, we expect, however, a lower recall because of the lower grammatical coverage of shallow parsers, in particular with respect to those syntactic constructions responsible for a long distance between the items of candidate pairs.

Although we did not perform a thorough evaluation against methods based on shallow parsing, we made a preliminary analysis of the collocations identified with a shallow parser for English. We carried out a case study on the V-O and S-V collocations with the noun *preference* that were extracted from the BNC corpus with the Sketch Engine. The Sketch Engine (Kilgarriff et al., 2004) is a state-of-the-art extractor that identifies collocation candidates of several syntactic types by relying on shallow parsing implemented as pattern matching over POS tags. The association measure used to rank candidates is an adaptation of MI that gives more weight to the co-occurrence frequency.

Among the 201 V-O pair types with *preference* obtained without applying a frequency cutoff, a number of 15 were grammatically incorrect (i.e., 7.5%). Several such pairs are shown in Example 18 below, together with a corpus instance for each. Another 4 pairs used a majority of incorrect instances, and thus got artificially promoted to higher ranks (e.g., the pairs in Example 19).

(18)   a.   *vote preference* (rank 20) - we asked about *voting preferences*

       b.   *focus preference* (rank 24) - *focus preferences* were taken to be strong

       c.   *elect preference* (rank 39) - most voters will find that a candidate for whom they have expressed some *preference* will have been *elected*

       d.   *peak preference* (rank 55) - could produce a sharply *peaked preference*

(19)   a.   *decide preference* (rank 47) - As they walked towards the hotel, she gave him the rates on an ascending scale and spat her gum into the kerbside as if she had already *decided* what his *preference* would be.

       b.   *count preference* (rank 51) - votes of lower *preference* are *counted* only when transfers have to be made.

Similarly, from the 63 S-V pair types returned by the Sketch Engine, a number of 10 pair types (15.9%) were incorrect, among which the pairs in Example 20 below. A number of 5 other S-V pairs used incorrect instances, like the pair in Example 21.

(20)   a.   *preference prejudice* (rank 1) - if compliance with the *preference* would *prejudice*

       b.   *preference support* (rank 6) - The proposal is a clear expression of local *preference supported* by local planning authorities.

---

[45] In this case, however, the argument of language independence and ease of implementation does not hold anymore, as shallow parser are also relatively difficult to develop.

(21)   *preference lead* - the existence of these *preferences* would clearly *lead* ulti-
        mately to a situation

Although the results obtained in this case study are not entirely conclusive due
to the small size of data evaluated, they suggest that the extraction based on shallow
parsing leaves considerable room for improvement, which, in our opinion, can be
achieved by deep parsing.

4.7 Summary

This chapter presented the core of our collocation extraction methodology. We
showed how our system relies on deep syntactic parsing of source corpora to opti-
mize the selection of candidate pairs from text. With respect to similar parsing based
extractors that we described in some detail, our extractor is built to try to fill a number of gaps related to robustness, precision, the number of syntactic configurations
taken into account, and, more importantly, to the type of syntactic transformations
handled. We showed how the Fips multilingual parser (Wehrli, 1997, 2004, 2007)
with its wide grammatical coverage permits the robust and fast syntactic analysis
of large text corpora and plays an essential role in the quality of the extraction
results.

After describing the extraction procedure proper, we focused on the contrastive
evaluation of the proposed method against the sliding window method, a standard
syntax-free extraction method based on the linear proximity of words. Our evaluation study was motivated by several concerns about the efficiency of extraction
based on deep parsing which are widely dismissed by researchers in computational
linguistics as too time-consuming and unreliable on unrestricted data as opposed to
syntax-free approaches that are considered readily available, robust, and able to produce acceptable results when applied to large data. In order to compare these methods, two evaluation experiments were performed with different settings (i.e., corpus
domain, corpus size, source languages, test data design, annotation categories). The
results obtained were consistent: in both experiments, for all languages supported
by our extractor, the syntax-based method outperformed the window method by a
large extent. In particular, we found that a high percentage of the window method
results, with the exception of the pairs situated in the very top of the significance list,
are erroneous. In contrast, the syntax-based method achieves high grammatical precision on both higher and lower levels in the significance list. In addition, we found
that the quality and the interpretability of window results suffer from the inescapable
mix of "true" and "false" instances identified in the source text for the output pairs.
In contrast, the pairs extracted with parsing contain syntactic information and most
of their instances are correct. These results have important, far reaching, positive
implications for the use of syntax based methods for lexicographic or NLP tasks. In
addition, the strong syntactic filter applied to candidate pairs facilitates the statistical
computation of score in the second extraction stage, whereas the window method
generates huge candidate data sets which are much more difficult to process.

As in the case of grammatical precision, MWE and collocational precision were also found to be higher for the syntax-based method. In Experiment 1 that evaluated the MWE precision on the top 500 results, the increase obtained with parsing is 9% (from 56.9 to 65.9%). Experiment 2 was concerned with several levels of the output list. Syntactic methods showed an increase of 2.5:1 in MWE precision (from 17.2 to 43.2%), and of 2.6:1 in collocational precision (from 12.8 to 32.9%), on average for all levels and languages considered.

In line with previous evaluation studies that quantified the impact of using parsing for collocation extraction (Breidt, 1993; Smadja, 1993; Lin, 1999; Krenn, 2000b; Zajac et al., 2003), our study concluded that the syntactic information makes a substantial contribution to the precision of results. Whereas previous studies have generally focused on a single language, our study provided a cross-lingual evaluation involving data in four languages. The data consisted of a relatively large number of pairs that have been selected from both the best-scored and the lower-scored results and annotated by at least two human judges. It also provided a detailed qualitative analysis of results of the methods compared which revealed possible causes for the differences observed in the pair rankings and in the number of instances retrieved, and highlighted the relative strengths of one method versus another depending on the particularities of the text.

Chapter 5
Extensions

5.1 Identification of Complex Collocations

The first extension considered for our method was aimed at the extraction of collocations made up of more than two items. In spite of the fact that theoretical studies consider collocations as made up of two *or more* words (see Chapter 2 and, in particular, Section 2.3), in practice the collocation extraction work focuses almost exclusively on binary collocations. The main reason for this is the manner in which collocations are generally modelled, as pairs of words which show an affinity for each other (Section 3.2.1), and which can be detected in corpora by using association measures designed for two variables (Section 3.2.4). To overcome this limitation related to the length of the collocations retrieved, several solutions could be considered, as described below.

1. Extending the existing association measures to more than two items (Villada Moirón, 2005)[1] or proposing new measures that cope with unrestricted length (Blaheta and Johnson, 2001; Dias, 2003).
2. Using a cyclic extraction strategy, in which previous results of syntax-based extraction are incorporated into future extraction, so that an already-known collocation is treated as a single item. This solution—which is already implemented in our extraction system, as discussed in Section 4.3.1—conveniently accounts for the recursive nature of collocations noted by researchers like Heid (1994, 232). However, it is difficult to put into practice because it requires human intervention in order to validate the extraction output and update the lexicon of the parser.
3. Post-processing the extraction output in order to automatically infer longer collocations from the binary combinations identified (Smadja, 1993; Kim et al., 1999, 2001).

In this section, we describe a method for extracting collocations of length higher than two (hereafter, *complex collocations* or *n-grams*)[2] that adopts the third

---

[1] Villada Moirón (2005) extends MI and χ^2 in order to deal with candidates of length 3.

[2] For the sake of simplicity, we will use the terms of *bigram*, *trigram*, and in general that of *n-gram* in order to indicate the arity of collocations, even if the component items are not adjacent.

solution. Given the binary collocations (*bigrams*) extracted as described in the previous chapter, it creates *collocation chains*[3] of unrestricted length, by joining bigrams whenever they are found together in the same sentence so that they share common items. For instance, once the bigrams *play role* and *important role* are extracted from a sentence and *role* is the very same token in that sentence, we can infer the trigram *play important role*. The process can be continued by adding a new item to the current chain, so that we will obtain, for instance, the 4-gram *play a critically important role*, given that the bigram *critically important* was also extracted from the same sentence and the token *important* is the exactly the one considered before.

A specific practical motivation for extracting such collocations with our method is that, among the resulting binary associations, one can find incomplete subparts of complex collocations. Some of the pairs proposed make no sense in isolation, because they are fragments of more complex collocations. For instance, *vote – take* is an incorrect result that was proposed by our extractor, and is a fragment of the subject-verb collocation *vote – take place*. This problem has been more acutely perceived in the field of terminology extraction: as Frantzi et al. (2000) show, a term like *soft contact lens* cannot be decomposed into fragments like *soft lens* or *soft contact*, but must be recovered in its entirety. Insofar as collocation extraction is concerned, the issue of fragments has recently been discussed in Kilgarriff et al. (2010). In their evaluation of Sketch Engine, Kilgarriff et al. (2010) decide to consider a partial collocation as a true positive, arguing that it is enough to signal the presence of the longer collocation to a lexicographer. However, this "was not a decision that human evaluators were comfortable with" (Kilgarriff et al., 2010).

Another motivation is that, even if some binary combinations cannot be considered as fragments because they occur autonomously, there is a strong preference for them to be used in conjunction with other words in order to acquire a syntactically complete status. Consider, for instance, the case of the collocation *stand in contrast*. In many contexts, the noun *contrast* requires a modifier that would complete this expression; in fact, the modifier which is the most commonly used is *stark*. Therefore, a lexicographer might find it useful to record the whole expression *stand in stark contrast*, rather than (or in addition to) the individual subparts alone, *stand in contrast* and *stark contrast*. Another example of a nested collocation is *mass destruction*. A lexicographer may decide that, in addition to the binary combination, it would also be useful to store larger collocations that contain it, for instance: *weapons of mass destruction, proliferation of weapons of mass destruction, treaty on the non-proliferation of weapons of mass destruction*.

5.1.1 The Method

In this section, we describe how we adapted our extraction methodology used for binary collocations, in order to obtain complex collocations of unrestricted length.

---

[3] An in-depth discussion on collocation chains can be found in Ramos and Wanner (2007).

The algorithm starts with the set of bigrams extracted by our system, where each bigram contains information regarding the lexical items involved, the syntactic type, and the source context (as described in Section 4.3.2).

In each iteration, n-grams are combined into $(n+1)$-grams, which is to say that longer collocation chains are obtained from the chains of maximal length built up to that point. The newly-constructed chains are stored, and iteration continues until no new combinations are generated. The maximum length reached is determined by the length of source sentences. The termination of the procedure is guaranteed, since the length of sentences is limited.

There are multiple ways of combining shorter chains into longer ones that may lead to the same results. For instance, one could obtain a 4-gram like *play (an) important role in* by combining a trigram with a bigram (*play important role, play in*), three bigrams (*play role, important role, play in*), or two trigrams (*play important role, play role in*). We opted for the combination of chains of equal, maximal length—i.e., as in the last option above—this is why the procedure exclusively uses n-grams for building $(n+1)$-grams. The choice is motivated by the simplicity and the uniformity in the description of the algorithm. In order to yield an $(n+1)$-gram, two n-grams are combined *iff* they share exactly $n - 1$ items; for these items, the source file and the file positions, which are stored in the fields `source` and `charlex1` or `charlex2`, respectively, must be identical.

The order of items in the resulting chain is most often determined by the canonical order of these items in the participating bigrams, as obtained from the sentence normalization provided by the parser. This allows the convenient grouping of all instances of the more syntactically versatile combinations under the same type. For instance, the following pairs:

(1)   *prendre décision*
      décision difficile

share the middle item in the resulting trigram, *prendre décision difficile*, and the order of the participating items is unambiguous. This (canonical) order is unique for all the corresponding instances. Thus, both instances shown in Example 2 are identified as belonging to the trigram type *prendre décision difficile*, even if the textual order for the second is different (*décision difficile prendre*).

(2)   a.   Le fait est que nous devons *prendre* des *décisions difficiles*.

      b.   Nous ne voulons pas que les fabriquants de produits du tabac profitent de
           la *décision difficile* que nous avons *prise* aujourd'hui.

In case of ambiguity, if the order cannot be inferred from the cannonical order of items in bigrams, it is decided by the source contexts (i.e., by the file position of items). For instance, for the bigrams in Example 3, it is not clear what the resulting trigram should be, *tenir référendum sur* or *tenir sur référendum*; therefore, it is the relative position of *référendum* and *sur* in the source text that is taken into account.[4]

(3)   *tenir référendum*
      tenir sur

A drawback of this combinatorial procedure is that for chains of length 4 and more it may lead to redundant results, because in certain cases the same chain can be built from distinct pairs of subchains. For instance, the 4-gram *démontrer grand ouverture de esprit* can be built from the following pairs of trigrams:

(4)   a.   *grand ouverture esprit - démontrer grand ouverture*

      b.   *démontrer ouverture esprit - grand ouverture esprit*

      c.   *démontrer ouverture esprit - démontrer grand ouverture.*

However, the procedure keeps track of the way in which an *n*-gram has been built and distinguishes between such redundant cases, in order to avoid reporting a false frequency for that *n*-gram. The frequency information is used in the subsequent extraction step, which ranks the generated candidates. On the basis of the obtained score, the different variants of a redundant *n*-gram could be decided between in order to retain only the most successful variant for the next iterations of the algorithm.[5]

In order to grade the association strength for the components in a complex collocation, we apply a classical two-variables association measure as described below. Since complex collocations can be regarded as recursively-embedded binary collocations sharing the base word,[6] it follows that the association measures which exist for binary collocations can be straightforwardly applied to collocations of arbitrary length in a recursive fashion, by treating complex lexical items like single words. In the corresponding contingency table, the frequency values that will be listed will be those of the complex items, computed from the corpus in the same manner as the frequencies of words (see Section 3.2.3). Table 5.1 illustrates the discussion.

As explained earlier in this section, in our method, a $(n + 1)$-gram is constructed from two *n*-grams. We compute the contingency values by taking into consideration the joint and marginal frequencies of these two *n*-grams. The log-likelihood ratio association measure (LLR) is then applied in the standard way, according to the formula shown in Section 3.2.4.2.

Table 5.1 Example of contingency table for the trigram *allgemeine Gültigkeit haben*

	(Gültigkeit, haben)	¬ (Gültigkeit, haben)
(allgemeine, Gültigkeit)	a	b
¬ (allgemeine, Gültigkeit)	c	d

---

[4] If more alternatives are possible, multiple types are generated accordingly.

[5] This filter is not implemented in the current version of our system.

[6] As illustrated by the trigram ((*allgemeine, Gültigkeit*), *haben*), composed of (*allgemeine, Gültigkeit*) and (*Gültigkeit, haben*), lit., "general validity have" (Heid, 1994, 232).

5.1.2 Experimental Results

This section reports on the multi-word collocations obtained by applying the extraction method described above on the bigrams previously extracted in Experiment 1 (Section 4.4.3). From the 370,932 total bigrams extracted, a number of 173,037 trigrams have been generated, that correspond to 143,229 trigram types. The combination of trigrams yielded, in turn, 146,032 4-grams instances and 140,138 types. The frequency distribution of trigram and 4-gram types is shown in Table 5.2.

Table 5.3 presents several examples of trigrams and 4-grams selected among the top results according to the LLR score. The results list the lemmas for the participating items, to which prepositions are added, depending on the syntactic configuration of the initial bigrams (refer to the list of configurations provided in Section 4.3.1).[7]

Tables 5.4 and 5.5 display some of the most frequent syntactic configurations for the obtained trigrams and 4-grams, as given by the configuration of the bigrams involved. Note that, due to the way the extraction procedure works, the words are currently shown in their base form, but in the future the inflected form could be considered for enhanced readability. To emphasize the fact that these complex

Table 5.2 Frequency distribution for the 3-grams and 4-grams extracted

Frequency	3-gram types	4-gram types
f = 1	131, 450	136, 842
f = 2	7, 337	2, 446
3 ≤ f ≤ 5	3, 344	691
6 ≤ f ≤ 10	694	96
f > 10	404	63

Table 5.3 Sample 3-grams and 4-grams among the top-scored results

3-gram	4-gram
accorder attention particulier	avoir effet négatif sur
attirer attention sur	créer grand nombre de emploi
avoir effet néfaste	être à prise avec taux de chômage
compter sur entier collaboration	franchir cap de milliard de dollar
donner bon résultat	jouer rôle de premier plan dans
être sur bon voie	jouer rôle important dans
jouer rôle important	jouer grand rôle dans
prendre décision difficile	poursuivre effort négociation avec
prendre engagement envers	présenter sincère félicitation pour
prendre mesure concret	question faire objet de examen
prêter oreille attentif	ramener partie à table de négociation
revêtir importance particulier	tirer bon profit possible
tirer coup de feu	trouver bon solution possible

---

[7] Note that some items constitute complex units in turn, e.g., *premier plan* in the fifth 4-gram shown. Also, as suggested by the last 4-grams in the list, our strategy that consists of systematically displaying lemmas rather than word forms led to an unusual presentation of some expressions (such as *trouver bon solution possible* instead of *trouver meilleur solution possible*).

Table 5.4 The most frequent combinations of syntactic types for 3-grams

Types	Structure	Frequency (tokens)	Example
S-V, V-O	(S-(V-O))	12,703	question revêtir importance
V-O, N-P-N	(V-(N-P-N))	10,926	améliorer qualité de vie
V-O, N-A	(V-(A-N))	8,483	avoir effet néfaste
N-P-N, N-P-N	(N-P-(N-P-N))	7,315	violation de droit de personne
N-P-N, N-A	(N-P-(N-A))	7,184	régime de assistance publique
V-O, V-P	((V-O)-P)	6,881	prendre engagement envers
V-O, V-P-N	((V-O)-P-N)	6,486	mettre terme à conflit
S-V, S-V	(S-(S-V))	6,433	argent servir financer
S-V, V-P-N	(S-(V-P-N))	5,752	frais élever à milliard
N-P-N, S-V	((N-P-N)-V)	5,533	taux de chômage situer

Table 5.5 The most frequent combinations of syntactic types for 4-grams

Types	Frequency (tokens)	Example
S-V, V-O, V-P	3,290	mesure stimuler entreprise dans
S-V, S-V, V-O	2,732	gouvernement tenter régler problème
N-A, S-V, S-V	2,704	argument principal être dire
N-P-N, S-V, S-V	2,540	taux de intérêt continuer baisser
S-V, V-O, N-P-N	2,519	projet faire objet de étude
S-V, V-O, V-P-N	2,465	comité axer travail sur question
V-O, A-N, N-P-N	2,428	coûter grand nombre de vie
S-V, V-O, N-A	2,160	carlement adopter mesure législatif
V-O, V-P, V-P	2,153	avoir débat avec au sujet
N-P-N, S-V, V-O	2,033	taux de chômage atteindre niveau

collocations are recursive, we also display the syntactic structure, showing the manner in which they are constructed from binary collocations (Table 5.3); note that this information is not explicitly available in our system and was added manually. Each binary structure reflects the base-collocate distinction made by theoretical descriptions (Section 2.5.1).

Although a thorough evaluation of the bigram composition method has not yet been carried out, the preliminary analysis of a small test set of randomly selected results (displayed in Tables 5.6 and 5.7) showed that it produces high-quality results in terms of grammaticality. The results also seem to indicate that the method is indeed able to retrieve good collocation candidates.

Overall, it can be noted that there are more numerous interesting candidates among the trigrams than among the 4-grams extracted. Indeed, as an effect of the higher fragmentation of data, the collocability strength is expected to decrease as the length of candidates increases. Also, many of the salient long associations discovered in this experiment are composed of collocational subparts, but to which a non-collocational item is added because it is characteristic of the domain (e.g., nouns like *ministre*, *député*, *gouvernement*, and so on), as in the trigram *ministre régler problème*. This inconvenience is caused by the choice of this particular source corpus, namely the Hansard corpus of parliamentary debates, but we expect the results on domain-independent corpora to be, for the main part, more interesting from a lexicographic point of view.

Table 5.6 Randomly selected trigram results

Rank	Keys	Types	Freq
87	loi (sur) protection (de) pêche	N-P-N, N-P-N	13
91	ancien gouvernement conservateur	A-N, N-A	18
98	base (de) force canadien	N-P-N, N-A	12
106	rehausser crédibilité (de) parlement	V-O, N-P-N	10
127	rapport (de) comité permanent	N-P-N, N-A	15
128	être bon chose	V-O, A-N	12
136	réintégrer marché (de) travail	V-O, N-P-N	10
162	économiser million (de) dollar	V-O, N-P-N	12
166	processus (de) négociation collectif	N-P-N, N-A	8
220	créer emploi à long terme	V-O, N-A	10
224	député exprimer opinion	S-V, V-O	9
234	faire objet (de) débat	V-O, N-P-N	10
240	connaître opinion sur	V-O, N-P	7
249	réduction (de) taxe (sur) cigarette	N-P-N, N-P-N	8
256	programme (de) nutrition prénatal	N-P-N, N-A	5
273	faire objet (de) examen	V-O, N-P-N	8
304	faire (de) choix difficile	V-P-N, N-A	6
307	nomination (de) nouveau président	N-P-N, A-N	6
319	créer comité spécial	V-O, N-A	8
330	faire bref commentaire	V-O, A-N	6
347	traverser période difficile	V-O, N-A	5
357	député retirer candidature	S-V, V-O	5
386	gouvernement prendre responsabilité	S-V, V-O	8
391	région (de) capitale national	N-P-N, N-A	4
410	prêter oreille attentif	V-O, N-A	4
457	ouvrir processus budgétaire	V-O, N-A	4
478	parti réformiste être	N-A, S-V	10
485	adresser (à) ministre (de) développement	V-P-N, N-P-N	15
487	commission (de) libération conditionnel	N-P-N, N-A	4
488	élaboration (de) politique gouvernemental	N-P-N, N-A	5

5.1.3 Related Work

Multi-word collocation extraction methods have generally been implemented so far on plain text or on POS-tagged data (Choueka et al., 1983; Smadja, 1993; Daille, 1994; Dias, 2003). They are affected by the rigidity and dispersion of the results retrieved, due the impossibility of dealing with syntactic variation. Compared to these methods, our method has the advantages of being able to abstract away from the specific text realization, to detect discontinuous items in the case of more syntactically versatile collocations, and to group various instances of a collocation type under the same canonical form.

The method of Choueka et al. (1983) identifies frequent sequences of at most 6 consecutive words, and is computationally expensive due to the high number of candidates that are generated from a corpus. In the second stage of Xtract, Smadja (1993) generates multi-word collocation candidates by analyzing the surrounding positions of already extracted bigrams. Rigid noun phrases and phrasal templates are thus identified (e.g., *The consumer price index*, *The NYSE's composite index*

Table 5.7 Randomly selected 4-gram results

Rank	Keys	Types	Freq
28	Chambre reprendre interrompre étude	S-V, V-O, V-O	10
59	programme (de) aide (à) remise (en) état	N-P-N, N-P-N, N-P-N	4
73	afficher liste (de) candidat dans	V-O, N-P-N, V-P	4
91	nomination (de) nouveau président (de) société	N-P-N, A-N, N-P-N	4
97	gouvernement être gouvernement méchant	S-V, V-O, N-A	4
99	représentant (de) bureau (de) régie interne	N-P-N, N-P-N, N-A	4
134	gouvernement devoir assumer responsabilité	S-V, S-V, V-O	4
138	bon accès (à) marché mondial	A-N, N-P-N, N-A	3
153	féliciter ministre (de) revenu national	V-O, N-P-N, N-A	3
176	rétablir confiance (de) Canadien dans	V-O, N-P-N, V-P	3
181	gouvernement devoir agir de	S-V, S-V, V-P	3
183	honorable député avoir parole	A-N, S-V, V-O	4
190	extension (de) régime (de) accession (à) propriété	N-P-N, N-P-N, N-P-N	3
232	gouvernement prendre engagement envers	S-V, V-O, V-P	3
236	ministre (de) Affaires étrangères aborder avec	N-P-N, S-V, V-P	3
237	féliciter honorable ministre pour	V-O, A-N, V-P	3
249	jouer rôle (de) premier plan dans	V-O, N-P-N, V-P	4
276	proposer (à) loi (sur) protection (de) pêche	N-P-N, N-P-N, N-P-N	3
352	trouver juste milieu entre	V-O, A-N, V-P	2
360	premier ministre pouvoir donner	A-N, S-V, S-V	3
414	être (à) prise (avec) taux (de) chômage	N-P-N, N-P-N, N-P-N	2
422	groupe demander révocation (de) député	S-V, V-O, N-P-N	2
453	être excellent joueur pour	V-O, A-N, V-P	2
460	injecter million (de) dollar (dans) économie	V-O, N-P-N, N-P-N	2
461	ministre avoir rencontre avec	S-V, V-O, V-P	2
471	trouver bon solution possible	V-O, A-N, N-A	2
479	lacune (dans) système (de) justice pénal	N-P-N, N-P-N, N-A	2
482	présider forum national sur	V-O, N-A, V-P	2
483	réforme (de) système (de) justice pénal	N-P-N, N-P-N, N-A	2

of all its listed common stocks *VERB* *NUMBER* to *NUMBER*), which are argued as being useful for language generation.

Another method is proposed by Dias (2003). It generates continuous or discontinuous candidate sequences within a 7-word window. These are still rigid, because they follow the linear order in the text. Multiword units are identified among these candidates by combining the association scores obtained for the sequence of words, on the one hand, and for the corresponding sequence of POS tags, on the other hand. Those sequences of length n whose score is greater than the score of all immediately subsuming and subsumed sequences (i.e., sequences of length $n+1$ and $n-1$) are retained as valid units. The system implemented was successfully used to extract English trigrams, but was reported to fail for longer sequences. The precision achieved is rather low, between 20 and 40%. Another drawback of this method is that it cannot deal with large bodies of text because it is too computationally intensive.

A linguistically-motivated method is adopted by Daille (1994), who deals with the problem of long compound nouns by enumerating the syntactic patterns defining them, and by listing the operations that can lead to their formation from shorter parts (juxtaposition, substitution, modification or coordination). As she acknowledges, it is hard to tell these operations apart. For instance, the N1-A-P-N2 term *réseau national à satellites* can be obtained either by substitution (in *réseau à satellites*, *réseau* is replaced by *réseau national*), or by modification (*réseau à satellites* is modified by the adjective *national*). Our approach takes the opposite direction: the relevant patterns do not have to be known beforehand, since they do not guide the extraction; multi-word collocations are found in an unconstrained way, based on the co-occurrence of their already identified subparts in the text. The patterns can be inferred later from the data extracted. This seems to be a more suitable approach, given the multitude of syntactic configurations in which the participating items can be found in a collocation. Note that the long compound nouns that Daille (1994) deals with are, in comparison, much more restricted from the point of view of syntax.

The (very few) methods that extract long candidates from syntactically parsed text deal with specific types of trigrams, such as multi-word verbs containing a verb and two particles, e.g., *look forward to* (Blaheta and Johnson, 2001), or A-N-V combinations in German, like *rote Zahlen schreiben* (lit. *red numbers write*, "be in the red") (Zinsmeister and Heid, 2003). Both configurations correspond to particular sequences of types that were also identified in the experiments run with our method (note that the counterpart of A-N-V in our system is (V-O, N-A)).

A method which uses an approach more similar to ours is presented in Kim et al. (1999, 2001). It retrieves *n*-grams from Korean text by creating clusters of bigrams having similar values for relative entropy and Dice coefficient. Since no syntactic criterion is used to link the bigrams, it is not clear whether the combinations obtained are indeed grammatical, as suggested by examples translated as *white sneakers wear* and *give birth to a child*, or the items in the obtained sets just happen to co-occur in the same sentence as a consequence of the fact that both measures rely heavily on co-occurrence frequency.

5.2 Data-Driven Induction of Syntactic Patterns

A crucial issue that collocation extraction systems have to address from the very beginning is the definition of the accepted POS combinations, because the quality of their results—in particular, the recall—depends heavily on this initial choice. In our case, since the extraction is based on syntactic parsing, the question we have to answer is what syntactic configurations are adequate for describing collocations.

Often, extraction systems are designed for a single configuration, like V-O, P-N-V, or P-N-P, or they consider only the several most representative

Table 5.8 Patterns used for collocations in the literature

	A-N	N-N	N-P-N	S-V	V-O	V-P	V-P-N	Adv-A	V-Adv
Benson et al. (1986a)	✓		P = *of*	✓	✓		✓	✓	✓
Hausmann (1989)	✓	✓	✓	✓	✓			✓	✓
Smadja (1993)	✓	✓		✓	✓	✓			✓
Basili et al. (1994)	✓	✓	✓	✓		✓			
Lin (1998)	✓	✓		✓	✓				
Kilgarriff and Tugwell (2001)	✓	✓	✓	✓	✓	✓			
Goldman et al. (2001)	✓	✓	✓	✓	✓	✓	✓		

configurations, as in Lin (1998, 1999) (see the review in Section 3.4). As a matter of fact, the POS combinations or the syntactic configurations (which we call *patterns* in short) are highly divergent from one system to another, as can be seen from the synoptic view provided in Table 5.8.[8] One reason for this high divergence is, arguably, the lack of consensus in the morpho-syntactic descriptions of collocations, as discussed in Section 2.5.2.[9]

In our opinion, the definition of the collocationally relevant patterns cannot rely exclusively on linguistic intuitions, but has to be supported by a corpus-based investigation of empirical data. This section presents an experiment aimed at the data-driven acquisition of patterns in a semi-automatic way, that has been conducted on both English and French text corpora.

5.2.1 The Method

We address the problem of finding a set of collocationally relevant patterns that is as exhaustive as possible by adopting a corpus-based approach. The identification method consists of two main steps. In the first step, all the productive patterns in a language are detected, then in the second step, the patterns judged as most interesting are eventually retained.

More precisely, in the first step the method extracts collocations from the source corpora by relaxing the syntactic constraints that apply to the candidate data. As explained in Section 4.3.1, candidate pairs are identified, in our system, from partial or complete parse trees built for the source sentences by the Fips parser. Several constraints are imposed on these candidates, which have to be, first of all, syntactically bound, then they must conform to a specific configuration from a set of predefined

---

[8] This table displays for Benson et al. (1986a) only the lexical collocations listed in the preface of the BBI dictionary. Also, the system of Smadja (1993) deals with the following additional types: V-V, N-P, N-D. Similarly, Basili et al. (1994) state that about 20 patterns were used, while our table displays only those that were explicitly mentioned in their publication.

[9] Some of the most representative patterns that are currently supported by our extraction system are shown in Table 4.1. As mentioned in Section 4.3.1, the complete list of patterns is actually longer, and is evolving as more and more data is inspected.

configurations. For our purpose, we now only impose the syntactic criterion, and consider any possible POS combination as relevant a priori. Given $[_{XP}$ L X R], a syntactic structure built by Fips (refer to Section 4.2 for the relevant details), the set of candidates is built by retaining all the combinations between the current head X, and the heads of the left and right subconstituents L and R. The procedure continues by collecting such pairs from the substructures L and R, recursively.

All the lexical categories considered by Fips are allowed, and therefore the initial set of patterns is very permissive. Each combination of two (not necessarily distinct) categories is, in principle, allowed as collocationally relevant. However, some combinations, like P-V or N-Adv, are obviously impossible due to the grammar rules defined in Fips.

In the second step of the method, the identified candidates are ranked using LLR. The most salient pairs that correspond to the productive combinations undergo a process of manual analysis, that decides the "interestingness" of each pattern and therefore its inclusion in the actual list of patterns used by the extraction system.

5.2.2 Experimental Results

Two different pattern induction experiments have been carried out using the method described above on English and French corpora of newspaper articles. The English corpus contains online articles from the journal "The Economist", and the French data belongs to the corpus "Le Monde" distributed by the Linguistic Data Consortium.[10]

Several extraction statistics are displayed in Table 5.9: the size of the source corpora[11], the total number of pairs extracted, and the number of distinct pairs for each language (rows 1–3).

The number of productive patterns found is shown in the last row of Table 5.9. The results indicate that a high number of POS combinations are actually productive. Some of these patterns contain very numerous pair instances (e.g., D-N, P-D, N-P, P-N), others very few (Conj-N, V-Conj, V-V). Tables 5.10 and 5.11 list some of the new collocationally relevant patterns found for English and French, in addition to those already used in our extraction system and that are shown in Table 4.1.

Table 5.9 Statistics for the pattern induction experiment

Experimental data	English	French
Words (approx.)	0.5 M	1.6 M
Extracted pairs (tokens)	188,527	748,592
Extracted pairs (types)	65,853	171,584
Productive POS combinations	60	57

---

[10] URL: http://www.ldc.upenn.edu/, accessed June, 2010.

[11] Since the experiments are not comparative and were conducted independently, the two corpora are of different sizes.

Table 5.10 Some interesting patterns discovered for English and their equivalents in the BBI dictionary

Pattern	Example	BBI code	BBI example
N-P	*Decision on*	G1: N-P	*Apathy towards*
N-conj	*Recognition that*	G3: N-that	*Agreement that*
P-N	*Under pressure*	G4: P-N	*In advance*
A-P	*Essential to*	G5: A-P	*Angry at*
A-conj	*Necessary for*	G7: A-that	*Afraid that*
V-conj	*Judge whether*	–	–
Adv-adv	*Much more*	–	–
Adv-P	*Together with*	–	–
Adv-conj	*Rather than*	–	–
P-P	*From near*	–	–

Table 5.11 Some interesting patterns discovered for French

Pattern	Example
N-P	*précaution quant*
N-conj	*idée que*
P-N	*sur mesure*
A-P	*déterminé comme*
A-conj	*probable que*
V-conj	*faire ainsi que*
Adv-adv	*bien au contraire*
Conj-adv	*ou bien*
Adv-conj	*d'autant plus que*
P-P	*jusque sur*
P-adv	*depuis longtemps*

These new patterns are commonly ignored by extraction systems, since they include function words. In the BBI dictionary (Benson et al., 1986a), however, such patterns are widely represented. They are called *grammatical collocations*, as opposed to *lexical collocations* which only contain open-class words. The preface of the dictionary provides a classification of the grammatical patterns, identified by a series of codes; the last column of Table 5.10 displays, for each pattern identified with our method, the corresponding code in the BBI classification, whenever a match is found.

Note that some of the patterns discovered may suggest an overlap between the notions of collocation and subcategorization. Some insights on this phenomenon are provided in Rögnvaldsson (2010); see also the discussion in Section 2.5.2.

5.2.3 Related Work

In trying to strike the right balance between precision and recall, extraction systems face the problem of choosing an appropriate set of patterns that describe the type of pairs sought. In order to increase the precision—and also the tractability—of systems, combinations that include functional categories (e.g., D, P, Conj) are usually excluded from the list of accepted patterns. But this choice leads to the failure of systems to capture a whole range of collocational phenomena which, as advocated particularly in van der Wouden (2001), are nonetheless important. An exception is the work of Smadja (1993), which discusses the collocational relevance of patterns like N-P (*accordance with, advantage of, agreement on, allegations of, anxiety about*) and N-D (*some people*). Lexicographic interest in such patterns is proven by the large amount of grammatical collocations listed in specific dictionaries like BBI (Benson et al., 1986a).

We adhere to the views expressed by Fontenelle (1992) and van der Wouden (2001), according to which lexical items of any category can show collocational effect. This is why, in our attempt to induce patterns from data, we considered any possible POS combination as relevant a priori. Then we narrowed down the obtained set of productive patterns (about 60 in English and in French) through an analysis of the pair instances found. This led to the discovery of a relatively reduced number of new patterns (about 20 per language) that could indeed be useful for future extraction. Part of the patterns found are combinations made up exclusively of closed-class categories, plus adverbs (e.g., Adv-Adv, Adv-Conj, Conj-Adv, P-P, P-Adv). These patterns are perhaps less useful for extraction, because, although highly frequent, they represent very few pair types, which can be exhaustively listed and known in advance. On the contrary, the patterns that include an open class category are very useful, as they permit the automatic discovery of the collocational properties of a large number of words.

Pursuing the same goal of solving the problem of pattern definition, Dias (2003) also proposes a data-driven approach, in which the relevant sequences of POS tags are identified with an association measure called Mutual Expectation.[12] As this method refers to the surface of the text, the patterns produced reflect the order of words in the text; they are affected by dispersion and rigidity, and are not guaranteed to be grammatically well-formed.

On the contrary, the patterns detected with our parse-based method are independent of the surface word order and they are grammatically well-formed. The method we proposed can be applied to any language supported by the parser in order to detect collocationally relevant configurations of length two; these, in turn, can be used to extract longer collocations with the method presented in Section 5.1. However, the full customization of our collocation extraction system for a new language should also take into account factors such as differences in lexical distribution across languages, because these are responsible for the performance of association measures when applied to a specific pattern. For instance, in English there are numerous V-P pairs which constitute phrasal verbs and verb-particle constructions, whereas

---

[12] More precisely, multi-word units are then identified in Dias (2003) by: (a) applying this measure on both sequences of words and on the corresponding sequences of POS tags; (b) combining the scores obtained, and (c) retaining only the local maxima candidates as valid, according to the method briefly explained in Section 5.1.3.

in French there are fewer such pairs. Therefore, a measure that is suitable to this pattern in English might be less suitable to the same pattern in French.[13]

5.3 Corpus-Based Collocation Translation

Due to their massive presence in language and their idiomatic encoding, collocations play a crucial role in NLP applications focused on text production, such as machine translation. Although collocations are at first sight semantically transparent and therefore similar to regular constructions, many of them cannot be translated literally. The choice of the "right word" to use in the target language is often a subtle process, with crucial implications on the translation quality. For example, apparently harmless combinations, like *grande attention*, *grande diversité*, *grande vitesse* in French, will lead to inadequate formulations in English if translated literally: **big attention, *big diversity, *big speed*. The right translations, *great attention*, *wide range* and *high speed*, illustrate the necessity of using collocations in the target language: the same adjective, *grande* ("big"), is translated in three different ways, depending on the noun that it modifies. Knowledge of collocations is considered indispensable for producing a more acceptable translation output (Orliac and Dillinger, 2003). This section describes a method that automatically finds translation equivalents for collocations by exploiting translation archives, like those represented by the available parallel corpora.

5.3.1 The Method

The method developed is based on a "deep" syntactic approach, in which collocations in the source language and their potential translations are identified in parallel corpora by relying on the multilingual parser Fips (Wehrli, 2007). The translation procedure consists of the following sequence of steps:

1. Extracting collocations from the source language corpora, by using the syntax-based method described in Chapter 4;
2. For each collocation pair, selecting a limited number of sentence contexts amongst all its contexts of occurrence in the source corpus (in our present experiments, we considered a maximum of 50 contexts for each pair);
3. Aligning the source sentences and obtaining a list of corresponding sentences in the target language;
4. Extracting collocations from the target sentences using the same method as in Step 1;

---

[13] In Seretan and Wehrli (2006) we discuss in detail the problems a (syntax-based or syntax-free) collocation extraction system faces when ported from English to a new language with a richer morphology and more flexible word order.

5. Matching the source collocation with its potential translation in the list of collocations extracted for the target language.

The sentence alignment method used in Step 3 is an in-house method described in Nerima et al. (2003). In Step 5, the selection of the potential translation is made by applying a series of filters on the pairs extracted in Step 4. Their role is to gradually reduce the number of candidate translations until a single candidate is eventually retained, which will be proposed as translation. These filters are described below.

Syntactic filter: Only those pairs are retained as potential translations that have a compatible syntactic type. At first, we made the simplifying assumption that collocations preserve their syntactic structure across languages, therefore the only target syntactic type allowed was the source syntactic type: for example, it was supposed that the English equivalent of a French verb-object collocation was a verb-object collocation, and so on. While this assumption is definitely too strong, it was shown to hold in the majority of cases (Lü and Zhou, 2004).
In a subsequent implementation, however, the condition of syntactic isomorphism was relaxed and instead of a single target type, we considered one-to-many mappings to account for the syntactic divergence between languages. Thus, language-dependent mapping sets were defined, in which the target configurations were ordered according to pre-determined weights.

Dictionary filter: A further strategy for narrowing the search space was to use bilingual dictionaries, when available, in order to retain only the target-language pairs that contain specific words. This filter is based on the base-collocate dichotomy in collocations (see Section 2.4.3), and assumes that the base—i.e., the semantic head of the collocation—preserves its meaning across languages, whereas the collocate does not. For instance, when the French collocation *gagner argent* is translated into English, the base preserves its meaning and is translated literally (*argent*, "money"), contrary to the collocate (*gagner*, "make"; compare *make money* with the literal translation **win money*, which is an anti-collocation[14]). The translation procedure first identifies the base word of the source collocation, which can be determined unequivocally given the syntactic type. Then, it searches for translations of that word in the bilingual dictionary, and retains only those target-language pairs which actually contain one of the translations proposed for the base.
The application of this filter might be problematic if the coverage of the bilingual dictionaries is insufficient. When a dictionary entry does not propose enough translation alternatives, it may happen that valid translation candidates are ruled out with this filter, and no solution is found. For instance, our French-English dictionary contained the following translations for the noun *remarque*: *remark, comment, note*. The translation method failed to find an English equivalent for the French collocation *faire une remarque*, because the valid candidate found in

---

[14] Term introduced by Pearce (2001a).

the corpus, *to make a point*, was excluded by the dictionary filter since *point* was not proposed as a translation for *remarque*. In the subsequent refinements of our method, we overcame this dictionary coverage problem by requiring that, whenever the search fails because of the dictionary filter, the search space is restored and the procedure continues without applying this filter.

Frequency filter: The final decision for choosing the target collocation among the remaining pairs is based on frequency. The pair with the highest number of occurrences in the target sentences is returned by the algorithm as the translation of the source collocation. In fact, due to the manner in which the target sentences have been selected (as equivalents of sentences in which the source collocation appears), the frequency of pairs in these sentences is a good indicator for the target collocation. In case of tied frequency values, no translation was initially proposed, as our experiments have shown that the inclusion of all of the top pairs affects the precision of the translation method. In later implementation, however, we succeeded in increasing the coverage of the method by proposing to take into account the association score in order to decide between candidate pairs, in case of equal frequencies.

5.3.2 Experimental Results

Collocation translation experiments have been run on the data used in Experiment 2, containing parallel texts in four languages—English, French, Spanish and Italian—from the Europarl corpus (Section 4.4.5). First, the basic translation method, which excludes the improvements mentioned in the description provided in the previous section, was applied on the top 500 verb-object collocations extracted. The translation involved all of the 12 possible language pairs.

Table 5.12 illustrates some of the translations obtained for French-English and English-French. The equivalents shown are all non-literal translations of the source collocations. Randomly selected results for the other language pairs considered are provided in Seretan and Wehrli (2007). An evaluation was conducted on two thirds of the results—i.e., 4,000 translation equivalents—for 8 language pairs from the 12 considered. It showed a precision of 89.9% and a coverage (percentage of collocation pairs for which a translation was proposed) of 70.9%.

The evaluation also showed that there is no marked difference in precision among the collocations with a high, medium, and low frequency, i.e., between collocations with 31–50 instances, 16–30 instances, and 1–15 instances, respectively. The precision is 95.6% for the first group, 93.3% for the second, and 89.8% for the third. However, the translation coverage is more affected by the decrease in frequency: from 75.8% for the first group it descends to 70.7% for the second and to 58.3% for the low-frequency group.

We also assessed the impact of the dictionary on the performance of the translation method, and found that this is not crucial for the quality of results. The collocation translation method we proposed produces good results even in the absence of bilingual dictionaries. The average precision for the language pairs for which a

Table 5.12 Sample collocation translation results for the basic method

French-English	English-French
accomplir progrès - make progress	breathe life - donner vie
accorder importance - attach importance	bridge gap - combler lacune
accuser retard - experience delay	broach subject - aborder sujet
atteindre but - achieve goal	devote attention - accorder attention
combler fossé - bridge gap	draw conclusion - tirer conclusion
commettre erreur - make mistake	draw distinction - établir distinction
consentir effort - make effort	draw list - dresser liste
constituer menace - pose threat	face challenge - relever défi
demander asile - seek asylum	foot bill - payer facture
donner avis - issue advice	fulfil criterion - remplir critère
effectuer visite - pay visit	give example - citer exemple
établir distinction - draw distinction	give support - apporter soutien
exercer pression - put pressure	have difficulty - éprouver difficulté
faire pas - take step	have reservation - émettre réserve
fixer objectif - set objective	hold discussion - avoir discussion
jeter base - establish basis	hold presidency - assurer présidence
lancer appel - make appeal	learn lesson - tirer leçon
lever obstacle - remove obstacle	lend support - apporter soutien
mener débat - hold debate	make effort - déployer effort
mener discussion - have discussion	make sense - avoir sense
opérer distinction - draw distinction	pose threat - constituer menace
porter fruit - bear fruit	reach compromise - trouver compromis
poser question - ask question	reap benefit - récolter fruit
prendre distance - keep distance	run risk - courir risque
prononcer discours - make speech	set precedent - créer précédent
remplir condition - meet condition	shoulder responsibility - assumer responsabilité
remporter succès - have success	strike balance - trouver équilibre
rendre hommage - pay tribute	take place - avoir lieu
respecter principe - uphold principle	take stand - prendre position
traiter question - address issue	wage war - faire guerre

bilingual dictionary was used is 92.9%; for the others, 84.5%. The difference in coverage is even smaller (71.7% vs. 69.5%).

The refinements made to the basic method contributed to a substantial increase in coverage. Measured on the English-French language pair, the coverage raised from 71.4 to 94.2%. In exchange for this increase, the precision decreased from 94.4 to 84.1%. On balance, the overall performance of the method reported in terms of F-measure[15] was found to raise from 78.6 to 81.6%. Table 5.13 provides examples of translations that do not preserve the syntactic structure in the target language.

---

[15] The F-measure is the harmonic mean of precision and recall: $F = 2PR/(P+R)$. If we consider that the task to solve is to find exactly one translation for each source collocation, then the recall represents, in our case, the number of correct translations returned divided by the number of correct translations expected.

Table 5.13 Sample collocation translation results for the enhanced method

English (V-O) → French (V-P-N)		English (V-P-N)→ French (V-O)	
Answer question	répondre à question	Adhere to deadline	respecter délai
Attend meeting	assister à réunion	Bring to attention	attirer attention
Have access	bénéficier de accès	Bring to end	mettre terme
Lose sight	perdre de vue	Come to decision	prendre décision
Meet demand	satisfaire à exigence	Comply with legislation	respecter législation
Meet need	répondre à besoin	Lead to improvement	entraîner amélioration
Reach compromise	parvenir à compromis	Meet with resistance	rencontrer résistance
Reach conclusion	aboutir à conclusion	Provide with opportunity	fournir occasion
Reach consensus	aboutir à consensus	Respond to challenge	relever défi
Stress need	insister sur nécessité	Touch on point	aborder point

5.3.3 Related Work

Corpus-based collocation translation has previously been dealt with in a number of works. One of the earliest is described by Kupiec (1993), and is focused on finding noun phrase correspondences between English and French from the sentence-aligned Hansard parallel corpus. Both source and target corpora are POS-tagged, then NPs are detected with a finite-state recognizer. The matching is done by using Expectation Maximization (EM), an iterative re-estimation algorithm. The precision reported is 90% for the top 100 translations obtained. A similar method was proposed by van der Eijk (1993) for the language pair Dutch-English. The matching method is done using two main heuristics: the target noun phrase is selected depending on (a) its frequency in the target sentences, and (b) its relative position in the source sentence. The reported performance was lower (68% precision and 64% coverage), and this difference was explained by the fact that the evaluation was performed on a larger test set of 1,100 noun phrases.

Also, Dagan and Church (1994) made use of word alignment to find candidate translations for noun phrases in parallel corpora. Once the source noun phrases have been identified, the text span between the alignments of the first and the last words of the phrase is proposed as a translation candidate. Candidates are sorted in the decreasing frequency order. Unlike the previous approaches, their system, Termight, has the advantage of finding translations even for infrequent terms. But like the preceding systems, it is limited to rigid constructions. Evaluation performed on 192 English-German correspondences showed a precision of 40%.

Champollion (Smadja et al., 1996) is the first proper collocation translation system. Built around Xtract (Smadja, 1993), Champollion can handle both rigid and flexible collocations in English, for which it detects a translation in the aligned French sentences from the Hansard corpus with the help of a statistical correlation metric, the Dice coefficient. The method used requires an additional post-processing step in which the order of words in a flexible collocation is decided, given that no syntactic analysis is performed on the target side. The system was evaluated by three annotators and showed a precision of 77 and 61%, respectively, on two different test sets of 300 collocations each. These collocations were randomly selected among the medium-frequency results; the difference in the precision obtained is explained by the lower frequency of collocations from the second set.

Finally, the work of Lü and Zhou (2004) can also deal with flexible collocations; moreover, these are well-formed since they are extracted using a parser. The syntactic types considered are verb-object, adjective-noun, and adverb-verb. Collocations are extracted from monolingual corpora in English and Chinese by applying the log-likelihood ratio measure on syntactically related pairs identified by a dependency parser. The match between a source and target collocation is performed by using a statistical translation model which estimates word translations with EM. The head and the dependent word are assigned uneven probabilities, while the dependency relation is considered to be preserved across languages. The method (whose reported coverage is 83.98%) was evaluated on a test set of 1,000 randomly selected collocations. It achieves between 50.85 and 68.15% accuracy, depending on the syntactic type. The availability and the quality of bilingual dictionaries are essential for the performance of this method.

Compared to the methods mentioned above, the method we proposed takes into account a wider range of syntactic configurations, it can handle both rigid and syntactically flexible constructions, both frequent and infrequent collocations, and is efficient both in the presence and the absence of bilingual dictionaries. We believe that its higher performance, obtained in spite of its simplicity, is mainly due to the availability of syntactic information for both the source and target languages.

5.4 Summary

This chapter provided solutions to several problems that are often overlooked in applied accounts of collocations.

The first problem addressed is the limitation of existing extraction work to collocations of length two. Binary collocation is only one facet of the much more complex phenomenon of word collocability (see Chapter 2). This is because "basic" binary collocations may be embedded within other binary collocations to form complex collocations containing a larger number of words. Our empirical investigation revealed that some of the binary collocations previously identified by our syntax-based method (presented in Chapter 4) occur significantly in combination with other such collocations. Therefore, we were able to extend the extraction method to cope with the systematic combination of collocations— either basic or complex which we call *collocation chains*—by relying on the concept of "collocation of collocations". The identification of complex collocations is particularly important in cases where a link in a collocation chain does not constitute a complete or autonomous phraseological unit by itself, but is only the fragment of a more complex unit. In coming up with a solution to the collocation chain problem, we related this problem to the problem of nested (fragmentary) terms, which is better known in the related field of terminology.

The second issue dealt with in this chapter was the problem of deciding which syntactic patterns are relevant for collocation extraction in a given language, a problem of relevance to shallow approaches that apply a POS pattern filter on extraction candidates as well as to syntax-based extraction approaches. Generally chosen in a rather arbitrary way, the syntactic patterns used in extraction are nonetheless essential for the quality of results. While combinations with closed-class words are of the greatest importance in lexicography and NLP, in the tradeoff between precision and recall, functional categories are usually disregarded in existing extraction work and only open-class words are retained. In contrast, in our data-driven pattern induction experiments, these combinations were found to constitute an important part of a newly-discovered pattern for English and French.

The third issue addressed was the automatic acquisition of collocation equivalents from parallel text corpora. Unlike the sustained efforts made to acquire monolingual collocations, relatively little has been done in the recent applied work to compile bilingual collocational resources needed for machine translation, which is the application that is most in need of collocational knowledge. However, with a few exceptions, the acquisition of translation equivalents has concentrated mainly on one category of collocations, noun phrases. We provided a more appropriate account for the less rigid collocations by introducing a method that detects collocation translations by relying on syntactic analysis of both source and target languages.

In all the extensions discussed in this chapter, we showed that considerable leverage can be gained from syntactic analysis of the input text. Deep parsing helps to abstract away from the particular surface text realization of collocation candidates, enables the convenient grouping of multiple instances belonging to the same collocation type, and permits the retrieval of discontinuous instances for the collocations that are syntactically flexible.

Chapter 6
Conclusion

6.1 Main Contributions

The phenomenon of *word collocation*, which was at the heart of the research described in this book, has received considerable attention in many fields, including corpus linguistics, computational lexicography, terminology, foreign language teaching and computational linguistics. In our review in Chapter 2, we attempted to guide the reader through the maze of the various, and often inconsistent, theoretical description provided for this phenomenon in the relevant literature. We described the manner in which collocations have been accounted for in several theoretical frameworks, and we identified the main collocation features that serve as the basis in our practical investigations.

Our work focussed specifically on *collocation extraction*, an established area of research in NLP which aims at providing methodologies for the automatic acquisition of collocations from text corpora. In Chapter 3, we introduced the backgrounds of extraction techniques that are in use nowadays; we discussed the role of linguistic preprocessing as a means to enhance the performance of these techniques; and we reviewed the practical work dedicated to collocation extraction. We attempted to provide a self-contained description that does not require expert knowledge to be understood, but is accessible to the reader not familiar with the topic. As further reading suggestions, we propose the general introductions provided by McKeown and Radev (2000), Evert (2008a), and Baroni and Evert (2008) on the topics of collocation, collocation extraction, and the relation with other research topics in NLP. A detailed description of collocations and other types of multi-word expressions from a practical perspective has recently been provided by Baldwin and Kim (2010). A picture of the current NLP research on multi-word expressions in general, and collocations in particular, can be found, for instance, in the proceedings of the ACL Workshops on Multiword Expressions, as well as in Grossmann and Tutin (2003), Villavicencio et al. (2005), and Rayson et al. (2010).

The main aim of the work described in this book was to propose a collocation extraction approach that integrates syntactic information as one of its essential ingredients. The underlying message of the book is that a syntax-based approach is one that succeeds to adequately model the collocation phenomenon and to account for

V. Seretan, *Syntax-Based Collocation Extraction*, Text, Speech and Language Technology 44, DOI 10.1007/978-94-007-0134-2_6,
© Springer Science+Business Media B.V. 2011

the high morpho-syntactic flexibility of collocations. As previously suggested by
other authors—e.g., Smadja (1993), Krenn (2000a), Pearce (2002), Evert (2004b)—
we argued that (full) deep syntactic parsing, whenever available, should be used for
preprocessing the text corpora as an alternative to shallow preprocessing based on
part-of-speech pattern matching.

As described in Chapter 4, in our work we used a multilingual parser developed
at the University of Geneva, and showed that a syntax-based extraction approach
is indeed feasible. A deep syntactic analysis was performed on large corpora of
unrestricted text in English, French, Spanish and Italian. The parser used has a broad
grammatical coverage and can handle complex constructions in which the individual
words of a collocation may appear far apart from each other due to various grammatical transformations (e.g., passivisation, relativisation, interrogation, clefting). Our
understanding of the collocation concept departs from the one used in the British tra-
dition, as words co-occurring "within a short space of each other in a text" (Sinclair,
1991, 170). We adopt a narrower, linguistically-motivated understanding, in line
with recent work that proposes the use of a different term (*co-occurrence*) for the
traditional understanding. Therefore, in our work we applied the syntactic proximity
instead of the linear proximity as a criterion in selecting collocation candidates in a
text.

The motivation for proposing a syntax-based approach for collocation extraction
came from encouraging results obtained by using syntactic parsing for other NLP
tasks, like term extraction (Maynard and Ananiadou, 1999), semantic role labelling
(Gildea and Palmer, 2002) and semantic similarity computation (Padó and Lapata,
2007). As in the case of the work cited above, syntactic information was found
to make a substantial contribution to the quality of collocation extraction results.
Our evaluation experiments compared our purposed extraction method based on
deep syntactic parsing against a baseline represented by the sliding window method
based on POS pattern matching. Syntactic information was found to lead to a substantial increase in extraction precision, both in a multilingual and in a cross-lingual
extraction setting. Some of the particular advantages of carrying out a preliminary
syntactic analysis of the text corpora are: the high reliability of results in terms
of grammaticality; the availability of syntactic information (which facilitates the
interpretation of results); the consolidation of the different instances of the same
collocation, even when they have a different morpho-syntactic realization (which
leads to less data sparsity problems and to a more reliable statistical inference); and
the drastic reduction of the number of candidates (which leads to a more tractable
computation when large corpora are processed).

Also, the syntax-based extraction approach proved very useful in extending our
practical account of collocation—as described in Chapter 5—in order to cover a
broader spectrum of collocational phenomena in text. We considered three research
directions that have been less explored in previous work: the extraction of collocation made up of more than two words, the semi-automatic induction of syntactic
patterns defining collocation in a given language, and the extraction of translation
equivalents for collocations. These explorations offer an outlook on promising directions for future research on collocation extraction.

There is, basically, a single counterargument to syntax-based collocation extraction, namely, the reduced availability of syntactic parsers for many languages. As the parsing field is making steady progress, especially through the development of language-independent frameworks for dependency parsing (Nivre, 2006), we expect that an ever increasing amount of collocation extraction work will be performed in the future by relying on parsing. The extraction methodology we proposed is not dependent on a specific parser, therefore it can be an inspiration to similar approaches.

6.2 Future Directions

Although throughout this book we attempted to cover the most important issues related to syntax-based extraction as comprehensively as possible, there are undoubtedly many issues that escaped our analysis or have only partly been addressed. For instance, the issue of portability of our extraction methodology across languages has only been partly addressed in the work described in this book. The extraction experiments described involved relatively similar languages and used practically the same set of syntactic patterns. In Chapter 5 we proposed a strategy for customising the extraction procedure to a new language, which consisted of inducing collocationally relevant syntactic patterns from generic dependency relations. However, we have not yet applied it on structurally different languages, like German, which exhibits specific features, possibly challenging our standard extraction method. Our preliminary experiments on German collocation extraction made use of the same patterns, but finer tuning is supposedly required to meet the needs of extraction for lexicographic purposes.

A connected issue is that of evaluating the recall or extraction method. This has insufficiently been investigated in our present analysis, in which we only conducted a few case-study evaluations of recall. A more extensive evaluation is needed in order to identify which collocational phenomena fail to be captured by a syntax-based approach, compared to a syntax-free approach. Such an evaluation is currently difficult to perform, given the absence of large-scale reference resources.

Another investigation that should be extended is the comparative evaluation against extraction based on shallow-parsing approaches, which are much more common in current research than the traditional window method. In line with what has already been said in Chapter 4, it must be stressed out that many researchers are skeptical about whether deep parsing is really necessary for high-quality extraction, or shallow-parsing techniques are sufficient. In our work, we made a preliminary evaluation of the results obtained by a state-of-the-art extractor based on shallow parsing, the SketchEngine (Kilgarriff et al., 2004). The results are not entirely conclusive, because we only investigated the grammaticality of a small number of results in English. This evaluation suggested that there is room for improvement, and this improvement should be possible to achieve by using deep parsing. But a more thorough evaluation is required in order to better assess the difference in performance between the two approaches.

An issue which we did not explore yet is the exploitation of the alternative syntactic analyses proposed by a parser for a sentence, in the extraction process. Ambiguity, as is well-known, pervades languages, and as a matter of fact, syntactic parsers generally return more than one analysis for a sentence. As in related work, we only considered the first, most probable, analysis produced by the parser. The question that emerges is whether the other alternatives could lead to the discovery of more collocation types of tokens. This is a direction which we consider particularly worth pursuing in future investigations, because it could shed light on the complex interplay between collocations and parsing and, more generally, on the interrelation between lexicon and grammar.

Perhaps the relatively broad interpretation of the collocation concept we adopted in our work could also be seen as a limitation of our study. In fact, it covers any statistically significant combination of words in a syntactic relationship, and may overlap with particular subtypes of multi-word expressions that linguists normally try to tell apart (e.g., support-verb constructions, compounds, idioms, phrasal verbs). The finer-grained classification of multi-word expressions is an important, and very debated topic in the theoretical literature—see, for instance, the recent account of Leoni de Leon (2008). However, from a practical point of view such a distinction is less relevant, because regardless of their specific label, multi-word expressions pose similar processing problems. It is perhaps of higher importance to distinguish them from fully productive combinations, which can be processed in a regular way. In the NLP literature, there are numerous reports on practical attempts to distinguish compositional from non-compositional expressions, e.g., Bannard (2005), Fazly and Stevenson (2007), McCarthy et al. (2007), Cook et al. (2008), Diab and Bhutada (2009).

In our evaluation experiments, multi-word expressions have been classified in four categories: idiom, collocation, compound, and named entity. The annotated data produced (shown in Appendixes C.2 and E.1 and available online[1]) can serve as a basis for future investigations of this kind. For instance, it can be used for supervised classification, or for signalling researchers what are the borders between categories that are more difficult to define. In particular, our annotated data suggest that most of the ambiguity cases concern regular combinations and collocations, and there is less ambiguity between collocations and idioms. This finding is consistent with the report of Benson et al. (1986b), according to which collocations are more difficult to identify than idioms and compounds.[2]

Seen from a broader perspective, our work represents only one step towards a better treatment of collocations in a computational framework. The extraction can be further improved by complementary techniques applied either at the candidate

---

[1] URL: http://www.latl.unige.ch/personal/vseretan/data/annot/Exp1.html   and http://www.latl.unige.ch/personal/vseretan/data/annot/Exp2.html.

[2] "The critical problem for the lexicographer has been, heretofore, the treatment of collocations. It has been far more difficult to identify them than idioms or even compounds" (Benson et al., 1986b, 256).

selection or candidate ranking stage. For instance, as suggested in Chapter 3, more sophisticated text analysis modules (such as anaphora resolution) might prove useful for detecting more collocation types and instances; this is particularly desirable for lower frequency collocations, which make up the majority of collocations in a corpus. Other NLP techniques (e.g., paraphrase detection, nominalization interpretation) could also serve this goal and could be integrated in collocation extractors to perform a more complex linguistic preprocessing of the text. Lexical semantic resources (e.g., Wordnet, FrameNet, other thesauri and lexical ontologies) could also complement these techniques and allow for enhanced collocation extraction.[3]

In addition, novel association measures which are more adequate to language data and take into account the base-collocate distinction in collocations are expected to enhance extraction as well. The research on asymmetric measures has already been initiated by Michelbacher et al. (2007). As an alternative, other extraction techniques could by employed that do not rely on statistical inference, e.g., techniques based on data mining (Rajman and Besançon, 1998; Kurz and Xu, 2002), machine learning (Yang, 2003), or word alignment (Villada Moirón and Tiedemann, 2006; de Caseli et al., 2010). Data sparsity problems can be overcome by Web-based extraction (Pearce, 2001a; Zaiu Inkpen and Hirst, 2002; Keller and Lapata, 2003). Furthermore, the examples contained in many traditional mono-lexeme dictionaries constitute a rich source of collocational information, but, as far as we know, this has not yet been exploited for collocation extraction.

Last but not least, it must be mentioned that collocation extraction, although an independent area of research, is not a goal in itself. As shown in Chapters 1 and 3, collocation extraction results are used in a variety of NLP applications and in several lexicographic projects. Yet, their integration in more challenging tasks dealing with language production or in computer-assisted language learning systems cannot succeed without a more adequate contextual description. This is necessary in order to specify the allowed (or preferred) degree of morpho-syntactic flexibility, e.g., number variation for nouns, presence or absence of determiners, modification potential, voice for verbs. Such corpus-based analyses are the focus of current research (Tutin, 2004, 2005; Villada Moirón, 2005; Ritz, 2006; Heid and Weller, 2008; Weller and Heid, 2010). Another important research direction is the development of techniques for organising the extraction results according to semantic criteria in order to facilitate lexicographic studies and the practical use in other applications (L'Homme, 2003; Wanner et al., 2006). Whether these tasks could benefit from a syntax-based approach similar to the one we adopted for collocation extraction is a question that deserves close attention in future research on phraseological units.

---

[3] Semantic annotations have been used for multi-word expression extraction, for instance, in Piao et al. (2005).

Appendix A
List of Collocation Dictionaries

English

- BBI – The BBI Dictionary of English Word Combinations (Benson et al., 1986a)
- LDOCE – Longman Dictionary of Contemporary English (Procter, 1987)
- LLA – Longman Language Activator (Maingay and Tribble, 1993)
- A Dictionary of English Collocations (Kjellmer, 1994)
- COBUILD – Collins Cobuild English Dictionary (Sinclair, 1995)
- The LTP Dictionary of Selected Collocations (Hill and Lewis, 1997)
- OCDSE – Oxford Collocations Dictionary for Students of English (Lea and Runcie, 2002)
- English Collocations in Use (O'Dell and McCarthy, 2008)

French

- ECD – Dictionnaire explicatif et combinatoire du français contemporain (Mel'čuk et al., 1984, 1988, 1992, 1999)
- DiCo – Dictionnaire de Combinatoire (Polguère, 2000)
- LAF – Lexique actif du français (Polguère, 2000)
- Dictionnaire de cooccurrences (Beauchesne, 2001)
- DAFLES – Dictionnaire d'apprentissage du français langue étrangère ou seconde (Selva et al., 2002)
- Dictionnaire combinatoire du français: expressions, locutions et constructions (Zinglé and Brobeck-Zinglé, 2003)
- Les Voisins de *Le Monde* (Bourigault, 2005)
- Le Robert – Dictionnaire des combinaisons de mots: les synonymes en contexte (Fur et al., 2007)

Italian

- DICI – The Dictionary of Italian Collocations (Spina, 2010)

V. Seretan, *Syntax-Based Collocation Extraction*, Text, Speech and Language Technology 44, DOI 10.1007/978-94-007-0134-2,
© Springer Science+Business Media B.V. 2011

Polish

– The SyntLex Dictionary of Collocations (Vetulani et al., 2008)

Portugese

– COMBINA-PT – Word Combinations in Portuguese Language (Santos Pereira et al., 2002)

Russian

– CrossLexica (Bolshakov and Gelbukh, 2001)

Spanish

– DiCE – Diccionario de Colocaciones del Español (Alonso Ramos, 2004)

Appendix B
List of Collocation Definitions

1. Firth (1957, 181)

   Collocations of a given word are statements of the habitual and customary places of that word.

2. Firth (1968, 182)

   Collocations are actual words in habitual company.

3. Cowie (1978, 132)

   the co-occurrence of two or more lexical items as realizations of structural elements within a given syntactic pattern

4. Hausmann (1985)

   typical, specific and characteristic combination of two words

5. Cruse (1986, 40)

   The term *collocation* will be used to refer to sequences of lexical items which habitually co-occur, but which are nonetheless fully transparent in the sense that each lexical constituent is also a semantic constituent.

6. Kjellmer (1987, 133)

   a sequence of words that occurs more than once in identical form (...) and which is grammatically well structured.

7. Choueka (1988)

   a sequence of two or more consecutive words, that has characteristics of a syntactic and semantic unit whose exact and unambiguous meaning or connotation cannot be derived directly from the meaning or connotation of its components

8. Hausmann (1989, 1010)

   On appellera collocation la combinaison caractéristique de deux mots dans une des structures suivantes : (a) substantif + adjectif (épithète); (b) substantif + verbe; (c) verbe + substantif (objet); (d) verbe + adverbe; (e) adjectif + adverbe; (f) substantif + (prép.) + substantif." [We shall call collocation a characteristic combination of two words in a structure like the following: (a) noun + adjective (epithet); (b) noun + verb; (c) verb + noun (object); (d) verb + adverb; (e) adjective + adverb; (f) noun + (prep) + noun.]

9. Benson (1990)

   A collocation is an arbitrary and recurrent word combination.

10. Sinclair (1991, 170)

> Collocation is the cooccurrence of two or more words within a short space of each other in a text.

11. Fontenelle (1992, 222)

> The term *collocation* refers to the idiosyncratic syntagmatic combination of lexical items and is independent of word class or syntactic structure.

12. Smadja (1993, 143)

> recurrent combinations of words that co-occur more often than expected by chance and that correspond to arbitrary word usages

13. van der Wouden (1997, 5)

> Collocation: idiosyncratic restriction on the combinability of lexical items

14. Manning and Schütze (1999, 151)

> A collocation is an expression consisting of two or more words that correspond to some conventional way of saying things.

15. McKeown and Radev (2000, 507)

> Collocations (...) cover word pairs and phrases that are commonly used in language, but for which no general syntactic and semantic rules apply.

16. Polguère (2000, 518)

> The notion of COLLOCATION refers to semi-idiomatic expressions L1+L2 such that one of the components, the COLLOCATE, is chosen to express a given meaning, in a specific syntactic role, contingent upon the choice of the other component, called the BASE of the collocation.

17. Lea and Runcie (2002, vii)

> Collocation is the way words combine in a language to produce natural-sounding speech and writing

18. Sag et al. (2002, 7)

> Institutionalized phrases are semantically and syntactically compositional, but statistically idiosyncratic. (...) We reserve the term *collocation* to refer to any statistically significant cooccurrence, including all forms of MWE (...) and compositional phrases.

19. Evert (2004b, 17)

> A collocation is a word combination whose semantic and/or syntactic properties cannot be fully predicted from those of its components, and which therefore has to be listed in a lexicon.

20. Bartsch (2004, 76)

> lexically and/or pragmatically constrained recurrent co-occurrences of at least two lexical items which are in a direct syntactic relation with each other

21. Krenn (2008, 7)

> Collocations in our terms are lexically motivated word combinations that constitute phrasal units with restrictions in their semantic compositionality and morpho-syntactic flexibility.

Appendix C
Association Measures – Mathematical Notes

C.1 χ^2

$$\chi^2 = \sum_{i,j} \frac{(O_{ij} - E_{ij})^2}{E_{ij}} = \sum_{i,j} \frac{O_{ij}^2}{E_{i,j}} - 2\sum_{i,j} O_{i,j} + \sum_{i,j} E_{i,j}$$

$$= \sum_{i,j} \frac{O_{ij}^2}{E_{i,j}} - 2N + \frac{\sum_{i,j} R_i C_j}{N} = \sum_{i,j} \frac{O_{ij}^2}{E_{i,j}} - \frac{2N^2 - \sum_{i,j} R_i C_j}{N}$$

$$\tag{C.1}$$

Since $\displaystyle\sum_{i,j} R_i C_j = a^2 + b^2 + c^2 + d^2 + 2ab + 2ac + 2ad + 2bc + 2bd + 2cd = N^2$,
by substituting in (C.1) we obtain:

$$\chi^2 = \sum_{i,j} \frac{O_{ij}^2}{E_{i,j}} - N = \frac{Na^2}{(a+b)(a+c)} + \frac{Nb^2}{(a+b)(b+d)} + \frac{Nc^2}{(a+c)(c+d)}$$

$$+ \frac{Nd^2}{(c+d)(b+d)} - N$$

$$= \frac{N(a^2(c+d)(b+d) + b^2(a+c)(c+d) + c^2(a+b)(b+d) + d^2(a+b)(a+c))}{(a+b)(a+c)(b+d)(c+d)}$$

$$- \frac{N(a+b)(a+c)(b+d)(c+d)}{(a+b)(a+c)(b+d)(c+d)}$$

$$= \frac{N(a^2d^2 + b^2c^2 - 2abcd)}{(a+b)(a+c)(b+d)(c+d)} = \frac{N(ad-bc)^2}{(a+b)(a+c)(b+d)(c+d)}$$

C.2 Log-Likelihood Ratio

$$LLR = -2\log\frac{L(H_0)}{L(H_1)} = -2\log\frac{B(a; a+b, p)B(c; c+d, p)}{B(a; a+b, p_1)B(c; c+d; p_2)}$$

$$= -2\log\frac{B\left(a; a+b, \dfrac{a+c}{N}\right)B\left(c; c+d, \dfrac{a+c}{N}\right)}{B\left(a; a+b, \dfrac{a}{a+b}\right)B\left(c; c+d; \dfrac{c}{c+d}\right)}$$

$$= -2\log\frac{\dbinom{a+b}{a}\left(\dfrac{a+c}{N}\right)^a\left(1-\dfrac{a+c}{N}\right)^b\dbinom{c+d}{c}\left(\dfrac{a+c}{N}\right)^c\left(1-\dfrac{a+c}{N}\right)^d}{\dbinom{a+b}{a}\left(\dfrac{a}{a+b}\right)^a\left(1-\dfrac{a}{a+b}\right)^b\dbinom{c+d}{c}\left(\dfrac{c}{c+d}\right)^c\left(1-\dfrac{c}{c+d}\right)^d}$$

$$= -2\left(a\log\frac{a+c}{N} + b\log\frac{b+d}{N} + c\log\frac{a+c}{N} + d\log\frac{b+d}{N}\right.$$

$$\left. -a\log\frac{a}{a+b} - b\log\frac{b}{a+b} - c\log\frac{c}{c+d} - d\log\frac{d}{c+d}\right)$$

$$= -2(a\log(a+c) - a\log N + b\log(b+d) - b\log N + c\log(a+c)$$

$$-c\log N + d\log(b+d) - d\log N - a\log a + a\log(a+b)$$

$$-b\log b + b\log(a+b) - c\log c + c\log(c+d) - d\log d + d\log(c+d))$$

$$= -2((a+b)\log(a+b) + (a+c)\log(a+c)$$

$$+(b+d)\log(b+d) + (c+d)\log(c+d) - (a+b+c+d)\log N$$

$$-a\log a - b\log b - c\log c - d\log d)$$

$$= 2(a\log a + b\log b + c\log c + d\log d - (a+b)\log(a+b) - (a+c)\log(a+c)$$

$$-(b+d)\log(b+d) - (c+d)\log(c+d) + (a+b+c+d)\log(a+b+c+d))$$

Appendix D
Monolingual Evaluation (Experiment 1)

D.1 Test Data and Annotations

Test data and annotations used in Experiment 1 (Section 4.4.3). Labels: 0 = *erroneous pair*; 1 = *interesting pair*; 2 = *regular pair*. Common items in the two lists compared are underlined. The following marks are used: star (*) = *erroneous pair*; diamond (◇) = *interesting pair* (multi-word expression); question mark (?) = undecided (complete disagreement); no mark = *regular pair*.

Parse-based method

	Key1, Prep, Key2	Type	LLR	F	Labels
TS1					
◇	premier - ministre	A-N	4317.6	1047	1-1-1
◇	bloc - québécois	N-A	3946.1	429	1-1-1
◇	discours - de - trône	N-P-N	3894.0	426	1-1-1
◇	vérificateur - général	N-A	3796.7	460	1-1-2
◇	parti - réformiste	N-A	3615.0	474	1-1-1
	gouvernement - fédéral	N-A	3461.9	860	2-2-1
◇	missile - de - croisière	N-P-N	3147.4	323	1-1-1
	Chambre - de - commune	N-P-N	3083.0	430	1-1-2
◇	livre - rouge	N-A	2536.9	215	1-1-2
◇	secrétaire - parlementaire	N-A	2524.7	283	1-1-1
◇	question - adresser	S-V	2460.9	321	1-1-1
	opposition - officiel	N-A	2294.2	217	1-2-2
	programme - social	N-A	2165.7	394	1-1-1
◇	jouer - rôle	V-O	1909.5	199	1-1-1

Window method

	Key1, Key2	Type	LLR	F	Labels
◇	Monsieur - président	N-N	21138.1	2680	2-1-1
◇	premier - ministre	A-N	5571.0	1293	1-1-1
◇	madame - présidente	N-N	5279.2	419	2-1-1
*	Monsieur - présider	N-V	3804.6	385	2-0-0
◇	vérificateur - général	N-A	3403.9	447	1-1-1
◇	bloc - québécois	N-A	3124.3	407	1-1-1
◇	parti - réformiste	N-A	3083.0	462	1-1-1
◇	campagne - électoral	N-A	2905.3	306	1-1-1
◇	livre - rouge	N-A	2773.5	272	1-1-1
◇	discours - trône	N-N	2574.7	413	1-2-1
◇	gouvernement - fédéral	N-A	2395.2	896	1-1-1
	milliard - dollar	N-N	2364.8	483	2-1-2
	missile - croisière	N-N	2292.5	327	1-1-1
◇	secrétaire - parlementaire	N-A	2287.0	285	1-2-1

Parse-based method

Key1, Prep, Key2	Type	LLR	F	Labels
◊ poser - question	V-O	1877.1	282	1-1-1
milliard - de - dollar	N-P-N	1846.1	259	2-2-2
◊ créer - emploi	V-O	1709.5	261	1-1-1
◊ développement - de - ressource	N-P-N	1626.4	200	1-1-2
◊ prendre - décision	V-O	1607.4	278	1-1-1
◊ création - de - emploi	N-P-N	1552.3	245	1-1-1
◊ défense - national	N-A	1444.4	201	1-1-1
adresser - à - ministre	V-P-N	1397.1	238	2-1-2
◊ petit - entreprise	A-N	1378.3	204	1-1-2
◊ consentement - unanime	N-A	1333.8	101	1-1-1
◊ million - de - dollar	N-P-N	1258.5	215	2-2-2
◊ maintien - de - paix	N-P-N	1250.4	189	1-1-1
◊ président - suppléant	N-A	1216.4	115	2-1-1
- député - honorable	V-O	1194.0	118	0-1-2
◊ remercier - député	V-O	1186.9	200	2-1-2
rapport - de - vérificateur	N-P-N	1185.4	140	2-2-2
◊ comité - permanent	N-A	1184.0	157	1-1-1
◊ taux - de - chômage	N-P-N	1180.4	102	1-1-1
◊ compte - public	N-A	1170.3	143	1-1-1
◊ régler - problème	V-O	1091.6	161	1-1-1
◊ code - criminel	N-A	1081.1	90	1-1-1
◊ essai - de - missile	N-P-N	1073.9	158	2-2-2
vote - libre	N-A	1040.3	90	1-2-2
◊ chef - de - opposition	N-P-N	1032.8	145	1-1-1
◊ marché - de - travail	N-P-N	1018.3	120	1-1-2
◊ solliciteur - général	N-A	985.2	128	1-1-1
◊ ministre - de - Affaires étrangères	N-P-N	974.1	78	1-1-1
◊ Conseil - de - trésor	N-P-N	971.3	93	1-1-1

Window method

Key1, Key2	Type	LLR	F	Labels
◊ question - s'adresser	N-V	2086.2	313	1-1-1
◊ maintien - paix	N-N	2054.4	435	1-1-1
◊ ressource - humain	N-A	2053.9	318	1-1-1
million - dollar	N-N	1954.6	460	2-2-2
monsieur - président	N-N	1909.7	282	2-1-1
◊ tenir - compte	V-N	1869.2	282	1-1-1
opposition - officiel	N-A	1772.0	215	2-2-1
◊ programme - social	N-A	1763.2	562	1-2-1
◊ petit - entreprise	A-N	1588.0	269	1-1-1
◊ créer - emploi	V-N	1528.6	301	1-2-1
◊ s'adresser - ministre	V-N	1521.9	270	2-2-2
consentement - unanime	N-A	1379.4	108	1-2-1
◊ poser - question	V-N	1341.7	256	1-1-1
◊ Chambre - commune	N-N	1313.4	406	1-1-1
◊ création - emploi	N-N	1175.3	296	1-2-1
* petite - entreprendre	N-V	1164.1	123	0-2-0
◊ soin - santé	N-N	1125.9	225	1-1-1
◊ logement - social	N-A	1107.7	226	1-1-1
◊ essai - missile	N-N	1103.2	200	1-1-1
◊ défense - national	N-A	1075.0	175	1-1-1
dernier - année	A-N	1058.4	237	2-2-1
président - suppléant	N-A	1047.8	109	2-2-1
présidente - suppléant	N-A	1027.6	88	2-2-1
sécurité - social	N-A	1010.1	226	1-1-1
◊ jouer - rôle	V-N	998.8	135	1-1-1
personne - âgé	N-A	997.9	128	1-1-1
◊ comité - permanent	N-A	988.3	163	2-1-1
◊ code - criminel	N-A	963.7	88	1-1-1

Parse-based method

Key1, Prep, Key2	Type	LLR	F	Labels
député - d'en face	N-A	970.3	109	2-1-2
◇ prendre - mesure	V-O	951.1	228	1-1-1
dernier - année	A-N	950.0	233	2-1-2
développement - régional	N-A	936.3	127	1-2-2
◇ prendre - parole	V-O	931.6	182	1-1-1
gouvernement - précédent	N-A	930.0	196	2-1-2
◇ croissance - économique	N-A	908.9	142	1-1-1
◇ mesure - législatif	N-A	892.3	141	1-1-1

TS2

Key1, Prep, Key2	Type	LLR	F	Labels
* entreprendre - petite	V-O	888.7	88	0-0-0
◇ parti - libéral	N-A	873.5	190	1-1-1
ministre - chargé	N-A	861.2	96	2-1-2
◇ logement - social	N-A	850.8	135	1-1-1
semaine - dernier	N-A	841.0	96	2-1-2
◇ profiter - de - occasion	V-P-N	836.2	90	1-1-1
◇ plan - de - action	N-P-N	804.3	77	1-1-1
◇ certain - nombre	A-N	774.4	158	2-1-1
◇ invoquer - règlement	V-O	770.6	73	1-1-2
◇ honorable - député	A-N	752.1	140	2-1-1
◇ mettre - en - oeuvre	V-P-N	712.2	114	1-1-1
◇ avoir - intention	V-O	693.7	206	1-1-1
offre - final	N-A	689.3	56	2-1-2
- affaire - indien	N-A	678.6	76	1-0-2
◇ ministre - de - agriculture	N-P-N	657.4	53	1-1-1
◇ relever - défi	V-O	647.3	63	1-1-1
◇ côte - ouest	N-A	645.7	50	2-1-1
féliciter - député	V-O	623.2	125	2-2-2
ouvrage - de - franchissement	N-P-N	622.8	46	2-1-2

Window method

Key1, Key2	Type	LLR	F	Labels
◇ secteur - privé	N-A	936.7	146	1-1-1
◇ solliciteur - général	N-A	936.6	124	1-2-1
* essai - croisière	N-N	928.9	168	0-0-0
certain - nombre	A-N	925.4	157	2-2-1
◇ vote - libre	N-A	925.2	98	1-1-1
◇ parti - libéral	N-A	905.4	193	1-2-1
* développement - humain	N-A	884.5	179	0-0-1
◇ prendre - décision	V-N	851.2	205	1-1-1

TS2

Key1, Key2	Type	LLR	F	Labels
◇ prendre - parole	V-N	810.9	176	1-1-1
◇ régler - problème	V-N	807.4	149	1-1-1
◇ se rendre - compte	V-N	799.2	105	1-1-1
◇ chef - opposition	N-N	794.8	153	1-2-1
◇ guerre - froid	N-A	793.4	76	1-1-1
◇ mesure - législatif	N-A	771.3	146	1-1-1
◇ finance - public	N-A	747.4	131	1-1-1
◇ taux - chômage	N-A	737.4	119	1-1-1
◇ croissance - économique	N-A	731.8	138	1-1-1
◇ rendre - hommage	V-N	714.9	68	1-2-1
* Canada - gouvernement	N-N	714.2	44	0-0-0
* gouvernement - gouvernement	N-N	703.7	165	0-0-0
gouvernement - précédent	N-A	703.0	208	2-2-2
◇ deuxième - lecture	A-N	702.8	89	2-2-1
◇ profiter - occasion	V-N	694.6	84	1-1-1
◇ mettre - oeuvre	V-N	690.6	118	1-1-1
rapport - vérificateur	N-N	682.3	147	2-2-1
◇ Conseil - trésor	N-N	676.7	90	1-2-1
◇ ancien - Yougoslavie	A-N	671.2	79	1-1-1

Parse-based method

	Key1, Prep, Key2	Type	LLR	F	Labels
◇	atteindre - objectif	V-O	622.6	83	1-1-1
◇	avoir - occasion	V-O	611.6	172	1-1-1
◇	attirer - attention	V-O	604.0	53	1-1-1
◇	ministre - de - santé	N-P-N	591.5	63	1-1-1
◇	soulever - question	V-O	582.0	114	1-1-1
	autonomie - gouvernemental	N-A	579.8	72	2-2-1
◇	économie - de - ouest	N-P-N	578.4	74	2-2-2
◇	lésion - corporel	N-A	575.8	38	1-2-1
◇	résoudre - problème	V-O	572.9	77	1-1-1
◇	mettre - en - place	V-P-N	563.3	106	1-1-1
◇	soin - de - santé	N-P-N	561.1	88	1-1-1
◇	programme - de - infrastructure	N-P-N	560.5	120	2-1-1
◇	argent - de - contribuable	N-P-N	552.6	68	2-2-2
◇	fin - de - semaine	N-P-N	550.9	47	2-1-1
*	faible - revenir	S-V	550.1	40	0-0-0
◇	deuxième - lecture	A-N	549.1	86	2-1-1
◇	adopter - motion	V-O	543.0	83	1-1-1
◇	gouvernement - libéral	N-A	538.6	190	2-2-2
◇	bureau - fédéral	N-A	534.8	95	1-1-1
◇	prononcer - discours	V-O	522.8	57	1-1-1
◇	dépenser - argent	V-O	517.6	71	1-1-1
◇	double - emploi	A-N	517.4	62	1-1-1
◇	taux - de - intérêt	N-P-N	514.7	58	1-1-1
◇	commerce - international	N-A	508.6	55	2-1-1
◇	défendre - intérêt	V-O	507.5	66	1-2-1
◇	ministre - de - environnement	N-P-N	507.5	116	1-1-1
	ministre - responsable	N-A	505.6	67	2-1-2
	service - de - traversier	N-P-N	503.5	70	2-1-2

Window method

	Key1, Key2	Type	LLR	F	Labels
	développement - régional	N-A	663.8	123	2-2-1
◇	honorable - député	A-N	663.7	161	2-1-1
◇	payer - impôt	V-N	652.7	98	2-1-1
*	gouvernement - ministre	N-N	645.3	54	0-0-0
◇	ressource - naturel	N-A	639.1	99	1-2-1
	remercier - député	V-N	632.8	189	2-2-2
-	chargé - bureau	A-N	631.0	73	0-2-1
	semaine - dernier	N-A	628.8	102	2-2-2
*	gouvernement - député	N-N	623.8	53	0-0-0
◇	casque - bleu	N-A	619.2	54	1-1-1
◇	compte - public	N-A	616.8	145	1-1-1
◇	mettre - place	V-N	612.6	125	1-1-1
◇	invoquer - règlement	V-N	599.9	65	1-2-1
	M. - Michel	N-N	596.8	82	2-0-2
◇	développement - ressource	N-N	592.3	189	1-2-1
◇	avoir - besoin	V-N	591.3	253	1-1-1
◇	classe - moyen	N-A	579.4	59	1-1-1
◇	recherche - développement	N-N	578.9	148	1-1-1
◇	gouvernement - provincial	N-A	561.8	224	2-1-1
◇	avoir - besoin	V-N	560.0	264	1-1-1
◇	prochain - année	A-N	555.4	118	2-1-2
◇	casque - bleu	N-N	552.0	55	1-1-1
◇	affaire - indien	N-A	546.9	74	1-2-2
*	Canada - ministre	N-N	542.6	13	0-0-0
-	bureau - régional	N-A	540.6	82	0-2-1
◇	offre - final	N-A	539.9	53	1-1-1
◇	ministre des Finances - chargé	N-A	537.9	72	2-1-1
◇	question - supplémentaire	N-A	528.3	111	2-1-1

Parse-based method					Window method				
Key1, Prep, Key2	Type	LLR	F	Labels	Key1, Key2	Type	LLR	F	Labels
◇ régime - fiscal	N-A	502.2	91	1-1-1	* monsieur - présider	N-V	527.7	59	0-1-0
◇ affaire - intergouvernemental	N-A	499.7	48	1-1-1	◇ relever - défi	V-N	522.5	56	1-1-1
◇ être - cas	V-O	498.3	136	1-1-1	◇ côte - ouest	N-A	519.9	48	2-1-1
TS3									
◇ gouvernement - provincial	N-A	492.6	150	2-1-1	◇ attirer - attention	V-N	519.4	56	1-1-1
◇ évaluation - environnemental	N-A	487.4	53	1-1-2	◇ rapport - général	N-A	519.1	121	0-1-1
◇ réduire - déficit	V-O	486.0	73	2-1-1	◇ paiement - transfert	N-N	517.3	88	2-1-1
◇ gens - d'affaires	N-A	484.6	48	1-1-1	◇ jeune - contrevenant	A-N	514.5	50	2-1-1
◇ être - suivant	V-O	480.1	96	2-2-0	◇ faire - preuve	V-N	505.9	131	1-1-1
◇ monde - entier	N-A	474.9	50	2-1-1	◇ réduire - déficit	V-N	504.8	85	2-2-1
◇ trouver - solution	V-O	474.1	81	1-1-1	◇ Canada - atlantique	N-A	502.3	96	1-1-1
jeune - contrevenant	A-N	470.6	49	2-1-2	◇ avoir - intention	V-N	501.3	199	1-1-1
période - de - question	N-P-N	463.3	105	2-1-2	◇ ouvrage - franchissement	N-N	499.4	47	2-2-1
prochain - année	A-N	461.1	114	2-2-1	◇ filet - sécurité	N-N	497.6	80	1-1-1
◇ gouverneur - général	N-A	460.0	62	1-1-1	◇ formation - professionnel	N-A	495.4	61	1-1-1
◇ revenu - national	N-A	460.0	102	1-1-1	* Canada - député	N-N	493.7	18	0-0-0
◇ aide - humanitaire	N-A	453.0	54	1-1-1	* indien - nord	A-N	493.6	47	0-0-1
◇ assiette - fiscal	N-A	451.8	56	1-1-1	◇ autonomie - gouvernemental	N-A	492.0	70	2-2-1
modifier - loi	V-O	449.6	73	2-2-1	◇ arme - nucléaire	N-A	491.6	62	1-1-1
réduire - dépense	V-O	449.3	79	2-2-1	◇ député - d'en face	N-A	487.4	99	2-1-2
◇ assumer - responsabilité	V-O	446.2	56	1-1-1	◇ faire - partie	V-N	486.4	167	1-1-1
◇ agent - de - paix	N-P-N	439.6	60	1-1-1	◇ atteindre - objectif	V-N	486.2	72	1-1-1
◇ juste - part	A-N	436.3	46	1-1-1	* ministre - humain	N-A	483.5	177	0-0-0
◇ avoir - impression	V-O	426.9	65	1-1-1	◇ lésion - corporel	N-A	481.7	41	1-1-1
◇ représenter - circonscription	V-O	426.8	66	2-2-2	◇ assiette - fiscal	N-A	479.2	65	1-1-1
◇ fardeau - fiscal	N-A	425.9	62	1-1-1	◇ gouvernement - libéral	N-A	478.8	200	2-1-1
◇ faire - objet	V-O	423.4	74	1-1-1	* faible - revenir	N-V	476.7	40	0-0-0
◇ libération - conditionnel	N-A	421.1	28	1-1-1	◇ grand - nombre	A-N	467.1	146	1-1-1

Parse-based method

	Key1, Prep, Key2	Type	LLR	F	Labels
◊	comité - de - compte	N-P-N	415.0	95	1-1-2
◊	relance - économique	N-A	413.1	57	1-1-1
◊	député - de - bloc	N-P-N	410.1	91	2-1-2
◊	accord - de - libre-échange	N-P-N	405.4	40	1-1-1
◊	député - de - parti	N-P-N	402.4	140	2-1-1
	gouvernement - conservateur	N-A	401.3	98	2-2-1
	habitant - de - circonscription	N-P-N	394.8	68	2-2-2
◊	guerre - de - golfe	N-P-N	393.2	33	1-1-1
◊	répondre - à - besoin	V-P-N	390.1	59	1-1-1
◊	mettre - terme	V-O	388.0	47	1-1-1
◊	président - de - Conseil	N-P-N	387.9	63	1-1-1
◊	accession - à - propriété	N-P-N	386.5	33	1-1-1
◊	chef - de - parti	N-P-N	386.4	85	1-1-1
◊	participer - à - débat	V-P-N	385.9	75	2-2-2
◊	territoire - de - nord-ouest	N-P-N	384.3	33	2-1-1
◊	honorable - collègue	A-N	377.4	63	2-1-1
	ancien - gouvernement	A-N	375.4	80	2-1-2
◊	paiement - de - transfert	N-P-N	374.5	49	2-1-1
◊	ministre - de - diversification	N-P-N	368.4	61	1-1-2
◊	mettre - sur - pied	V-P-N	367.1	70	1-1-1
◊	relancer - économie	V-O	365.8	41	1-1-1
	service - gouvernemental	N-A	365.4	76	2-1-1
◊	grand - nombre	A-N	364.9	152	1-1-2
◊	équilibrer - budget	V-O	362.1	37	2-1-1
◊	député - nouveau	V-O	361.6	51	2-0-2
◊	filet - de - sécurité	N-P-N	358.5	36	1-1-1

Window method

	Key1, Key2	Type	LLR	F	Labels
◊	avoir - lieu	V-N	459.8	169	1-1-1
*	séance - h	N-N	458.4	47	0-0-0
◊	mettre - pied	V-N	457.9	80	1-1-1
◊	prendre - mesure	V-N	455.9	171	1-1-1
◊	régime - fiscal	N-A	453.4	113	1-1-1
◊	gouverneur - général	N-A	449.3	64	1-1-1
◊	résoudre - problème	V-N	443.5	71	1-1-1
◊	fonction - public	N-A	442.8	86	1-1-1
◊	aide - humanitaire	N-A	441.7	58	1-1-1
◊	évaluation - environnemental	N-A	435.3	57	2-1-1
◊	homme - femme	N-N	431.7	77	2-0-2
*	député - gouvernement	N-N	430.5	105	0-0-0
◊	réduire - dépense	V-N	430.1	88	2-1-1
◊	programme - infrastructure	N-N	427.7	182	1-2-1
◊	article - règlement	N-N	426.4	83	2-2-2
◊	faire - face	V-N	422.7	63	1-1-1
*	citoyenneté - immigration	N-N	422.7	50	1-0-0
◊	ministre - chargé	N-A	422.2	104	2-1-1
◊	fardeau - fiscal	N-A	420.2	69	1-1-1
◊	paiement - péréquation	N-N	419.1	73	1-1-2
◊	avoir - occasion	V-N	418.9	160	1-1-1
◊	ministre - Affaires étrangères	N-N	418.1	115	1-1-1
◊	plan - action	N-N	417.0	92	1-1-1
*	parlementaire - ministre	A-N	416.4	166	0-0-2
◊	table - rond	N-A	414.8	30	1-1-1
*	Canadien - Canadienne	N-N	412.3	105	2-0-0

Parse-based method					Window method				
Key1, Prep, Key2	Type	LLR	F	Labels	Key1, Key2	Type	LLR	F	Labels
TS4									
◊ abri - fiscal	N-A	354.5	43	1-1-1	* humain - diversification	A-N	411.0	45	0-0-0
contribuable - canadien	N-A	352.8	73	2-2-2	◊ assumer - responsabilité	V-N	408.2	58	1-1-1
◊ ministère - de - finance	N-P-N	351.7	56	1-1-1	◊ fond - public	N-A	401.2	64	1-1-1
◊ bureau - de - poste	N-P-N	351.0	33	1-1-1	◊ commerce - international	N-A	400.0	54	2-1-1
◊ prendre - engagement	V-O	348.3	91	1-1-1	◊ trouver - solution	V-N	399.5	83	1-1-1
payer - impôt	V-O	346.6	50	2-2-1	◊ ancien - combattant	N-N	399.0	44	1-1-1
◊ aborder - question	V-O	344.5	70	1-1-1	◊ défendre - intérêt	V-N	398.9	67	1-1-1
◊ politique - de - défense	N-P-N	343.6	70	2-1-1	* Canada - Chambre	N-N	398.7	15	0-0-0
◊ réduction - de - déficit	N-P-N	342.5	51	2-1-1	* nouveau - député	N-V	397.9	50	2-0-0
◊ attaquer - à - problème	V-P-N	342.5	58	1-1-0	◊ ministre - gouvernement	N-N	396.6	124	2-1-2
nouveau - parti	N-A	342.4	34	2-1-2	* programme - ministre	N-N	393.6	14	0-0-2
◊ développement - durable	N-A	341.4	49	1-1-1	◊ modifier - loi	V-N	392.3	82	2-1-1
◊ renvoyer - à - comité	V-P-N	340.4	41	2-1-2	◊ double - emploi	A-N	389.6	61	1-1-1
leader - de - gouvernement	N-P-N	339.6	65	2-1-2	◊ manque - gagner	N-V	388.7	35	1-1-1
construction - de - pont	N-P-N	339.0	43	2-1-2	* programme - député	N-N	385.5	13	0-0-0
entreprise - privé	N-A	339.0	45	1-1-1	◊ affaire - intergouvernemental	N-A	384.3	47	1-1-1
◊ poser - question	V-O	337.1	57	1-1-1	◊ chargé - développement	A-N	383.4	68	2-1-2
◊ service - de - santé	N-P-N	336.4	42	1-1-1	◊ revenu - national	N-A	382.9	105	1-1-1
◊ population - canadien	N-A	336.2	91	2-2-2	◊ libération - conditionnel	N-A	381.0	29	1-1-1
◊ droit - de - personne	N-P-N	335.2	67	1-1-1	contrebande - cigarette	N-N	373.5	69	2-2-2
causer - mort	V-O	333.8	28	1-1-1	gouvernement - conservateur	N-A	372.8	107	2-1-2
◊ répondre - à - question	V-P-N	331.7	87	2-1-1	◊ rôle - jouer	N-V	370.0	45	1-1-1
◊ paiement - de - péréquation	N-P-N	330.3	44	2-1-1	◊ taux - élevé	N-A	369.6	56	1-1-1
◊ électeur - de - circonscription	N-P-N	330.0	59	2-1-2	argent - contribuable	N-N	366.3	85	2-1-2
◊ personne - handicapé	N-A	328.5	29	1-1-1	renvoyer - comité	V-N	364.3	51	2-2-1
◊ ministre - de - travail	N-P-N	325.5	52	1-1-1	- président - gouvernement	N-N	363.9	11	2-1-0
◊ échappatoire - fiscal	N-A	325.1	41	1-1-1	◊ question - poser	N-V	363.8	72	1-0-1
◊ remettre - à - travail	V-P-N	320.3	39	1-1-2	◊ période - question	N-N	363.6	176	2-2-1

Parse-based method

	Key1, Prep, Key2	Type	LLR	F	Labels
◊	exprimer - opinion	V-O	317.0	43	1-1-1
	patrimoine - canadien	N-A	313.0	60	2-2-2
◊	même - chose	A-N	312.5	87	2-1-1
◊	ministre - de - citoyenneté	N-P-N	312.0	50	1-1-2
◊	région - rural	N-A	311.6	37	2-1-1
◊	société - canadien	N-A	311.3	97	2-1-2
◊	ligne - directeur	N-A	309.6	21	1-1-1
◊	pêche - côtier	N-A	309.0	29	2-1-1
◊	sécurité - de - vieillesse	N-P-N	306.2	35	1-1-2
◊	présenter - projet de loi	V-O	306.1	58	1-1-2
◊	respecter - loi	V-O	305.3	60	1-1-1
◊	solution - de - rechange	N-P-N	304.5	28	1-1-1
◊	transport - de - grain	N-P-N	302.4	40	2-2-2
◊	comité - spécial	N-A	302.4	63	2-2-1
◊	grave - problème	A-N	300.0	48	1-2-1
◊	Conseil - privé	N-A	298.3	35	1-1-1
◊	prendre - parole	V-O	296.5	42	1-1-1
◊	justice - pénal	N-A	294.6	22	1-1-1
◊	respecter - engagement	V-O	292.9	56	1-1-1
◊	régime - de - retraite	N-P-N	291.2	25	1-1-1
◊	assistance - public	N-A	287.3	35	1-1-1
*	entreprendre - moyenne	V-O	286.7	28	0-0-0

TS5

	Key1, Prep, Key2	Type	LLR	F	Labels
◊	développement - économique	N-A	286.6	87	2-1-1
◊	ministre - de - développement	N-P-N	281.1	121	1-1-2
◊	séance - lever	S-V	280.8	22	1-1-1

Window method

	Key1, Key2	Type	LLR	F	Labels
◊	question - suivant	N-A	363.6	90	2-1-1
*	Canada - question	N-N	361.5	21	0-0-0
*	député - Canada	N-N	358.1	47	0-0-0
*	Chambre - gouvernement	N-N	357.0	83	0-1-0
*	question - gouvernement	N-N	356.8	81	0-0-2
◊	poser - question	V-N	356.4	69	1-1-1
◊	mauvais - gestion	A-N	355.5	48	1-1-1
◊	avoir - impression	V-N	352.3	62	1-1-1
◊	M. - Pierre	N-N	352.2	49	2-1-2
◊	motion - adopter	N-V	352.0	61	1-0-1
◊	rôle - jouer	N-V	350.0	54	1-1-1
*	financement - établi	N-A	347.8	42	0-1-0
◊	même - chose	A-N	346.8	83	2-1-1
◊	Canada - Canada	N-N	346.5	58	0-0-0
◊	marché - travail	N-N	345.9	117	1-1-1
*	diversification - ouest	N-N	345.4	51	0-0-0
◊	M. - Paul	N-N	345.0	51	2-1-2
*	pays - gouvernement	N-N	344.3	19	0-0-0
◊	gens - d'affaires	N-A	342.6	47	1-1-1
◊	province - nanti	N-A	342.2	46	1-2-1
◊	relance - économique	N-A	339.8	58	1-1-1
◊	Québécois - Québécoise	N-N	339.5	42	2-0-2

	Key1, Key2	Type	LLR	F	Labels
◊	statut - réfugié	N-N	338.8	43	1-1-1
◊	juste - part	A-N	336.6	43	1-1-1
◊	filet - social	N-A	335.9	61	1-1-0

Parse-based method

Key1, Prep, Key2	Type	LLR	F	Labels
◇ ministre - de - industrie	N-P-N	279.4	90	1-1-1
taxe - sur - cigarette	N-P-N	273.4	41	2-2-2
◇ réforme - parlementaire	N-A	272.2	51	1-2-1
◇ mettre - accent	V-O	271.7	30	1-1-1
◇ système - de - sécurité	N-P-N	270.9	45	1-2-1
centaine - de - millier	N-P-N	270.7	36	2-2-2
solution - à - problème	N-P-N	268.3	50	2-2-1
semaine - prochain	N-A	266.4	35	2-2-1
◇ arbitrage - de - offre	N-P-N	265.8	24	1-1-2
modification - constitutionnel	N-A	265.6	35	2-2-1
coûter - million	V-O	265.6	36	2-2-2
norme - national	N-A	265.2	49	2-2-1
gouvernement - être	S-V	264.4	75	2-2-0
programme - établi	N-A	262.7	46	2-1-2
débat - de - aujourd'hui	N-P-N	261.6	41	2-2-2
an - prochain	N-A	260.7	25	2-2-1
◇ avoir - difficulté	V-O	260.2	46	1-1-1
crédit - de - impôt	N-P-N	259.8	27	2-1-2
processus - de - évaluation	N-P-N	259.7	23	2-2-1
◇ faire - travail	V-O	259.0	79	1-2-1
◇ avoir - chance	V-O	259.0	61	1-2-1
côté - de - Chambre	N-P-N	258.7	68	1-2-2
◇ tenir - promesse	V-O	256.4	33	1-1-1
◇ prendre - à - sérieux	V-P-N	254.7	27	1-1-1
◇ réduction - de - taxe	N-P-N	252.7	47	2-1-1
remercier - de - question	V-P-N	252.3	82	2-1-2
◇ exprimer - point de vue	V-O	251.2	37	1-2-1
remercier - collègue	V-O	250.9	46	2-2-2
◇ groupe - de - travail	N-P-N	250.3	33	1-1-1

Window method

Key1, Key2	Type	LLR	F	Labels
◇ communauté - internationale	N-N	335.8	66	2-1-1
* gouvernement - président	N-N	335.3	16	0-0-0
◇ ouest - canadien	N-A	335.0	69	1-2-1
◇ représenter - circonscription	V-N	332.4	79	2-1-1
◇ député - réformiste	N-A	331.9	124	2-1-1
◇ moyen - entreprise	A-N	330.8	66	1-1-1
◇ langue - officiel	N-A	330.2	43	1-1-1
pêche - océan	N-N	328.5	51	2-0-2
* ministre - national	N-A	326.4	177	0-1-0
◇ faire - objet	V-N	326.3	77	1-1-1
* gouvernement - question	N-N	326.2	91	0-0-0
◇ monde - entier	N-N	326.2	46	1-1-1
◇ économie - souterrain	N-A	323.8	39	1-1-1
causer - mort	V-N	323.4	31	1-1-1
◇ féliciter - député	V-N	323.4	134	2-2-2
être - mesure	V-N	323.2	90	1-1-1
* petite - moyenne	N-N	323.1	43	2-0-0
remercier - question	V-N	322.9	122	2-0-2
* Chambre - ministre	N-N	322.4	28	0-0-0
* Canada - programme	N-N	320.4	31	0-0-0
crème - glacé	N-A	320.1	22	1-1-1
◇ soulever - question	V-N	317.6	96	1-1-1
accord - libre-échange	N-N	317.4	47	0-1-1
secrétaire - ministre	N-N	317.3	163	2-0-2
service - traversier	N-N	315.8	78	2-2-1
◇ décision - prendre	N-V	312.0	90	1-0-1
coûter - dollar	V-N	311.1	56	2-2-2
territoire - nord-ouest	N-N	310.0	39	1-2-2
* député - ministre	N-N	309.4	57	0-0-0

Parse-based method

Key1, Prep, Key2	Type	LLR	F	Labels
◇ ligne - de - conduite	N-P-N	248.9	17	1-1-1
soldat - canadien	N-A	248.8	52	2-2-2
◇ déployer - effort	V-O	247.3	25	1-1-1
rénovation - résidentiel	N-A	246.8	17	2-1-2
◇ avoir - droit	V-O	245.3	69	1-2-1
◇ cours - de - année	N-P-N	244.6	45	1-1-2
◇ régime - de - assistance	N-P-N	243.5	28	2-1-2
◇ faire - doute	V-O	243.0	44	1-1-1
◇ frai - partagé	N-A	242.9	18	1-1-0
◇ élargir - assiette	V-O	242.5	19	1-1-2
◇ activité - économique	N-A	242.1	54	2-2-1
◇ temps - de - parole	N-P-N	242.1	28	1-1-1
◇ contestation - judiciaire	N-A	241.8	18	2-1-1
◇ dépense - gouvernemental	N-A	240.8	60	2-2-1
◇ élever - à - milliard	V-P-N	240.4	24	2-1-2
◇ ministre - de - justice	N-P-N	240.1	59	1-1-1
◇ assemblée - législatif	N-A	239.4	33	1-1-1
◇ fin - de - guerre	N-P-N	236.8	25	2-1-2

TS6

Key1, Prep, Key2	Type	LLR	F	Labels
◇ moment - donné	N-A	235.8	23	1-1-1
◇ opération - de - maintien	N-P-N	234.1	43	2-1-2
◇ ministre - de - affaire	N-P-N	233.7	76	1-1-1
◇ produit - de - tabac	N-P-N	233.6	31	2-2-2
◇ agence - de - promotion	N-P-N	233.5	20	2-1-1
◇ ministre - de - patrimoine	N-P-N	233.0	47	1-1-2
* ministre - de - ancien	N-P-N	233.0	41	0-1-0
◇ reprendre - étude	V-O	231.3	33	2-1-1
◇ loi - de - impôt sur le revenu	N-P-N	229.0	31	1-1-2

Window method

Key1, Key2	Type	LLR	F	Labels
◇ honorable - collègue	A-N	308.8	63	2-1-1
◇ comité - spécial	N-A	306.5	72	1-2-1
◇ échappatoire - fiscal	N-A	306.4	45	1-2-1
* bureau - fédéral	N-A	305.3	93	1-1-1
◇ seconde - mondial	N-A	305.1	32	0-0-0
* ticket - modérateur	N-A	303.3	19	1-1-1
* ministre des Finances - bureau	N-N	301.6	66	0-0-0
◇ programme - Chambre	N-N	299.1	13	0-0-0
* gouvernement - Monsieur	N-N	299.0	4	0-0-0
◇ présenter - projet de loi	V-N	295.6	66	1-1-1
◇ accession - propriété	N-N	295.6	33	1-2-1
◇ transfert - province	N-N	295.3	99	2-2-2
◇ opération - maintien	N-N	294.4	80	1-2-1
* fédéral - développement	A-N	294.0	104	0-2-0
◇ lésion - grave	N-A	292.9	35	1-2-1
* député - programme	N-N	292.8	32	0-0-0
◇ recette - fiscal	N-A	292.3	56	1-1-1
* leader - commune	N-N	291.8	65	0-0-2
◇ répondre - besoin	V-N	289.2	52	1-1-1
centaine - millier	N-N	288.9	47	2-1-2
* parlementaire - leader	A-N	288.7	41	0-0-0
◇ abri - fiscal	N-A	287.2	44	1-1-1
◇ taxe - cigarette	N-N	285.5	64	2-2-2
◇ denier - public	N-A	285.4	43	1-1-1
◇ développement - durable	N-A	284.7	52	1-0-1
* programme - question	N-N	284.6	15	0-2-0
◇ avoir - été	V-N	279.9	86	0-2-2

Parse-based method

	Key1, Prep, Key2	Type	LLR	F	Labels
◇	bateau - de - pêche	N-P-N	226.2	23	1-1-1
◇	honorable - députée	A-N	224.8	33	2-1-1
◇	éprouver - difficulté	V-O	224.5	24	1-1-1
◇	revêtir - importance	V-O	224.2	23	1-1-1
◇	ouvrir - séance	V-O	223.3	21	1-1-1
◇	retirer - troupe	V-O	222.7	24	2-1-1
◇	maintenir - paix	V-O	222.3	32	1-1-1
◇	ministre - de - revenu	N-P-N	221.9	87	1-1-2
◇	prise - de - décision	N-P-N	221.8	23	1-1-1
◇	avoir - honneur	V-O	220.7	74	1-2-1
◇	représenter - électeur	V-O	220.2	41	2-2-2
◇	accomplir - travail	V-O	219.5	30	1-1-1
	autre - pays	A-N	219.2	100	2-2-2
◇	poursuite - de - essai	N-P-N	218.2	29	2-1-1
	présenter - pétition	V-O	218.1	32	1-2-2
	ouvrir - à - heure	V-P-N	218.1	21	2-2-1
	secrétaire - de - Etat	N-P-N	217.0	20	1-1-1
	aller - de - avant	V-P-N	217.0	24	1-1-1
◇	féliciter - collègue	V-O	216.9	40	2-2-2
	peuple - autochtone	N-A	216.7	29	2-1-1
	exploitation - forestier	N-A	214.6	18	1-2-1
◇	membre - de - famille	N-P-N	214.5	20	1-2-1
◇	groupe - de - intérêt	N-P-N	213.2	42	1-1-1
	Chambre - reprendre	S-V	212.3	34	2-2-0
◇	recours - à - force	N-P-N	211.6	21	1-1-1
◇	ministre - de - défense	N-P-N	210.7	83	1-1-1
	prochain - budget	A-N	210.1	38	2-2-2
◇	régime - de - pension	N-P-N	209.6	32	1-1-1
◇	rôle - important	N-A	208.6	44	1-2-1

Window method

	Key1, Key2	Type	LLR	F	Labels
	comité - public	N-A	279.6	119	0-2-2
	construction - pont	N-N	278.9	51	2-2-2
◇	relancer - économie	V-N	278.2	38	1-1-1
	économie - ouest	N-N	275.5	70	2-2-2
	équilibrer - budget	V-N	275.0	33	2-2-1
	région - rural	N-A	275.0	45	2-2-1
◇	nord - canadien	N-A	273.7	58	1-2-1
	mission - paix	N-N	273.7	83	0-2-1
-	transport - grain	N-N	273.5	45	2-2-2
*	Chambre - programme	N-N	273.4	18	0-0-0
◇	dépenser - argent	V-N	273.3	50	1-1-1
◇	agent - paix	N-N	273.2	67	1-1-1
	contribuable - canadien	N-A	272.6	80	2-2-2
*	moyenne - entreprendre	N-V	272.3	32	0-1-0
*	question - Canada	N-N	272.0	42	0-0-0
◇	diversification - économie	N-N	271.1	59	1-2-1
◇	cercle - vicieux	N-A	270.4	17	1-1-1
◇	cour - suprême	N-A	269.9	25	1-1-1
	patrimoine - canadien	N-A	269.9	62	2-1-2
	chambre - commune	N-A	269.0	33	1-1-1
◇	participer - débat	V-N	267.9	73	1-1-1
*	paix - gouvernement	N-N	267.5	2	0-0-0
◇	poser - question	V-N	267.4	77	1-1-1
	gain - capital	N-N	267.2	39	1-1-1
◇	prendre - part	V-N	267.1	47	1-1-1
*	national - combattant	A-N	264.7	43	0-0-0
◇	gardien - paix	N-N	263.7	54	1-1-1
	économie - canadien	N-A	263.1	124	2-2-2
	bureau - développement	N-N	263.0	82	1-2-2

Parse-based method

Key1, Prep, Key2		Type	LLR	F	Labels
◇	comité - parlementaire	N-A	208.4	66	1-1-1
◇	membre - de - parti	N-P-N	207.7	25	1-2-1
	année - dernier	N-A	207.3	31	2-2-1
	inviter - député	V-O	207.1	41	2-2-2
◇	palier - de - gouvernement	N-P-N	207.0	39	1-1-2
	ministre - dire	S-V	206.9	76	2-2-0
	remercier - députée	V-O	206.6	32	2-1-2
	force - susceptible	N-A	204.9	26	2-2-2
◇	pays - industrialisé	N-A	204.4	21	1-1-1
◇	perdre - emploi	V-O	204.0	36	1-1-1
◇	forum - national	N-A	203.5	28	1-1-1
	dernier - élection	A-N	202.2	44	2-2-2

TS7

Key1, Prep, Key2		Type	LLR	F	Labels
	informer - Chambre	V-O	202.1	20	2-2-2
	génération - futur	N-A	201.7	18	2-1-1
◇	qualité - de - vie	N-P-N	201.2	32	1-1-1
	province - nanti	N-A	200.6	21	1-2-2
	relation - de - travail	N-P-N	200.6	28	2-2-1
◇	courir - risque	V-O	200.3	17	1-1-1
	premier - discours	A-N	200.3	93	2-2-2
	autoriser - essai	V-O	199.3	23	2-2-2
	Chambre - ajourner	S-V	198.9	23	2-1-2
◇	renouveau - de - fonction	N-P-N	198.1	15	1-1-2
	féliciter - ministre	V-O	197.9	41	2-2-2
	trouver - moyen	V-O	197.9	43	1-1-1
	taxe - sur - tabac	N-P-N	197.2	33	2-2-1
◇	communauté - européen	N-A	196.4	22	1-1-1
	objectif - être	S-V	196.3	32	2-2-2

Window method

Key1, Key2		Type	LLR	F	Labels
*	pays - ministre	N-N	262.4	5	0-0-0
◇	exprimer - opinion	V-N	261.1	40	1-1-1
*	général - Canada	A-N	260.8	127	0-0-0
	coûter - million	V-N	260.6	45	2-2-2
	comité - compte	N-N	259.9	115	1-2-2
	habitant - circonscription	N-N	259.3	82	2-2-2
	vendredi - dernier	N-A	259.2	30	2-2-2
◇	assemblée - législatif	N-A	258.9	36	1-1-1
◇	ministre - environnement	N-N	258.9	167	1-2-1
◇	s'attaquer - problème	V-N	257.5	59	1-1-1
	groupe - spécial	N-A	257.0	47	1-2-2
-	leader - Chambre	N-N	256.9	107	1-0-2
◇	aller - avant	V-N	256.8	29	1-1-1
◇	répondre - question	V-N	256.4	84	2-1-2
*	ministre - programme	N-N	256.2	45	0-0-0
◇	ancien - combattant	A-N	255.9	38	1-1-1
*	arbitrage - final	N-A	255.7	24	0-0-2
◇	ligne - directeur	N-A	254.7	21	1-1-1
◇	pension - vieillesse	N-N	254.4	34	1-0-1
◇	comité - plénier	N-A	254.2	36	1-2-1
◇	développement - économique	N-A	253.0	103	1-2-1
◇	guerre - golfe	N-N	251.8	32	1-2-1
*	national - ancien	A-N	250.5	33	0-0-0
◇	respecter - engagement	V-N	250.3	49	1-1-1
◇	respecter - loi	V-N	248.1	62	1-1-1
◇	service - gouvernemental	N-A	247.7	79	1-1-1
*	pays - député	N-N	247.1	6	0-0-0

Parse-based method

	Key1, Prep, Key2	Type	LLR	F	Labels
◇	réponse - à - question	N-P-N	196.3	53	2-1-1
	écouter - discours	V-O	195.1	34	2-2-1
◇	région - de - pays	N-P-N	194.8	57	2-2-2
	crime - organisé	N-A	194.8	16	1-1-1
◇	financement - de - programme	N-P-N	194.3	59	2-2-1
	vaste - consultation	A-N	193.5	24	1-2-2
◇	force - causer	S-V	193.1	20	1-2-1
◇	étude - de - motion	N-P-N	192.5	32	1-2-2
◇	gardien - de - paix	N-P-N	192.3	27	1-1-1
-	membre - de - comité	N-P-N	192.1	54	1-2-0
◇	offrir - service	V-O	189.5	30	1-2-1
◇	décision - difficile	N-A	188.9	30	2-2-2
◇	être - avec - plaisir	V-P-N	188.1	24	1-1-1
◇	statut - de - réfugié	N-P-N	187.7	17	1-2-1
	autre - province	A-N	187.6	65	2-2-2
◇	processus - décisionnel	N-A	187.5	19	1-2-1
◇	choix - difficile	N-A	187.0	21	2-2-2
◇	prévention - de - crime	N-P-N	186.4	17	1-2-1
◇	preuve - de - leadership	N-P-N	186.4	20	1-2-2
◇	être - de - avis	V-P-N	186.0	36	1-1-1
◇	répondre - à - besoin	V-P-N	185.8	30	1-1-1
◇	gardien - de - paix	N-P-N	185.3	21	1-1-1
◇	avoir - effet	V-O	184.2	71	1-1-1
◇	réponse - à - discours	N-P-N	184.2	44	2-2-2
◇	ministère - de - défense	N-P-N	183.9	47	1-1-1
◇	comité - mixte	N-A	183.6	23	1-1-1
◇	école - secondaire	N-A	183.4	15	1-1-1
◇	fameux - livre	A-N	183.3	19	2-1-2
◇	lire - projet de loi	V-O	183.2	31	2-1-2

Window method

	Key1, Key2	Type	LLR	F	Labels
*	commune - général	N-A	246.4	47	0-0-2
*	Canada - président	N-N	246.0	6	0-0-0
◇	présenter - pétition	V-N	244.3	35	1-2-1
*	chef - parti	N-N	244.3	94	1-1-1
*	commune - solliciteur	N-N	240.9	49	0-0-0
	se féliciter - nomination	V-N	240.8	26	2-2-1
◇	séance - suspendre	N-V	240.6	20	1-0-1
*	gouvernement - pays	N-N	240.2	44	0-0-2
*	chef - réformiste	N-A	239.6	49	0-0-2
	ministre - ressource	N-N	239.2	215	1-2-2
◇	dernier - élection	A-N	238.4	49	2-2-2
◇	défi - relever	N-V	237.1	30	1-0-1
◇	démuni - société	A-N	236.7	35	1-0-1
◇	entreprise - privé	N-A	236.0	52	1-1-1
◇	cotisation - assurance-chômage	N-N	236.0	40	1-1-1
◇	grave - problème	A-N	235.9	52	1-1-1
*	ministre - député	N-N	233.6	82	0-0-0
*	question - premier	N-A	233.0	120	0-0-0
*	emploi - ministre	N-N	232.9	2	0-0-0
*	gouvernement - paix	N-N	232.0	7	0-0-0
◇	prendre - sérieux	V-N	230.8	25	1-1-1
*	Québec - gouvernement	N-N	230.6	39	0-0-0
*	Canadien - député	N-N	230.2	16	0-0-0
-	ministre - diversification	N-N	230.1	90	1-0-2
*	programme - gouvernement	N-N	230.1	131	0-0-1
*	Canadien - ministre	N-N	230.0	18	0-0-0
◇	cher - collègue	A-N	229.4	24	2-1-1
◇	pâte - papier	N-N	229.2	18	1-1-1
◇	norme - national	N-A	229.1	49	1-2-1

Parse-based method

Key1, Prep, Key2	Type	LLR	F	Labels
◇ joindre - bout	V-O	183.1	11	1-1-1
◇ faire - commentaire	V-O	183.0	44	1-1-1
◇ accord - parallèle	N-A	182.3	16	1-1-2
loi - sur - contrevenant	N-P-N	182.3	23	2-1-2
◇ apporter - modification	V-O	182.1	24	1-1-1
grand - ministre	A-N	181.9	1	1-2-2

TS8

Key1, Prep, Key2	Type	LLR	F	Labels
◇ conclure - accord	V-O	181.4	22	1-1-1
◇ donner - parole	V-O	181.0	37	1-1-1
◇ occuper - place	V-O	180.4	21	1-1-1
◇ compression - budgétaire	N-A	180.2	18	1-1-1
◇ précédent - gouvernement	A-N	179.9	28	2-2-2
◇ sincère - condoléances	A-N	179.9	14	1-1-1
◇ remettre - en - question	V-P-N	179.7	41	1-1-1
◇ coup - de - feu	N-P-N	179.0	12	1-1-1
◇ bref - délai	A-N	178.8	18	1-1-2
◇ secteur - agricole	N-A	178.6	27	1-1-1
◇ conclure - entente	V-O	178.6	21	1-1-1
◇ régime - de - accession	N-P-N	178.4	26	1-1-1
◇ participer - à - processus	V-P-N	178.3	36	2-2-2
◇ attention - particulier	N-A	177.7	18	1-2-1
◇ taux - de - imposition	N-P-N	177.3	21	1-1-1
◇ ordonner - impression	V-O	176.9	18	2-2-2
◇ négociation - collectif	N-A	176.5	20	2-1-2
- bonne - parti	N-A	176.2	18	1-2-0
◇ territoire - canadien	N-A	176.0	42	2-1-2
◇ député - ministériel	N-A	175.8	31	1-1-1
◇ donner - exemple	V-O	175.5	36	1-1-1
◇ exercice - de - fonction	N-P-N	174.6	17	1-1-1

Window method

Key1, Key2	Type	LLR	F	Labels
◇ personne - handicapé	N-A	228.9	29	1-1-2
société - canadien	N-A	228.4	106	2-0-2
ministre - développement	N-N	227.6	250	1-2-2
- opération - paix	N-N	227.3	77	0-2-1
◇ solution - problème	N-N	226.9	92	1-2-1
loi - modifier	N-V	226.0	46	2-2-1
◇ élargir - assiette	V-N	225.7	21	1-2-1
libre-échange - nord-américain	N-A	224.9	18	2-2-2
nouveau - parti	N-A	224.9	32	2-2-1
◇ procureur - général	N-A	224.8	29	1-1-1
◇ modification - constitutionnel	N-A	224.7	37	1-2-1
* Monsieur - gouvernement	N-N	224.3	17	0-0-0
◇ produit - intérieur	N-A	223.9	26	1-1-1
◇ réforme - parlementaire	N-A	223.3	53	1-2-1
◇ revêtir - importance	V-N	223.2	24	1-1-1
◇ être - cas	V-N	223.1	156	1-2-1
◇ rénovation - résidentiel	N-A	222.8	17	1-2-1
◇ Canada - anglais	N-A	221.5	44	1-2-1
* fédéral - province	A-N	221.1	103	0-0-0
◇ travail - public	N-A	221.1	85	1-1-1
◇ dernier - campagne	A-N	220.3	51	2-1-2
◇ question - se poser	N-V	219.3	39	1-2-1
ministre - responsable	N-A	219.1	78	2-2-2
◇ secrétaire - état	N-N	218.4	45	1-1-1
◇ fin - semaine	N-N	218.2	50	1-2-1
◇ frappe - aérien	N-A	217.9	20	1-1-1
* emploi - député	N-N	217.8	3	0-0-0
◇ système - sécurité	N-N	217.5	101	1-1-1

Parse-based method

	Key1, Prep, Key2	Type	LLR	F	Labels
◊	ouverture - de - esprit	N-P-N	174.4	16	1-1-1
	motif - raisonnable	N-A	173.1	17	2-2-2
◊	conseil - de - administration	N-P-N	173.0	16	1-1-1
◊	soulever - point	V-O	172.4	29	1-1-1
◊	assainissement - de - finance	N-P-N	172.2	16	1-1-1
	proposer - amendement	V-O	171.6	26	1-2-2
◊	consultation - public	N-A	171.4	30	2-1-1
	déposer - rapport	V-O	171.0	28	1-2-2
◊	écouler - temps	V-O	170.5	17	1-1-1
	question - suivant	N-A	170.4	37	2-2-1
◊	modifier - article	V-O	169.9	27	2-2-1
	terminer - guerre	V-O	169.6	16	2-2-2
	peuple - fondateur	N-A	169.5	16	2-1-2
◊	gain - en - capital	N-P-N	169.0	20	1-1-1
	cher - collègue	A-N	168.7	18	2-2-1
◊	tenir - débat	V-O	168.6	33	1-1-1
◊	droit - inhérent	N-A	168.4	19	1-1-2
◊	appareil - gouvernemental	N-A	168.0	26	1-1-2
◊	liberté - de - expression	N-P-N	167.9	13	1-1-1
◊	rehausser - crédibilité	V-O	167.7	13	1-1-2
◊	crédibilité - de - parlement	N-P-N	167.7	18	2-2-2
◊	entier - collaboration	A-N	167.2	16	2-2-2
◊	utiliser - force	V-O	166.6	27	1-2-1
	institution - financier	N-A	166.4	32	2-2-1
	dernier - campagne	A-N	165.7	29	2-2-2
◊	accès - à - capital	N-P-N	165.6	26	1-1-2
◊	élargissement - de - assiette	N-P-N	165.5	11	1-1-2
◊	réduction - de - dépense	N-P-N	164.4	42	2-2-1

Window method

	Key1, Key2	Type	LLR	F	Labels
◊	régie - interne	N-A	216.2	17	1-2-1
◊	séance - lever	N-V	215.9	20	1-0-1
	pêche - côtier	N-A	215.8	26	2-2-1
◊	tenir - coeur	V-N	215.3	25	1-1-1
◊	solution - rechange	N-N	214.7	29	1-1-1
*	Chambre - Canada	N-N	214.5	61	0-0-2
◊	faire - preuve	V-N	214.1	60	1-1-1
	dernier - législature	A-N	212.8	49	2-2-2
◊	venir - aide	V-N	212.7	26	1-1-1
◊	remettre - travail	V-N	212.3	38	1-1-1
	premier - discours	A-N	211.8	101	2-2-2
	électeur - circonscription	N-N	211.6	85	2-2-2
*	ministre - intergouvernemental	N-A	211.4	46	0-0-2
◊	redonner - espoir	V-N	210.7	30	1-1-1
◊	dépense - public	N-A	210.6	98	1-1-1
*	emploi - gouvernement	N-N	210.4	33	0-0-0
◊	politique - défense	N-N	210.3	85	1-2-1
	arbitrage - offre	N-N	210.1	25	2-2-1
-	honorable - députée	A-N	209.5	37	2-0-1
*	gouvernement - Canadien	N-N	208.4	71	0-0-2
◊	faire - plaisir	V-N	208.0	32	1-1-1
◊	régime - pension	N-N	207.8	52	1-2-1
◊	élargissement - assiette	N-N	207.8	19	1-1-1
*	ministre - dire	N-V	207.0	75	2-0-2
*	pays - Chambre	N-N	206.5	4	0-0-0
*	défense - combattant	N-N	205.1	39	0-0-2
	taxe - tabac	N-N	205.0	45	2-2-2
◊	ajourner - heure	V-N	204.9	20	2-2-0

Parse-based method

TS9

	Key1, Prep, Key2	Type	LLR	F	Labels
◇	séance - suspendre	S-V	164.3	13	1-2-1
◇	tour - de - scrutin	N-P-N	164.2	13	1-1-1
◇	réintégrer - marché	V-O	163.9	10	1-1-2
	sécurité - de - revenu	N-P-N	163.4	39	2-2-1
◇	étroit - collaboration	A-N	162.8	14	1-2-1
◇	parti - à - pouvoir	N-P-N	162.4	15	1-2-1
◇	féliciter - députée	V-O	162.2	26	2-2-2
	contrebande - de - cigarette	N-P-N	162.0	24	2-2-1
◇	occuper - poste	V-O	161.5	17	1-1-1
◇	être - à - courant	V-P-N	161.5	45	1-1-1
◇	renvoyer - projet de loi	V-O	160.8	21	1-1-1
◇	adopter - résolution	V-O	160.6	22	1-1-1
◇	table - de - négociation	N-P-N	160.6	16	1-1-1
◇	construire - pont	V-O	160.2	17	2-2-2
◇	corriger - situation	V-O	159.2	22	2-1-2
◇	stimuler - croissance	V-O	158.7	20	2-1-1
	adresser - à - ministre des Finances	V-P-N	158.3	32	2-2-2
◇	situation - financier	N-A	158.3	43	2-2-1
◇	préparation - de - budget	N-P-N	157.5	21	2-1-2
◇	avoir - répercussion	V-O	157.5	41	1-1-1
	automne - dernier	N-A	156.6	17	2-2-1
◇	politique - monétaire	N-A	156.5	20	1-1-1
◇	répondre - à - besoin	V-P-N	156.5	25	1-1-1
◇	signer - accord	V-O	156.4	18	1-2-1
	féliciter - gouvernement	V-O	156.4	27	2-1-2
◇	cas - présent	N-A	155.2	14	1-1-1
◇	tueur - en - série	N-P-N	155.2	15	1-1-1
	nouveau - gouvernement	A-N	154.5	82	2-2-2

Window method

	Key1, Key2	Type	LLR	F	Labels
◇	aborder - question	V-N	204.8	63	1-1-1
◇	moment - donné	N-A	204.6	22	1-1-1
◇	vivre - pauvreté	V-N	204.3	31	1-1-1
◇	reprendre - séance	V-N	204.2	24	1-1-1
◇	discours - prononcer	N-V	204.2	32	1-0-1
	pays - question	N-N	204.0	4	2-0-2
*	diversification - canadien	N-A	203.4	43	0-0-2
*	susceptible - mort	A-N	203.0	20	0-0-2
-	donner - suite	V-N	202.9	36	1-1-1
	président - député	N-N	202.8	11	0-1-2
	population - canadien	N-A	201.1	101	2-2-2
◇	prendre - note	V-N	201.0	39	1-1-1
	mardi - février	N-N	201.0	24	2-2-2
-	affaire - nord	N-N	200.9	44	1-0-2
*	Canada - Monsieur	N-N	200.7	2	0-0-0
*	président - programme	N-N	200.7	3	0-0-0
	premier - fois	A-N	200.6	71	2-2-2
◇	seuil - pauvreté	N-N	200.3	26	1-2-1
◇	président - Conseil	N-N	200.1	81	1-2-1
	prochain - budget	A-N	199.9	41	2-2-2
◇	question - soulever	N-V	199.8	64	1-2-1
	collègue - d*en - face	N-A	199.3	34	2-2-1
*	Québec - député	N-N	199.2	11	0-0-0
*	justice - procureur	N-N	198.6	25	0-0-0
	semaine - prochain	N-A	198.2	39	2-2-2
	octobre - dernier	N-A	197.7	26	2-2-2
	programme - établi	N-A	197.7	55	2-2-1
◇	communauté - européen	N-A	197.6	23	1-1-1

Parse-based method

Key1, Prep, Key2	Type	LLR	F	Labels
◇ capital - de - risque	N-P-N	153.8	20	1-1-1
◇ apporter - changement	V-O	153.8	23	1-2-1
◇ document - de - orientation	N-P-N	153.6	11	1-1-2
bande - indien	N-A	152.9	14	2-1-2
◇ groupe - spécial	N-A	152.7	27	1-2-1
force - canadien	N-A	152.6	71	2-2-2
◇ aller - dans - sens	V-P-N	151.7	15	2-1-1
principe - de - projet de loi	N-P-N	151.4	28	2-2-2
◇ employer - force	V-O	151.4	19	1-1-1
◇ exercer - influence	V-O	151.2	15	1-1-1
◇ politique - gouvernemental	N-A	151.0	41	1-1-1
ministre - pouvoir	S-V	150.4	230	2-2-0
représentant - élu	N-A	149.5	13	1-2-2
◇ étape - de - lecture	N-P-N	148.9	18	2-2-2
◇ raid - aérien	N-A	148.6	12	1-2-1
troupe - canadien	N-A	148.4	35	2-2-2
◇ vie - humain	N-A	148.2	20	1-2-1
◇ affaire - extérieur	N-A	147.7	19	1-1-1
◇ base - militaire	N-A	147.4	21	1-1-1
◇ pêche - illégal	N-A	147.3	18	2-2-2
◇ prestation - de - assurance-chômage	N-P-N	146.9	22	1-1-1
◇ assisté - social	N-A	146.6	23	1-1-1

TS10

Key1, Prep, Key2	Type	LLR	F	Labels
autre - ministre	A-N	146.6	9	2-2-2
chômage - élevé	N-A	146.5	18	2-2-0
◇ député - de - opposition	N-P-N	145.9	64	2-1-1
redonner - à - Canadien	V-P-N	145.9	29	2-2-0

Window method

Key1, Key2	Type	LLR	F	Labels
M. - Philippe	N-N	197.5	25	2-0-2
* président - Canada	N-N	197.4	15	0-0-2
bateau - étranger	N-A	196.9	23	2-2-2
* mort - corporel	N-A	196.9	19	0-0-2
◇ produit - brut	N-A	196.7	23	1-2-1
mettre - terme	V-N	196.3	51	1-1-1
◇ gestion - offre	N-N	196.3	38	1-2-1
aller - sens	V-N	196.1	22	1-1-1
◇ peuple - autochtone	N-A	196.0	28	1-1-1
ministère - national	N-A	195.6	61	0-2-2
* ministre - combattant	N-N	195.3	70	0-0-2
* programme - Canada	N-N	195.3	68	0-0-2
bon - chance	A-N	195.2	37	1-1-1
avoir - effet	V-N	195.1	103	1-1-1
◇ partie - intégrant	N-A	195.0	22	1-1-1
* travail - gouvernement	N-N	194.9	19	0-0-2
◇ tour - scrutin	N-N	194.8	20	1-1-1
◇ autoroute - électronique	N-A	194.7	15	1-1-1
◇ haut - fonctionnaire	A-N	194.5	26	1-1-1
◇ contestation - judiciaire	N-A	194.5	17	1-2-1
devoir - être	V-N	193.8	31	2-2-2
◇ prendre - parole	V-N	193.7	39	1-1-1

TS10

Key1, Key2	Type	LLR	F	Labels
force - susceptible	N-A	193.7	29	2-2-1
◇ avoir - raison	V-N	193.7	114	1-1-1
* programme - président	N-N	193.7	4	0-0-2
ministre - Canada	N-N	193.5	108	2-0-2

Parse-based method

Key1, Prep, Key2	Type	LLR	F	Labels
◇ revenu - moyen	N-A	145.4	23	1-1-1
présence - de - casque	N-P-N	144.9	17	2-2-2
processus - de - consultation	N-P-N	144.6	23	2-2-1
◇ bureau - de - régie	N-P-N	144.5	13	1-1-2
modifier - constitution	V-O	144.2	20	2-2-1
jeu - de - tueur	N-P-N	144.2	15	2-2-2
valoir - peine	V-O	143.7	14	1-1-1
◇ président - de - élection	N-P-N	143.5	25	1-0-0
ministre - de - commerce	N-P-N	142.9	37	1-1-1
payer - part	V-O	141.9	25	1-2-2
◇ système - de - guidage	N-P-N	141.3	9	1-1-1
◇ problème - grave	N-A	141.3	23	1-2-1
◇ vote - de - confiance	N-P-N	141.1	14	1-1-1
manutention - de - grain	N-P-N	140.9	14	1-2-2
◇ emploi - à - long terme	N-A	140.8	24	1-1-1
◇ viser - objectif	V-O	140.5	25	1-1-1
◇ bout - de - ligne	N-P-N	139.9	14	1-1-1
◇ poser - question	V-O	139.7	20	1-1-1
◇ amendement - constitutionnel	N-A	139.4	16	1-2-1
dizaine - de - millier	N-P-N	139.3	17	2-2-2
soutenir - concurrence	V-O	139.3	13	2-1-2
◇ entrer - en - vigueur	V-P-N	139.1	16	1-1-1
◇ déposer - projet de loi	V-O	139.1	27	1-1-1
◇ petit - entrepreneur	A-N	138.8	23	1-1-2
◇ entendre - député	V-O	138.6	33	2-2-2
aide - à - rénovation	N-P-N	138.4	16	2-2-2
économie - canadien	N-A	138.1	59	2-2-2
◇ force - de - dissuasion	N-P-N	138.0	9	1-1-1
◇ secteur - de - activité	N-P-N	137.6	13	1-1-1

Window method

Key1, Key2	Type	LLR	F	Labels
* fleuve - Saint-Laurent	N-N	193.2	18	0-0-2
* nouveau - démocratique	N-A	193.1	29	0-1-0
◇ Chambre - ajourner	N-V	192.8	28	1-2-1
◇ trouver - moyen	V-N	192.7	49	1-1-1
◇ entrer - vigueur	V-N	192.4	21	1-1-1
◇ avoir - honneur	V-N	192.2	81	1-1-1
autre - pays	A-N	191.6	131	2-2-2
* femme - enfant	N-N	190.7	58	2-0-0
◇ Conseil - privé	N-A	190.7	33	1-2-1
* Québec - Chambre	N-N	190.4	4	0-0-0
◇ vaste - consultation	A-N	190.0	27	1-2-1
◇ être - fois	V-N	189.5	45	2-2-0
- bref - délai	A-N	189.3	18	1-1-1
◇ dette - déficit	N-N	188.9	55	2-0-1
ministre - finance	N-N	188.7	59	1-2-2
ministre - pays	N-N	188.7	19	2-0-2
M. - Gaston	N-N	188.7	26	2-1-2
* emploi - Chambre	N-N	188.6	1	0-0-0
◇ accord - nord-américain	N-A	188.2	23	1-2-2
◇ réduction - déficit	N-N	188.2	53	1-2-1
◇ exprimer - point de vue	V-N	188.1	31	1-1-1
◇ soldat - canadien	N-A	187.0	55	2-2-2
* chambrer - séance	V-N	186.6	20	0-0-0
◇ justice - pénal	N-A	186.1	20	1-1-1
* député - député	N-N	185.9	96	0-0-0
◇ service - jeunesse	N-N	185.9	45	1-2-1
◇ comité - examiner	N-V	185.8	48	2-2-0
◇ reprendre - étude	V-N	185.7	31	1-2-1
◇ fin - froid	N-A	185.7	24	0-2-2

Parse-based method

	Key1, Prep, Key2	Type	LLR	F	Labels
◇	dire - mot	V-O	137.3	21	1-1-2
◇	fonds - de - investissement	N-P-N	137.0	20	1-1-1
◇	poser - question	V-O	136.7	23	1-1-1
◇	débattre - question	V-O	136.4	28	1-1-2
◇	former - comité	V-O	136.3	23	1-2-1
◇	adresser - à - ministre	V-P-N	136.3	18	2-2-2
◇	poser - geste	V-O	135.7	19	1-1-1
◇	commettre - crime	V-O	135.6	11	1-1-1
◇	confier - mandat	V-O	135.6	15	1-1-1
◇	mise - en - chantier	N-P-N	135.5	9	1-1-1
◇	acquisition - de - arme à feu	N-P-N	135.4	13	2-2-2
◇	gagner - vie	V-O	135.2	19	1-1-1
◇	retombée - économique	N-A	135.1	24	1-1-1
◇	assurer - sécurité	V-O	134.9	19	1-1-1
◇	rester - à - feuilleton	V-P-N	134.9	13	2-2-2
◇	aborder - sujet	V-O	134.2	18	1-1-1
◇	service - de - police	N-P-N	134.2	10	1-1-1

Window method

	Key1, Key2	Type	LLR	F	Labels
*	étape - deuxième	N-A	185.3	22	0-2-0
*	Canada - Canadien	N-N	185.1	31	0-0-2
◇	bureau - poste	N-N	185.1	40	1-1-1
◇	dépense - gouvernemental	N-A	185.1	70	1-2-1
-	développement - gouvernement	N-N	184.7	12	1-0-2
◇	assistance - social	N-A	184.0	46	1-1-1
*	région - gouvernement	N-N	183.7	5	0-0-2
◇	tenir - promesse	V-N	183.7	34	1-1-1
*	Québec - ministre	N-N	183.1	16	0-0-0
◇	frai - partagé	N-A	182.9	17	1-2-1
*	faire - part	V-N	182.8	50	1-2-1
◇	représentant - élu	N-A	182.6	21	2-2-1
*	gouvernement - travail	N-N	182.5	22	0-0-2
*	dollar - ministre	N-N	182.5	3	0-0-0
◇	réforme - social	N-N	182.5	22	1-2-1
◇	revenu - garanti	N-A	180.5	72	1-2-1
◇	leader - solliciteur	N-N	180.5	25	2-1-2

D.2 Results

Graphical display of the results obtained in Experiment 1 (Section 4.4.3).

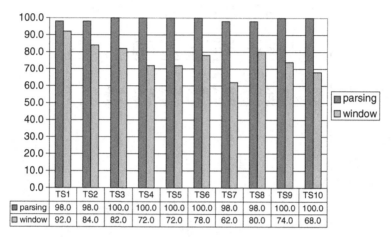

Fig. D.1 Results of Experiment 1: Grammatical precision for each test set

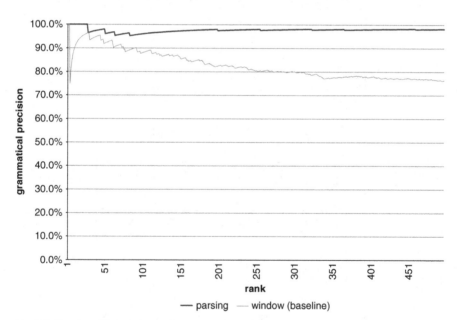

Fig. D.2 Results of Experiment 1: Grammatical precision on the entire test data (n-best precision curve)

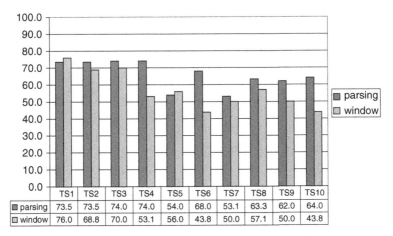

Fig. D.3 Results of Experiment 1: MWE precision for each test set

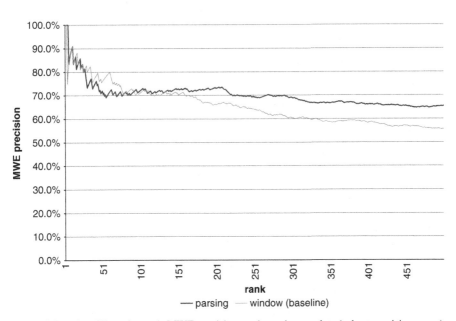

Fig. D.4 Results of Experiment 1: MWE precision on the entire test data (*n*-best precision curve)

Appendix E
Cross-Lingual Evaluation (Experiment 2)

E.1 Test Data and Annotations

Test data and annotations used in Experiment 2 (Section 4.4.5). Labels: 0 = *erroneous pair*; 1 = *regular pair*; 2 = *named entity*; 3 = *collocation*; 4 = *compound*; 5 = *idiom*. Common items in the output of the two methods compared are underlined. The following marks are used: star (*) = *erroneous pair*; diamond (◇) = *collocation* (i.e., true positive); NE = *named entity*; CP = *compound*; ID = *idiom*; question mark (?) = *undecided* (disagreement); no mark = *regular pair*.

Parse-based method

	Key1, Prep, Key2	Type	LLR	F	Labels
	English, TS1				
◇	take - place	V-O	5254.0	852	3-3
	next - item	A-N	4887.1	530	1-1
	amendment - no	N-N	4754.2	718	1-1
CP	same - time	A-N	4511.0	803	4-4
?	honourable - member	A-N	3805.4	379	1-3
	Swedish - presidency	A-N	3413.0	427	1-1
◇	close - debate	V-O	3230.8	411	3-3
	Belgian - presidency	A-N	3090.8	356	1-1
	candidate - country	N-N	3012.0	398	1-1
◇	play - role	V-O	3005.4	340	3-3
◇	internal - market	A-N	2949.6	373	3-3
◇	adopt - resolution	V-O	2945.7	422	3-3
◇	sustainable - development	A-N	2875.5	338	3-3
NE	court - of - auditor	N-P-N	2844.5	264	2-2
	item - be	S-V	2640.6	518	1-1

Window method

	Key1, Key2	Type	LLR	F	Labels
	lady - gentleman	N-N	25176.7	2036	1-1
	Mr. - president	N-N	18141.5	4217	1-1
	Mr. - President	N-N	13939.8	2845	1-1
	madam - president	N-N	9466.7	1408	1-1
◇	to take - place	V-N	4794.4	976	3-3
CP	same - time	A-N	4622.2	868	4-4
	next - item	A-N	4149.1	533	1-1
?	honourable - member	A-N	4123.4	502	1-3
◇	debate - to close	N-V	3624.0	408	3-3
	Swedish - presidency	A-N	3578.2	453	1-1
◇	to take - account	V-N	3348.5	647	3-3
	amendment - no	N-N	3300.4	877	1-1
◇	sustainable - development	A-N	3219.8	474	3-3
	Belgian - presidency	A-N	3182.5	374	1-1
◇	internal - market	A-N	2997.2	476	3-3

	Parse-based method						Window method				
	Key1, Prep, Key2	Type	LLR	F	Labels		Key1, Key2	Type	LLR	F	Labels
◇	draw - attention	V-O	2528.8	225	3-3	CP	medium - to size	N-V	2994.4	233	4-4
	madam - president	N-N	2441.8	238	1-1	CP	white - paper	A-N	2898.8	275	4-4
NE	vote - take	S-V	2181.3	325	1-1	*	member - to state	N-V	2873.9	534	0-0
NE	rule - of - procedure	N-P-N	2098.9	293	2-2		item - to be	N-V	2775.5	526	1-1
NE	united - nation	A-N	2000.6	193	2-2	*	commission - commission	N-N	2716.9	78	0-0
NE	common - position	A-N	1966.0	317	1-1	◇	to play - role	V-N	2628.5	333	3-3
?	rule - of - law	N-P-N	1955.5	209	3-4	◇	to adopt - resolution	V-N	2354.3	431	3-3
?	civil - society	A-N	1943.8	205	4-1	*	human - to right	N-V	2319.9	231	0-0
NE	European - council	A-N	1925.8	456	2-2	?	civil - society	A-N	2270.7	305	4-1
NE	court - of - justice	N-P-N	1860.5	180	2-2	*	member - to state	N-V	2218.9	372	0-0
	question - no	N-N	1820.7	324	1-1	◇	to draw - attention	V-N	2190.4	241	3-3
NE	European - commission	A-N	1791.2	365	2-2	*	vote - to take	N-V	2188.1	408	3-3
CP	great - deal	A-N	1761.6	229	4-4		country - commission	N-N	2166.3	19	0-0
	commission - proposal	N-N	1676.5	311	1-1	◇	common - position	A-N	2144.8	416	1-1
◇	apply - to	V-P	1637.6	592	3-3	NE	court - auditor	N-N	2095.9	314	2-2
	legislative - resolution	A-N	1623.2	186	1-1	NE	united - nation	A-N	2002.6	218	2-2
◇	table - amendment	V-O	1538.9	223	3-3	?	madam - President	N-N	1950.6	409	1-2
◇	free - movement	A-N	1506.7	142	3-3	◇	amendment - to table	N-V	1916.7	321	3-3
CP	point - of - order	N-P-N	1499.9	135	4-4	?	developing - country	A-N	1913.0	339	3-4
◇	right - direction	A-N	1485.8	159	3-3	*	commission - country	N-N	1844.3	66	0-0
NE	Kyoto - protocol	N-N	1478.5	156	2-2	◇	to bear - mind	V-N	1832.5	190	3-3
?	foot-and-mouth - disease	N-N	1466.6	145	3-4	?	parliament - to adopt	N-V	1819.9	502	1-1
?	take - into	V-P	1451.1	496	1-3	?	motion - resolution	N-N	1819.1	350	3-0
◇	solve - problem	V-O	1406.9	182	3-3	◇	to traffic - human being	V-N	1785.8	164	3-3
◇	legal - basis	A-N	1402.7	222	3-3	?	third - country	A-N	1727.9	417	4-3
◇	agree - with	V-P	1399.7	392	3-3		next - year	A-N	1710.9	417	1-1
?	cut - speaker	V-O	1378.5	97	5-3	?	legal - basis	A-N	1699.3	318	3-3
◇	enter - into	V-P	1365.4	235	3-3	◇	common - policy	A-N	1634.7	551	1-1

Parse-based method

	Key1, Prep, Key2	Type	LLR	F	Labels
NE	green - paper	A-N	1360.7	106	2-2
*	like - president	V-O	1335.3	173	0-0
◊	suspend - sitting	V-O	1317.7	107	3-3
◊	take - account	V-O	1315.6	242	3-3
?	crime - organize	S-V	1304.7	116	3-0
	oral - amendment	A-N	1232.6	136	1-1
◊	reach - agreement	V-O	1226.1	191	3-3

English, TS2

	Key1, Prep, Key2	Type	LLR	F	Labels
◊	cancellation - of - debt	N-P-N	62.1	5	3-3
◊	listen - to - voice	V-P-N	62.1	7	3-3
?	definitive - solution	A-N	62.1	10	1-3
?	country - national	N-N	62.1	27	4-3
?	wheel - vehicle	N-N	62.0	5	3-4
?	European - research	A-N	62.0	42	2-1
◊	lay - rule	V-O	62.0	14	3-3
◊	seal - of - approval	N-P-N	62.0	5	3-3
	number - of - death	N-P-N	62.0	22	1-1
?	open - door	V-O	61.9	8	3-5
◊	fulfil - mandate	V-O	61.9	9	3-3
◊	achieve - level	V-O	61.9	22	3-3
◊	particular - concern	A-N	61.9	17	3-3
?	mine - operation	V-O	61.9	6	1-0
	farming - community	N-N	61.9	17	1-1
◊	criminal - act	A-N	61.9	9	3-3
?	increase - premium	V-O	61.9	11	1-3
◊	renewal - of - agreement	N-P-N	61.8	11	3-3
?	key - player	A-N	61.8	11	4-3

Window method

	Key1, Key2	Type	LLR	F	Labels
	candidate - country	N-N	1578.6	639	1-1
CP	great - deal	A-N	1577.6	242	4-4
CP	small - medium	A-N	1573.2	182	4-4
	mutual - recognition	A-N	1562.1	149	1-1
	intergovernmental - conference	A-N	1557.8	164	1-1
	to accept - amendment	V-N	1550.6	334	3-3
◊	illegal - immigration	A-N	1537.9	178	1-1
?	union - action	N-N	73.1	15	0-1
	to begin - work	V-N	73.1	30	1-1
*	point - service	N-N	73.1	2	0-0
	service - point	N-N	73.1	2	1-1
*	service - matter	N-N	73.1	4	0-0
*	budget - decision	N-N	73.1	12	0-0
*	measure - house	N-N	73.1	5	0-0
	confidence - Mr.	N-N	73.1	1	1-1
?	to like - thank you	V-N	73.1	17	0-1
*	report - fight	N-N	73.1	11	0-0
*	change - debate	N-N	73.0	1	0-0
	animal - infected	N-A	73.0	9	1-1
*	environment - regulation	N-N	73.0	1	0-0
*	commission - opposition	N-N	73.0	1	0-0
*	year - requirement	N-N	73.0	3	0-0
	member - competition	N-N	73.0	3	0-0
	future - action	N-N	73.0	2	1-1
*	European Union - dialogue	N-N	73.0	10	0-0
	second - phase	A-N	73.0	17	1-1

Parse-based method

	Key1, Prep, Key2	Type	LLR	F	Labels
◇	face - dilemma	V-O	61.8	7	3-3
◇	maintain - position	V-O	61.8	22	3-3
◇	deserve - recognition	V-O	61.7	9	3-3
◇	have - chance	V-O	61.6	34	3-3
◇	face - difficulty	V-O	61.6	14	3-3
	sugar - regime	N-N	61.6	9	1-1
	chair - by	V-P	61.6	17	1-1
?	partnership - agreement	N-N	61.6	17	1-3
◇	research - fund	N-N	61.6	17	3-3
◇	dramatic - event	A-N	61.5	9	3-3
◇	entail - cost	V-O	61.5	9	3-3
?	contain - in	V-P	61.5	148	3-1
◇	be - debate	V-O	61.5	258	1-1
?	scientific - assessment	A-N	61.5	11	1-3
◇	set - priority	V-O	61.4	16	3-3
NE	Coptic - Christian	N-N	61.4	4	2-2
◇	know - as	V-P	61.4	16	3-3
?	balanced - participation	A-N	61.4	8	1-3
?	combat - exclusion	V-O	61.4	8	1-3
	Finnish - presidency	A-N	61.4	10	1-1
◇	switch - to - euro	V-P-N	61.4	6	1-1
?	affected - area	A-N	61.4	9	1-3
?	present - system	A-N	61.4	25	1-3
?	range - of - measure	N-P-N	61.4	17	1-3
◇	thorough - analysis	A-N	61.3	9	3-3
◇	put - emphasis	V-O	61.3	13	3-3
?	main - priority	A-N	61.3	16	1-3
*	gross - domestic	A-N	61.3	4	0-0

Window method

	Key1, Key2	Type	LLR	F	Labels
◇	convention - to ratify	N-V	73.0	16	3-3
?	to want - go	V-N	73.0	14	1-0
CP	community - law	N-N	73.0	202	4-4
?	medium - term	N-N	73.0	40	3-4
*	position - parliament	N-N	73.0	54	0-0
	report - nation	N-N	73.0	2	1-1
◇	stability - country	N-N	73.0	16	3-3
	energy - issue	N-N	73.0	9	1-1
*	European Parliament - protection	N-N	73.0	9	0-0
*	European Union - consultation	N-N	73.0	2	0-0
?	economic - stability	A-N	73.0	34	3-1
NE	valentine - day	N-N	73.0	9	2-2
*	strategy - directive	N-N	73.0	5	0-0
◇	to raise - point	V-N	73.0	39	3-3
*	presidency - people	N-N	72.9	1	0-0
*	mechanism - Mr.	N-N	72.9	2	0-0
*	reform - number	N-N	72.9	1	0-0
*	transport - union	N-N	72.9	2	0-0
*	research - measure	N-N	72.9	5	0-0
*	take - European	N-N	72.9	2	0-0
*	change - community	N-N	72.9	8	0-0
*	limit - council	N-N	72.9	3	0-0
*	council - limit	N-N	72.9	3	0-0
◇	to exceed - limit	V-N	72.9	11	3-3
*	government - interest	N-N	72.9	8	0-0
◇	amendment - fund	N-N	72.9	4	0-0
?	resolution - committee	N-N	72.9	28	0-0
◇	clean - energy	A-N	72.9	12	3-3

Parse-based method

	Key1, Prep, Key2	Type	LLR	F	Labels
◇	lose - credibility	V-O	61.3	9	3-3
◇	defend - against	V-P	61.3	17	3-3
ID	hit - nail	V-O	61.3	4	5-5

English, TS3

	Key1, Prep, Key2	Type	LLR	F	Labels
?	do - wish	V-O	25.2	4	1-0
◇	realize - importance	V-O	25.2	5	3-3
?	member - of - family	N-P-N	25.2	11	1-3
◇	table - draft	V-O	25.2	5	3-3
?	have - initiative	V-O	25.2	7	3-1
CP	postal - address	A-N	25.2	2	4-4
◇	surprise - at	V-P	25.2	9	3-3
?	member state - of - council	N-P-N	25.2	1	2-1
?	animal - product	N-N	25.2	8	1-3
◇	material - stream	A-N	25.2	2	3-3
◇	need - reform	V-O	25.2	13	1-1
?	short - route	A-N	25.2	4	1-5
?	freight - container	N-N	25.2	2	1-4
?	worker - involvement	N-N	25.2	3	1-3
?	proportional - representation	A-N	25.2	2	1-1
◇	petty - attempt	A-N	25.2	2	3-3
◇	collect - public	V-O	25.2	2	3-3
?	weight - of - ship	N-P-N	25.2	3	1-1
?	stance - on - issue	N-P-N	25.2	6	3-3
?	provide - overview	V-O	25.2	5	1-3
?	draw - version	V-O	25.2	4	1-0
?	remove - breeding-ground	V-O	25.2	3	5-3
◇	reform - system	V-O	25.2	8	3-3
?	beef - premium	V-O	25.2	2	1-3

Window method

	Key1, Key2	Type	LLR	F	Labels
*	policy - business	N-N	72.9	9	0-0
	other - amendment	A-N	72.9	71	1-1
*	problem - public	N-N	72.9	3	0-0
?	requirement - state	N-N	31.3	2	0-1
**	aim - question	N-N	31.3	1	0-0
	creation - committee	N-N	31.3	7	1-1
?	control - basis	N-N	31.3	3	0-1
?	basis - control	N-N	31.3	3	1-0
*	duty-free - product	A-N	31.3	4	0-0
	work - Mrs.	N-N	31.3	16	0-0
?	well - to document	N-V	31.3	5	0-1
	force - employment	N-N	31.3	1	1-1
*	level - idea	N-N	31.3	1	0-0
*	measure - list	N-N	31.3	1	0-0
	US - senator	A-N	31.2	3	1-1
*	head - proposal	N-N	31.2	1	0-0
*	port - EU	N-N	31.2	3	0-0
	concentration - ozone	N-N	31.2	5	1-1
	proportional - representation	A-N	31.2	3	1-1
	proportional - taxation	A-N	31.2	3	1-1
	holder - to await	N-V	31.2	3	1-1
*	pollution - to live	N-V	31.2	5	0-0
*	right - business	N-V	31.2	5	0-0
*	business - part	N-N	31.2	5	0-0
?	council - to remind	N-V	31.2	11	1-0
*	matter - national	N-N	31.2	1	0-0
*	worker - information	N-N	31.2	4	0-0

Parse-based method

	Key1, Prep, Key2	Type	LLR	F	Labels
◇	sound - cooperation	A-N	25.2	7	3-3
?	recipient - country	N-N	25.2	5	1-3
?	flax - case	N-N	25.2	3	1-3
?	advocate - rejection	V-O	25.2	3	1-3
?	quantity - of - waste	N-P-N	25.2	4	1-3
◇	sack - employee	V-O	25.1	2	3-3
?	small - company	A-N	25.1	10	4-3
NE	Balkan - war	A-N	25.1	3	2-2
	benefit - club	V-O	25.1	3	1-1
?	well-known - saying	A-N	25.1	2	1-3
?	sovereignty - of - food	N-P-N	25.1	4	1-3
?	life - risk	S-V	25.1	3	0-3
?	take - effect	S-V	25.1	3	3-3
◇	outcome - of - summit	N-P-N	25.1	7	1-3
?	European - statute	A-N	25.1	11	2-1
◇	escape - justice	N-N	25.1	2	3-3
◇	suicide - attack	N-N	25.1	2	3-3
?	sport - event	V-O	25.1	3	1-3
◇	giant - step	A-N	25.1	3	3-3
	know - book	V-O	25.1	2	1-1
	Mr. - ask	S-V	25.1	6	1-1
	Mr. - bring	S-V	25.1	6	1-1
	favour - of - committee	N-P-N	25.1	1	0-3
?	high - value	A-N	25.1	9	1-3
?	reconstruction - plan	N-N	25.1	5	1-3
?	group - in - country	N-P-N	25.1	2	1-1

Window method

	Key1, Key2	Type	LLR	F	Labels
*	target - community	N-N	31.2	2	0-0
*	rise - policy	N-N	31.2	1	0-0
?	solution - view	N-N	31.2	1	1-0
◇	restrictive - rule	A-N	31.2	9	3-3
*	provision - basis	N-N	31.2	3	0-0
*	access - concern	N-N	31.2	2	0-0
	nuts - bean	A-N	31.2	2	1-1
*	time - agency	N-N	31.2	2	0-0
*	authority - conclusion	N-N	31.2	1	0-0
*	proposal - association	N-N	31.2	8	0-0
*	country - farming	N-N	31.2	3	0-0
*	part - agriculture	N-N	31.2	2	0-0
	level - control	N-N	31.2	4	1-1
?	to support - process	V-N	31.2	44	3-1
◇	grey - area	A-N	31.2	5	3-3
*	European Union - loss	N-N	31.2	1	0-0
*	conference - people	N-N	31.2	4	0-0
◇	scientific - study	A-N	31.2	8	3-3
*	human - area	N-N	31.2	2	0-0
*	committee - threat	N-N	31.2	1	0-0
*	woman - dialogue	N-N	31.2	1	0-0
*	dialogue - woman	N-N	31.2	1	0-0
*	commission - manufacturer	N-N	31.2	3	0-0
	different - way	A-N	31.2	8	1-1
	price - to reflect	N-V	31.2	7	1-1
*	text - people	N-N	31.2	3	0-0

	Parse-based method					Window method					
	Key1, Prep, Key2	Type	LLR	F	Labels		Key1, Key2	Type	LLR	F	Labels
English, TS4											
?	end - put	S-V	17.3	4	0-3	?	to allow - transfer	V-N	19.8	4	1-1
	Turkish - prison	N-N	17.3	2	1-1	?	tragedy - September	N-N	19.8	10	4-3
?	give - to - proposal	V-P-N	17.3	18	3-0	*	force - fishery	N-N	19.8	1	0-0
?	impact - of - terrorist	N-P-N	17.3	3	0-1	*	fishery - force	N-N	19.8	1	0-0
?	connect - with - citizen	V-P-N	17.3	2	1-3	*	institution - September	N-N	19.8	1	0-0
	employ - assistant	V-O	17.3	2	1-1	*	September - institution	N-N	19.8	1	0-0
◇	cope - with - pressure	V-P-N	17.3	3	3-3	*	will - September	N-N	19.8	1	0-0
	new - way	A-N	17.3	5	1-1	*	general - community	N-N	19.8	10	0-0
	sixth - action	A-N	17.3	5	1-1	*	argument - parliament	N-N	19.8	3	0-0
	wait - from	V-P	17.3	8	1-1	*	justice - form	N-N	19.8	2	0-0
?	argue - against	V-P	17.3	5	3-1	*	board - community	N-N	19.8	3	0-0
*	weekend - address	S-V	17.3	2	0-0	*	commission - safeguard	N-N	19.8	4	0-0
	meet - representative	V-O	17.3	6	1-1	ID	to pull - weight	V-N	19.8	2	5-5
◇	lack - will	V-O	17.3	4	3-3		threatening - letter	A-N	19.8	2	1-1
?	fund - operation	V-O	17.3	4	3-1	*	report - comment	N-N	19.8	7	0-0
?	principle - of - discrimination	N-P-N	17.3	8	3-1	*	reality - agreement	N-N	19.8	1	0-0
?	irony - be	S-V	17.3	3	3-1	?	involvement - president	N-N	19.8	1	0-3
?	group - group	N-P-N	17.3	1	1-0	*	sea - part	N-N	19.8	1	0-0
◇	competitiveness - of - business	N-P-N	17.3	4	3-3	*	right - sea	N-N	19.8	1	0-0
	difficult - period	A-N	17.3	6	1-1	*	part - sea	N-N	19.8	1	0-0
◇	constitute - risk	V-O	17.3	6	3-3	?	situation - Yugoslav	N-A	19.8	6	1-0
	need - for - member	N-P-N	17.3	1	1-1	?	situation - adoption	N-N	19.8	2	0-1
	exclude - donation	V-O	17.3	2	1-1	*	adoption - situation	N-N	19.8	2	0-0
*	preparation - of - annual	N-P-N	17.3	2	0-0	*	start - member	N-N	19.8	1	0-0
?	interest - of - transparency	N-P-N	17.3	8	1-3	*	plant - member	N-N	19.8	1	0-0
	phase-out - of - textile	N-P-N	17.3	1	1-1	*	member - point of view	N-N	19.8	1	0-0

Parse-based method

	Key1, Prep, Key2	Type	LLR	F	Labels
?	connivance - of - Greek	N-P-N	17.3	1	1-0
	murderer - of - daughter	N-P-N	17.3	1	1-1
	attraction - for - hooligan	N-P-N	17.3	1	1-1
	purchase - of - plot	N-P-N	17.3	1	1-1
	vocation - of - serving	N-P-N	17.3	1	1-1
	episode - with - statue	N-P-N	17.3	1	1-1
?	wonder - of - wonder	N-P-N	17.3	1	3-4
	market - of - member country	N-P-N	17.3	1	1-1
	barrage - of - targeting	N-P-N	17.3	1	0-0
*	surface - of - square	N-P-N	17.3	1	0-1
?	third - report	A-N	17.3	13	1-1
◇	crude - form	A-N	17.3	2	3-3
?	treaty - ratify	S-V	17.3	4	0-3
◇	particular - regard	A-N	17.3	3	3-3
*	interest - annual	V-O	17.3	2	0-0
	demonstrate - by	V-P	17.3	12	1-1
◇	national - identity	A-N	17.3	5	3-3
◇	settle - problem	V-O	17.3	6	3-3
	unwanted - message	A-N	17.3	2	1-1
◇	stand - opposite	V-P	17.3	1	3-3
◇	arrogate - unto	V-P	17.3	1	3-3
◇	hijack - conference	V-O	17.3	2	3-3
?	possibility - offer	S-V	17.3	3	0-3
	coherent - manner	A-N	17.3	4	1-1

English, TS5

	army - carry	S-V	11.9	2	1-1
	such - complexity	A-N	11.9	2	1-1
◇	formulate - plan	V-O	11.9	3	3-3

Window method

	Key1, Key2	Type	LLR	F	Labels
*	system - culture	N-N	19.8	2	0-0
*	social security - to fund	N-V	19.8	4	0-0
	to list - article	V-N	19.8	5	1-1
?	health - to be	N-V	19.8	64	1-0
◇	to shut - door	V-N	19.8	2	3-3
?	opportunity - to be	N-V	19.8	52	0-1
*	task - case	N-N	19.8	1	0-0
*	Nice - debate	N-N	19.8	5	0-0
◇	fundamental - shift	A-N	19.8	4	3-3
*	case - task	N-N	19.8	1	0-0
◇	to achieve - success	V-N	19.8	5	3-3
*	convention - discussion	N-N	19.8	3	0-0
*	fact - attention	N-N	19.8	7	0-0
?	resistance - disobedience	N-N	19.8	2	0-1
?	executive - body	A-N	19.8	5	4-3
◇	to set - ceiling	V-N	19.8	5	3-3
*	agreement - challenge	N-N	19.8	2	0-0
	date - January	N-N	19.8	9	1-1
	conflict - Eritrea	N-N	19.8	4	1-1
*	mechanism - time	N-N	19.8	4	0-0
*	election - time	N-N	19.8	4	0-0
*	double - juice	A-N	19.8	2	0-0
?	religion - conscience	N-N	19.8	4	3-1
?	biotechnology - gene	N-N	19.8	4	0-1

*	to behave - democrat	V-N	11.9	1	0-0
	inspection - vessel	N-N	11.9	5	1-1
	to bury - monument	V-N	11.9	1	1-1

Parse-based method

	Key1, Prep, Key2	Type	LLR	F	Labels
?	be - hindrance	V-O	11.9	3	3-1
?	be - impediment	V-O	11.9	3	3-1
ID	be - straw	V-O	11.9	3	5-5
	Turkish - population	A-N	11.9	4	1-1
?	enter - by	V-P	11.9	8	0-1
*	force - delusion	V-O	11.9	1	0-0
?	process - vegetable	V-O	11.9	1	1-0
?	discipline - staff	V-O	11.9	1	1-3
*	process - schizophrenic	V-O	11.9	1	0-0
?	travel - intellectual	V-O	11.9	1	0-1
*	preserve - intellectual	V-O	11.9	1	0-0
	be - growth	V-O	11.9	3	1-1
	industry - recover	S-V	11.9	2	1-1
	son - die	S-V	11.9	1	1-1
◇	river - flow	S-V	11.9	1	3-3
?	coalition - hope	S-V	11.9	1	0-1
*	taxation - flow	S-V	11.9	1	0-0
?	private - flow	S-V	11.9	1	1-0
?	confidence - betray	S-V	11.9	1	0-3
?	deadline - freight	S-V	11.9	1	0-0
*	extension - minimize	S-V	11.9	1	1-1
	constraint - pave	S-V	11.9	1	0-0
*	go - wrong	S-V	11.9	1	1-1
*	laboratory - handle	S-V	11.9	1	0-0
*	cover - provision	S-V	11.9	1	0-0
*	course - inspire	S-V	11.9	1	0-0
CP	school - child	N-N	11.9	2	4-4
	declaration - acknowledge	S-V	11.9	2	1-1
?	support - violence	A-N	11.9	1	1-3

Window method

	Key1, Key2	Type	LLR	F	Labels
*	accession - society	N-N	11.9	1	0-0
?	society - accession	N-N	11.9	1	0-1
	to return - Argentina	V-N	11.9	1	1-1
	to treat - contempt	V-N	11.9	1	1-1
*	to sell - dealer	V-N	11.9	1	0-0
*	present - need	N-N	11.9	1	0-0
*	report - coin	N-N	11.9	3	0-0
*	group - line	N-N	11.9	10	0-0
?	explicit - mandate	A-N	11.9	2	1-0
	nation - invulnerable	N-A	11.9	1	1-1
*	nation - atavistic	N-A	11.9	1	0-0
	cooperation - association	N-N	11.9	4	1-1
*	claim - capital	N-A	11.9	1	0-0
*	liable - average	A-N	11.9	1	0-0
?	latent - seeker	A-N	11.9	1	1-3
*	alert - day after	A-N	11.9	1	0-0
?	memorable - trip	A-N	11.9	1	1-3
?	privatization - to rescue	N-V	11.9	1	0-0
*	petrol - to go	N-V	11.9	1	0-0
*	headway - to seem	N-V	11.9	1	0-0
*	footing - castle	N-N	11.9	1	0-0
	element - to add	N-V	11.9	1	1-1
?	to control - multinational	V-N	11.9	3	1-0
*	to control - lot	V-N	11.9	2	0-0
?	to truncate - single	V-N	11.9	2	0-3
*	to supervise - single	V-N	11.9	1	0-0
*	company - side	N-N	11.9	1	0-0
?	sea - fleet	N-A	11.9	2	4-1
*	Belgian - to refuel	N-V	11.9	1	0-0

Parse-based method

	Key1, Prep, Key2	Type	LLR	F	Labels
◇	conditional - release	A-N	11.9	1	3-3
?	visible - manifestation	A-N	11.9	1	1-3
	unbelievable - discrimination	A-N	11.9	1	1-1
ID	give - presidency	V-O	11.9	5	1-1
?	same - umbrella	A-N	11.9	2	5-5
?	originate - community	V-O	11.9	2	0-1
	UN - target	N-N	11.9	4	1-1
?	achieve - profitability	V-O	11.9	2	3-1
?	achieve - turnover	V-O	11.9	2	3-1
?	sail - round	V-P	11.9	1	1-3
?	frightening - statistic	A-N	11.9	1	3-1
	know - shortage	A-N	11.9	1	1-1
?	cruel - shortage	A-N	11.9	1	3-5
?	indiscriminate - sale	A-N	11.9	1	1-3
?	gigantic - holding	A-N	11.9	1	1-3
	sincere - appreciation	A-N	11.9	1	3-3
◇	encourage - bank	V-O	11.9	2	1-1
◇	savings - in - cost	N-P-N	11.9	2	3-3

French, TS1

	Key1, Prep, Key2	Type	LLR	F	Labels
◇	jouer - rôle	V-O	5913.8	600	3-3
	cher - collègue	A-N	4479.1	488	1-1
CP	pays - tiers	N-A	4265.8	484	4-4
	présidence - suédois	N-A	4112.9	485	1-1
◇	attirer - attention	V-O	4006.4	350	3-3
◇	développement - durable	N-A	3821.7	461	3-3
	million - de - euro	N-P-N	3810.8	535	1-1
	présidence - belge	N-A	3323.4	383	1-1

Window method

	Key1, Key2	Type	LLR	F	Labels
	armoury - armed forces	N-N	11.9	1	1-1
	pathway - contamination	N-N	11.9	1	1-1
*	feature - to face up	N-V	11.9	1	0-0
*	net - nitrogen	A-N	11.9	1	0-0
	to speak - minutes	V-N	11.9	3	1-1
*	indigenous - subcontinent	A-N	11.9	1	0-0
	to remove - debris	V-N	11.9	1	1-1
*	to remove - fluid	V-N	11.9	1	0-0
	to remove - heartbeat	V-N	11.9	1	1-1
*	to remove - innovator	V-N	11.9	1	0-0
*	debilitating - belief	A-N	11.9	1	0-0
◇	to submit - ratification	V-N	11.9	3	3-3
*	tight - stocking	A-N	11.9	1	0-0
◇	tight - speed-limit	A-N	11.9	1	3-3
*	representative - to negotiate	N-V	11.9	4	0-0
?	case - administration	N-N	11.9	1	0-1
?	to deploy - jurisprudence	V-N	11.9	1	0-1
?	to lobby - lawyer	V-N	11.9	1	1-1

	Key1, Key2	Type	LLR	F	Labels
?	Monsieur - président	N-N	44725.5	6682	1-3
◇	madame - présidente	N-N	18902.2	2031	3-3
	cher - collègue	A-N	13390.0	1240	1-1
*	Monsieur - présider	N-V	11627.8	874	0-0
?	état - membre	N-N	9774.5	4132	1-4
?	Monsieur - commissaire	N-N	6761.4	1518	1-3
◇	jouer - rôle	V-N	4411.1	564	3-3
◇	tenir - compte	V-N	4286.5	605	3-3

Parse-based method

	Key1, Prep, Key2	Type	LLR	F	Labels
◇	clore - débat	V-O	3157.7	364	3-3
?	certain - nombre	A-N	3124.9	529	1-3
?	conseil - européen	N-A	2986.3	747	2-4
CP	position - commun	N-A	2929.3	487	1-1
CP	être - cas	V-O	2914.7	784	4-4
◇	adopter - résolution	V-O	2859.1	416	3-3
◇	faire - objet	V-O	2734.0	415	3-3
◇	année - dernier	N-A	2732.6	355	1-1
?	droit - fondamental	N-A	2717.9	430	3-4
CP	affaire - intérieur	N-A	2691.5	325	4-4
?	accepter - amendement	V-O	2567.9	457	3-1
CP	plan - de - action	N-P-N	2329.3	263	4-4
?	cour - de - justice	N-P-N	2327.6	213	2-4
	année - prochain	N-A	2326.7	261	1-1
CP	droit - de - homme	N-P-N	2311.3	429	4-4
◇	atteindre - objectif	V-O	2214.9	323	3-3
?	cour - de - compte	N-P-N	2214.5	283	2-4
◇	résoudre - problème	V-O	2176.1	308	3-3
◇	prendre - décision	V-O	2155.6	399	3-3
?	base - juridique	N-A	2147.3	311	1-4
CP	société - civil	N-A	2133.3	248	4-4
◇	égalité - de - chance	N-P-N	2065.6	158	3-3
	conférence - intergouvernemental	N-A	2029.2	185	1-1
◇	mandat - de - arrêt	N-P-N	1999.4	171	3-3
	dernier - année	A-N	1972.0	424	1-1
ID	mettre - en - place	V-P-N	1967.6	347	5-5
◇	pays - en - développement	N-P-N	1949.4	258	3-3
◇	prendre - mesure	V-O	1914.3	410	3-3

Window method

Key1, Key2		Type	LLR	F	Labels
présidence - suédois		N-A	4193.6	519	1-1
commission - commission	*	N-N	3746.9	231	0-0
marché - intérieur	CP	N-A	3564.1	598	4-4
présidence - belge		N-A	3520.0	425	1-1
certain - nombre	?	A-N	3498.8	534	1-3
santé - public	?	N-A	3408.9	527	4-3
débat - clore	◇	N-V	3371.0	358	3-3
développement - durable	◇	N-A	3282.0	522	3-3
avoir - lieu	?	V-N	3212.1	1001	3-5
attirer - attention	◇	V-N	3156.9	376	3-3
pays - tiers	CP	N-A	3141.7	551	4-4
pays - commission	*	N-N	2898.7	16	0-0
Mesdames et Messieurs - député		N-N	2743.7	295	1-1
droit - fondamental	?	N-A	2645.1	528	3-4
accepter - amendement	?	V-N	2521.6	539	3-1
commission - pays	*	N-N	2517.4	67	0-0
position - commun	?	N-A	2510.8	540	4-1
ordre du jour - appeler	◇	N-V	2481.7	274	3-3
prendre - considération	◇	V-N	2436.6	458	3-3
faire - objet	◇	V-N	2186.2	490	3-3
état - commission	*	N-N	2167.8	65	0-0
justice - intérieur	*	N-A	2146.6	299	0-0
adopter - résolution	◇	V-N	2109.2	417	3-3
million - euro		N-N	2081.9	577	1-1
dernier - année		A-N	2081.2	473	1-1
libre - circulation	?	A-N	2041.1	213	3-4
affaire - intérieur	CP	N-A	2025.0	355	4-4
base - juridique	?	N-A	1941.5	340	3-4

Parse-based method

	Key1, Prep, Key2	Type	LLR	F	Labels
CP	affaire - étranger	N-A	1911.9	240	4-4
	parlement - national	N-A	1905.3	295	1-1
◇	poser - question	V-O	1881.0	285	3-3
?	livre - vert	N-A	1879.0	136	2-1
◇	personne - handicapé	N-A	1844.5	185	3-3
◇	pacte - de - stabilité	N-P-N	1814.7	171	3-3
?	revêtir - importance	V-O	1804.0	199	3-5
	semaine - dernier	N-A	1800.2	193	1-1
?	sécurité - alimentaire	N-A	1779.4	272	1-3
	féliciter - rapporteur	V-O	1771.6	206	1-1
◇	fond - structurel	N-A	1742.8	199	3-3
?	changement - climatique	N-A	1691.0	148	1-3
?	lutte - contre - terrorisme	N-P-N	1682.5	231	1-3
?	nom - de - groupe	N-P-N	1638.3	278	1-0

French, TS2

	Key1, Prep, Key2	Type	LLR	F	Labels
	second - phase	A-N	76.1	17	1-1
◇	mener - campagne	V-O	76.1	11	3-3
	provenir - de - donneur	V-P-N	76.1	8	1-1
	territoire - de - union	N-P-N	76.0	20	1-1
	commercialiser - engrais	V-O	76.0	5	1-1
◇	paiement - forfaitaire	N-A	76.0	8	3-3
?	argent - public	N-A	76.0	15	3-1
?	associer - à - remerciement	V-P-N	76.0	7	3-1
◇	annuler - vol	V-O	76.0	6	3-3
?	ressource - supplémentaire	N-A	75.9	22	1-3
	instrument - financier	N-A	75.9	35	1-1
◇	adresser - message	V-O	75.9	10	3-3

Window method

	Key1, Key2	Type	LLR	F	Labels
	année - dernier	N-A	1940.6	390	1-1
*	Union européenne - commission	N-N	1902.9	28	0-0
?	conférence - intergouvernemental	N-A	1899.6	196	3-1
?	pays - candidat	N-N	1848.2	811	1-4
◇	mettre - place	V-N	1826.5	413	3-3
*	charte - fondamental	N-A	1811.1	225	0-0
CP	livre - blanc	N-A	1809.8	176	4-4
CP	être - humain	N-A	1805.3	297	4-4
◇	ordre du jour - appeler	N-V	1802.1	197	3-3
ID	ligne - directeur	N-A	1801.7	175	5-5
?	compagnie - aérien	N-A	1796.9	209	3-4
NE	traité - Nice	N-N	1781.7	410	2-2
?	parlement - adopter	N-V	1752.8	420	3-1
*	commission - Union européenne	N-N	1747.8	51	0-0

	Key1, Key2	Type	LLR	F	Labels
*	Europe - conclusion	N-N	77.9	1	0-0
*	recherche - personne	N-N	77.9	7	0-0
*	asile - parlement	N-N	77.9	1	0-0
*	parlement - asile	N-N	77.9	1	0-0
*	lutte - sexuel	N-A	77.9	19	0-0
?	démocratie - parlementaire	N-A	77.9	19	1-3
?	projet - domaine	N-N	77.9	14	3-1
*	autorité - question	N-N	77.8	4	0-0
*	personne - nécessité	N-N	77.8	2	0-0
*	place - question	N-N	77.8	3	0-0
◇	recourir - instrument	V-N	77.8	18	3-3
*	judiciaire - membre	A-N	77.8	31	0-0

Parse-based method

	Key1, Prep, Key2	Type	LLR	F	Labels
◇	mettre - en - application	V-P-N	75.9	34	3-3
?	parlementaire - européen	N-A	75.9	29	1-4
	conflit - violent	N-A	75.9	10	1-1
◇	prêter - attention	V-O	75.9	8	3-3
	dissémination - de - OGM	N-P-N	75.9	6	1-1
	critère - de - pureté	N-P-N	75.9	7	1-1
	exprimer - vote	V-O	75.8	19	3-3
◇	groupe - confédéral	N-A	75.8	8	1-5
?	norme - élevé	N-A	75.8	18	3-1
?	cher - ami	A-N	75.8	14	1-1
	propre - peuple	A-N	75.8	16	1-1
◇	répondre - à - besoin	V-P-N	75.8	13	3-3
◇	approuver - projet	V-O	75.8	26	3-3
	rapporteur - dire	S-V	75.8	21	1-1
?	démocrate - chrétien	N-A	75.7	7	2-4
	secteur - de - viande	N-P-N	75.7	21	1-1
?	dictature - militaire	N-A	75.6	9	1-4
*	commission - règlement	N-P-N	75.6	2	0-0
	présent - directive	A-N	75.6	16	1-1
◇	accueillir - réfugié	V-O	75.6	9	3-3
?	organiser - séminaire	V-O	75.6	8	1-3
?	prise - accessoire	N-A	75.6	5	3-1
?	date - de - entrée	N-P-N	75.6	10	3-0
?	parti - conservateur	N-A	75.6	10	2-3
ID	assigner - à - résidence	V-P-N	75.5	5	5-5
?	titre - de - exemple	N-P-N	75.5	15	4-5
	montant - total	N-A	75.5	13	1-3
?	être - pour - pays	V-P-N	75.5	2	1-0

Window method

	Key1, Key2	Type	LLR	F	Labels
*	emploi - marché	N-N	77.8	14	0-0
?	recherche - contrôle	N-N	77.8	1	1-0
*	Irlande - conseil	N-N	77.8	1	0-0
*	raison - commission	N-N	77.8	3	0-0
*	commission - délai	N-N	77.8	17	0-0
*	chance - rapport	N-N	77.8	1	0-0
*	Union européenne - sommet	N-N	77.8	12	0-0
◇	tirer - conséquence	V-N	77.8	21	3-3
*	niveau - monde	N-N	77.8	3	0-0
?	tribune - officiel	N-A	77.8	8	3-1
◇	critique - formuler	N-V	77.8	11	3-3
◇	engin - mobile	N-A	77.8	7	3-3
*	secteur - nombre	N-N	77.7	6	0-0
*	pêche - programme	N-N	77.7	5	0-0
?	renforcement - proposition	N-N	77.7	1	3-1
?	négociation - action	N-N	77.7	2	1-0
*	enfant - travail	N-N	77.7	6	0-0
	discussion - Europe	N-N	77.7	10	1-1
*	Union - politique	N-N	77.7	11	0-0
*	activité - système	N-N	77.7	2	0-0
*	secteur - organisation	N-N	77.7	1	0-0
*	ONG - commission	N-N	77.7	2	0-0
*	régime - travail	N-N	77.7	4	0-0
*	Europe - est	N-N	77.7	8	0-0
?	citoyen - organisation	N-N	77.7	6	1-0
*	citoyen - utilisation	N-N	77.7	1	0-0
*	politique - navire	N-N	77.7	1	0-0
*	gouvernement - femme	N-N	77.7	4	0-0

Parse-based method

	Key1, Prep, Key2	Type	LLR	F	Labels
?	solution - satisfaisant	N-A	75.5	13	3-1
	été - dernier	N-A	75.4	20	1-1
◇	émettre - souhait	V-O	75.4	13	3-3
?	disparité - régional	N-A	75.4	10	3-1
?	facteur - essentiel	N-A	75.4	17	3-1
◇	infliger - amende	V-O	75.4	6	3-3
◇	délivrer - message	V-O	75.3	8	3-3
?	commercialiser - produit	V-O	75.3	9	1-3
	ajustement - structurel	N-A	75.3	10	1-1
*	être - accord	V-P-N	75.3	1	0-0

French, TS3

	Key1, Prep, Key2	Type	LLR	F	Labels
◇	causer - préjudice	V-O	29.9	3	3-3
	vote - majoritaire	N-A	29.9	4	1-1
	modèle - reposer	S-V	29.9	3	1-1
◇	définir - priorité	V-O	29.9	11	3-3
CP	droit - procédural	N-A	29.9	5	4-4
?	sécurité - de - travail	N-P-N	29.9	3	1-3
	remercier - Commission	V-O	29.9	6	1-1
?	explosion - de - violence	N-P-N	29.9	4	3-1
?	coalition - gouvernemental	N-A	29.9	4	1-4
	manière - explicite	N-A	29.9	8	1-1
	nécessiter - de - modification	V-P-N	29.9	3	1-1
?	texte - initial	N-A	29.9	7	1-1
?	progrès - décisif	N-A	29.9	7	3-1
	liberté - fondamental	N-A	29.9	5	3-4
*	commission - déclaration	N-P-N	29.9	1	0-0
*	commission - avec - déclaration	N-P-N	29.9	1	0-0

Window method

	Key1, Key2	Type	LLR	F	Labels
?	délégation - comité	N-N	77.7	44	1-0
*	situation - lieu	N-N	77.7	4	0-0
	réponse - Europe	N-N	77.7	3	1-1
*	Europe - amélioration	N-N	77.7	3	0-0
*	million - protection	N-N	77.7	2	0-0
	agriculteur - pays	N-N	77.7	4	1-1
?	soutien - niveau	N-N	77.7	5	3-0
?	document - développement	N-N	77.7	4	0-1
?	situation - liberté	N-N	77.7	4	1-0
*	Union européenne - réfugié	N-N	77.7	1	0-0
*	membre - sud	N-N	33.4	5	0-0
?	région - objectif	N-N	33.4	23	1-0
*	élément - affaire	N-N	33.4	1	0-0
*	calorique - graisse	A-N	33.4	2	0-0
*	Europe - immigration	N-N	33.4	7	0-0
*	intérêt - façon	N-N	33.4	2	0-0
*	proposition - équilibre	N-N	33.4	7	0-0
*	communication - communauté	N-N	33.4	2	0-0
*	annexer - Amsterdam	V-N	33.4	4	0-0
◇	panser - blessure	V-N	33.4	2	3-3
?	prise - M.	N-N	33.4	1	1-0
?	trèfle - luzerne	N-N	33.4	2	1-0
*	consommation - mesure	N-N	33.4	1	0-0
	répression - irrégulier	N-A	33.4	4	0-0
?	diminuer - émission	V-N	33.4	7	1-3
	expérimentation - cosmétique	N-N	33.4	4	1-1

Parse-based method

	Key1, Prep, Key2	Type	LLR	F	Labels
*	exiger - de - mesure	V-P-N	29.9	12	0-0
?	contrôle - à - frontière	N-P-N	29.9	12	1-3
?	aspect - sécuritaire	N-A	29.9	4	3-1
	proposition - originel	N-A	29.9	5	1-1
	refléter - coût	V-O	29.9	7	1-1
?	jeune - issu	N-A	29.9	4	1-0
◇	être - issu	V-O	29.9	12	3-3
?	preuve - scientifique	N-A	29.9	3	3-3
◇	espace - méditerranéen	N-A	29.9	7	3-1
?	fixer - pour	V-P	29.9	21	3-0
?	réunir - septembre	V-O	29.8	4	1-0
?	thème - sensible	N-A	29.8	6	1-3
?	avoir - permis	N-A	29.8	3	0-0
*	avoir - trouvé	N-A	29.8	3	0-0
?	recommander - octroi	V-O	29.8	3	1-3
?	langue - slovaque	N-A	29.8	4	1-4
?	avoir - dans	V-P	29.8	110	1-0
	service public - européen	N-A	29.8	8	1-1
	régime - de - sucre	N-P-N	29.8	7	1-1
?	acte - concret	N-A	29.8	12	1-3
◇	obligation - imposé	N-A	29.8	4	3-3
	redoublement - de - coque	N-P-N	29.8	2	1-1
◇	seuil - de - tolérance	N-P-N	29.8	2	3-3
◇	renforcer - capacité	V-O	29.8	10	3-3
	informer - population	V-O	29.8	6	1-1
?	étendre - règlement	V-O	29.8	6	1-3
◇	émettre - réserve	V-O	29.8	4	3-3
◇	prononcer - jugement	V-O	29.8	4	3-3

Window method

	Key1, Key2	Type	LLR	F	Labels
?	décès - blessure	N-N	33.4	4	3-0
*	prévention - UE	N-N	33.4	1	0-0
	soutien - Parlement européen	N-N	33.4	21	1-1
*	donnée - développement	N-N	33.4	3	0-0
◇	subir - pression	V-N	33.4	9	3-3
◇	mise - service	N-N	33.4	9	3-3
	point de vue - conseil	N-N	33.4	13	1-1
*	droit - possible	N-N	33.4	1	0-0
?	type - processus	N-N	33.4	3	0-1
*	pays - cycle	N-N	33.4	2	0-0
*	résolution - respect	N-N	33.4	3	0-0
*	chômage - pays	N-N	33.4	2	0-0
*	nom - débat	N-N	33.4	2	0-0
*	mettre - lieu	V-N	33.4	5	0-0
?	argent - marché	N-N	33.4	2	0-0
?	instrument - entreprise	N-N	33.4	2	0-0
?	entreprise - instrument	N-N	33.4	2	0-0
?	nombre - élargissement	N-N	33.4	3	0-0
?	élargissement - nombre	N-N	33.4	3	3-1
?	se vouloir - preuve	V-N	33.4	11	3-5
*	terme - autre	N-N	33.4	1	0-0
?	autre - terme	N-N	33.4	1	4-0
*	Conseil - soutien	N-N	33.4	4	0-0
*	être - compte	N-N	33.4	1	0-0
*	système - effet	N-N	33.4	6	0-0
◇	s*échouer - côte	V-N	33.4	3	3-3
*	point - compétence	N-N	33.4	2	0-0
*	être - formation	V-N	33.4	32	0-0

Parse-based method

	Key1, Prep, Key2	Type	LLR	F	Labels
?	rôle - fondamental	N-A	29.8	21	3-1
	disposition - contenu	N-A	29.8	7	1-1
	moderniser - administration	V-O	29.8	3	1-1
◊	sortir - misère	V-O	29.8	3	3-3
?	mode - de - vie	N-P-N	29.8	9	1-4
◊	aboutir - à - solution	V-P-N	29.8	8	3-3

French, TS4

	Key1, Prep, Key2	Type	LLR	F	Labels
?	transition - démocratique	N-A	19.4	4	1-4
	compatibilité - écologique	N-A	19.4	2	1-1
	occupation - de - terre	N-P-N	19.4	3	1-1
	faciliter - participation	V-O	19.4	5	1-1
?	billet - de - train	N-P-N	19.4	3	4-3
	préparation - de - conseil	N-P-N	19.4	15	1-1
?	améliorer - contrôle	V-O	19.4	10	1-3
◊	entraîner - répercussion	V-O	19.4	4	3-3
◊	réaffirmer - volonté	V-O	19.4	4	3-3
◊	formuler - avis	V-O	19.4	8	3-3
?	produit - viande	N-P-N	19.4	7	1-1
	problème - dans - domaine	N-P-N	19.4	1	1-1
	domaine - de - problème	N-P-N	19.4	1	1-1
?	mesure - immédiat	N-A	19.4	9	1-3
CP	confession - religieux	N-A	19.4	2	4-4
?	faire - évaluation	V-O	19.4	7	1-3
?	faire - économie	V-O	19.4	7	1-5
	coordonner - politique	V-O	19.4	6	1-1
?	obéir - à - logique	V-P-N	19.4	2	1-5
?	apporter - plus-value	V-O	19.4	3	3-1

Window method

	Key1, Key2	Type	LLR	F	Labels
*	homme - fond	N-N	33.4	1	0-0
*	fond - homme	N-N	33.4	1	0-0
?	salaire - minimum	N-A	33.4	4	1-4
	problème - participation	N-N	33.4	9	1-1
?	comité - se composer	N-V	33.4	4	1-3
*	principe - parti	N-N	33.4	2	0-0

	Key1, Key2	Type	LLR	F	Labels
*	chose - Europe	N-N	21.1	17	0-0
*	manière - financier	N-A	21.1	7	0-0
◊	acquitter - accusation	V-N	21.1	2	3-3
*	service - liste	N-N	21.1	1	0-0
*	stratégie - effet	N-N	21.1	1	0-0
	cas - fou	N-A	21.1	6	0-0
	manière - pragmatique	N-A	21.1	5	1-1
*	été - année	N-N	21.1	9	0-0
◊	conclusion - tirer	N-V	21.1	3	3-3
*	nouveau - aide	N-N	21.1	2	0-0
*	pouvoir - communication	N-N	21.1	1	0-0
	aide - état	N-N	21.1	2	1-1
?	document - voyage	N-N	21.1	13	4-3
*	aspect - environnement	N-N	21.1	4	0-0
*	mesure - recours	N-N	21.1	2	0-0
*	processus - fonds	N-N	21.1	3	0-0
*	fonds - processus	N-N	21.1	3	0-0
*	exercice - dire	N-V	21.1	4	0-0
*	préoccupation - traité	N-N	21.1	1	0-0
*	article - importance	N-N	21.1	5	0-0

Parse-based method

	Key1, Prep, Key2	Type	LLR	F	Labels
?	chose - facile	N-A	19.4	3	1-4
	nature - impérialiste	N-A	19.4	3	1-1
?	venir - de - être	V-P-N	19.4	5	1-0
	contribution - constructif	N-A	19.4	5	1-1
?	citer - extrait	V-O	19.4	2	1-3
?	lire - livre	V-O	19.4	3	1-3
	choisir - siège	V-O	19.4	3	1-1
	éloigner - de - autre	V-P-N	19.4	3	1-1
?	débuter - année	V-O	19.4	3	1-1
?	exil - fiscal	N-A	19.4	2	1-3
?	concurrence - fiscal	N-A	19.4	2	1-3
?	procédure - de - insolvabilité	N-P-N	19.4	4	6-4
◇	mettre - à - exécution	V-P-N	19.4	7	3-3
	million - de - livre sterling	N-P-N	19.4	3	1-1
	financement - de - travail	N-P-N	19.4	3	1-1
	consister - en - adoption	V-P-N	19.4	3	1-1
	inclure - disposition	V-O	19.4	7	1-1
?	accueillir - initiative	V-O	19.3	7	1-3
?	rendre - sur	V-P	19.3	16	3-0
◇	répondre - à - appel	V-P-N	19.3	4	3-3
◇	demande - parvenir	S-V	19.3	3	3-3
?	réalité - politique	N-A	19.3	11	1-4
?	être - bref	N-A	19.3	3	1-5
?	regretter - absence	V-O	19.3	2	1-3
	protéger - contre - intrusion	V-P-N	19.3	2	1-1
?	député - élu	N-A	19.3	3	1-3
	montrer - à - citoyen	V-P-N	19.3	5	1-1

Window method

	Key1, Key2	Type	LLR	F	Labels
*	titre - amendement	N-N	21.1	3	0-0
	investir - formation	V-N	21.1	4	1-1
	nationaliste - basque	N-A	21.1	2	1-1
	procédure - concurrence	N-N	21.1	6	1-1
*	austérité - entraîner	N-V	21.1	2	0-0
*	commissaire - conférence	N-N	21.1	4	0-0
	conseil - décider	N-V	21.1	18	1-1
*	décision - droit	N-N	21.1	3	0-0
◇	proposition - discuter	N-V	21.1	16	3-3
*	novembre - Union européenne	N-N	21.1	3	0-0
*	information - titre	N-N	21.1	1	0-0
?	an - sommet	N-N	21.1	3	1-0
?	explosion - périmètre	N-N	21.1	2	0-1
*	présidente - preuve	N-N	21.1	1	0-0
*	problème - concept	N-N	21.1	1	0-0
*	brin - lait	N-N	21.1	2	0-0
*	euro - cause	N-N	21.1	1	0-0
*	institution - victime	N-N	21.1	1	0-0
*	victime - institution	N-N	21.1	1	0-0
	avancée - désescalade	N-N	21.1	2	1-1
?	poisson - adulte	N-A	21.1	2	3-1
*	Nations unies - principe	N-N	21.1	2	0-0
?	présidence - jour	N-N	21.1	1	1-0
	harmonisation - s*avérer	N-V	21.1	4	1-1
?	Dieu - savoir	N-V	21.1	3	4-5
◇	dépasser - horaire	V-N	21.1	3	3-3
	améliorer - rapport	V-N	21.1	13	1-1

Parse-based method

	Key1, Prep, Key2	Type	LLR	F	Labels
?	assistance - mutuel	N-A	19.3	4	1-3
	gouvernance - mondial	N-A	19.3	5	1-1
?	débat - sur - proposition	N-P-N	19.3	4	1-3

French, TS5

	Key1, Prep, Key2	Type	LLR	F	Labels
	tolérer - séjour	V-O	12.4	1	1-1
*	prouver - été	V-O	12.4	1	0-0
	tolérer - laxisme	V-O	12.4	1	1-1
	annuler - mémoire	V-O	12.4	1	1-1
*	gouvernement - pour - rapport	N-P-N	12.4	1	0-0
	baser - emplacement	V-O	12.4	1	1-1
	exclure - paramilitaire	V-O	12.4	1	1-1
	entreposer - quantité	V-O	12.4	1	1-1
*	discipliner - énergie	V-O	12.4	1	0-0
*	noter - société	V-O	12.4	1	0-0
?	vouer - énergie	V-O	12.4	1	3-1
	exclure - turbine	V-O	12.4	1	1-1
	exclure - divulgation	V-O	12.4	1	1-1
	venir - opposition	V-O	12.4	1	0-0
*	répéter - vrai	V-O	12.4	1	0-0
*	succéder - catastrophe	V-O	12.4	1	0-0
?	devoir - décès	V-O	12.4	2	1-3
	censure - sur - imagination	N-P-N	12.4	1	1-1
?	bon - avec - occident	N-P-N	12.4	1	1-0
?	niveau - dans - hiérarchie	N-P-N	12.4	1	1-3
?	déni - de - génocide	N-P-N	12.4	1	1-3
*	plomb - de - résidu	N-P-N	12.4	1	0-0
	protéger - de - publicité	V-P-N	12.4	2	1-1

Window method

	Key1, Key2	Type	LLR	F	Labels
◇	importance - considérable	N-A	21.1	11	3-3
?	santé - économie	N-N	21.1	4	3-1
?	besoin - nécessité	N-N	21.1	2	1-0
*	présence - entreprise	N-N	12.0	1	1-1
*	inflation - fatidique	N-A	12.0	1	0-0
*	friction - écoulé	N-A	12.0	1	0-0
*	dernier - procédure	N-N	12.0	3	0-0
?	exister - risque	V-N	12.0	18	3-1
*	monstrueux - golfe	A-N	12.0	1	0-0
*	inoffensif - virus	A-N	12.0	1	0-0
*	ministre - avis	N-N	12.0	5	0-0
?	préoccuper - bulletin	V-N	12.0	1	1-0
*	préoccuper - Arizona	V-N	12.0	1	0-0
*	réducteur - voisinage	A-N	12.0	1	0-0
?	manque - citoyen	N-N	12.0	5	1-0
*	tenir - week-end	V-N	12.0	2	0-0
?	émission - radioactif	N-A	12.0	3	3-4
?	insérer - terme	V-N	12.0	3	3-1
*	mention - rapport	N-N	12.0	1	0-0
*	UE - revenu	N-N	12.0	1	0-0
?	être - espoir	V-N	12.0	25	3-1
*	UE - moi	N-N	12.0	1	0-0
*	manifestation - problème	N-N	12.0	1	0-0
	remercier - disponibilité	V-N	12.0	3	1-1
*	expliciter - homologue	V-N	12.0	1	0-0
?	éloigner - mafia	V-N	12.0	1	3-1

Parse-based method							Window method					
	Key1, Prep, Key2	Type	LLR	F	Labels			Key1, Key2	Type	LLR	F	Labels
?	protéger - contre - choc	V-P-N	12.4	2	1-3			détention - révéler	N-V	12.0	1	1-1
*	sou - de - forme	N-P-N	12.4	2	0-0			remercier - rapidité	V-N	12.0	5	1-1
?	impulser - à l*intérieur	V-P	12.4	1	1-0			brider - chercheur	V-N	12.0	1	1-1
?	flagrant - lacune	A-N	12.4	1	1-3		?	admission - regarder	N-V	12.0	1	0-1
?	provoquer - par - homme	V-P-N	12.4	2	1-3			arranger - actionnaire	V-N	12.0	1	1-1
?	éviter - gaspillage	V-O	12.4	2	1-3		*	presser - démocratisation	V-N	12.0	1	0-0
?	application - concret	N-A	12.4	2	1-3			communiste - regarder	N-V	12.0	1	0-1
	procéder - de - examen	V-P-N	12.4	1	1-1		?	hésitation - adoucissement	N-N	12.0	1	1-0
	prétendre - à - paiement	V-P-N	12.4	1	1-1		?	épidémie - juguler	N-V	12.0	1	3-3
	rajouter - à - pauvreté	V-P-N	12.4	1	1-1		◇	participer - nettoyage	V-N	12.0	2	1-1
◇	inculper - de - crime	V-P-N	12.4	1	3-3		*	se préparer - orgueil	V-N	12.0	1	0-0
	collaborer - avec - point	V-P-N	12.4	1	1-1			secrétaire - assurer	N-V	12.0	1	1-1
	soucier - de - Européen	V-P-N	12.4	1	1-1		*	engagement - gouvernement	N-N	12.0	16	0-0
◇	attaquer - à - question	V-P-N	12.4	5	3-3		*	avis - Union	N-N	12.0	3	0-0
	activité - exécutif	N-A	12.4	3	1-1		?	intervention - député	N-N	12.0	4	1-3
	combattant - kurde	N-A	12.4	1	1-1		?	député - intervention	N-N	12.0	4	1-3
	voix - contestataire	N-A	12.4	1	1-1		*	Chine - aide	N-N	12.0	1	0-0
?	ampoule - électrique	N-A	12.4	1	1-4		*	responsabilité - objet	N-N	12.0	2	0-0
	jeune homme - kurde	N-A	12.4	1	1-1		*	contrôle - route	N-N	12.0	1	0-0
?	humanisme - classique	N-A	12.4	1	1-3		*	route - contrôle	N-N	12.0	1	0-0
*	fait - incompréhensible	N-A	12.4	2	0-0		*	Parlement - façon	N-N	12.0	1	0-0
*	fait - inapproprié	N-A	12.4	2	0-0		*	autorité - durable	N-A	12.0	1	0-0
?	page - douloureux	N-A	12.4	1	5-3		*	surgir - incompréhension	V-N	12.0	1	0-0
*	vérification - donnant	N-A	12.4	1	0-0		?	hésitation - user	N-V	12.0	1	1-0
	nature - européen	N-A	12.4	1	1-1		?	sombrer - affrontement	V-N	12.0	1	3-1
?	nombre - augmenter	S-V	12.4	3	1-3			trafiquant - se sortir	N-V	12.0	1	1-1
	imaginer - misère	V-O	12.4	1	1-1		?	stress - désagrément	N-N	12.0	1	1-0

Parse-based method						Window method					
	Key1, Prep, Key2	Type	LLR	F	Labels		Key1, Key2	Type	LLR	F	Labels
Italian, TS1											
NE	unione - europeo	N-A	29489.5	6565	2-2		signora - presidente	N-N	55253.3	9380	1-1
NE	parlamento - europeo	N-A	10138.5	2865	2-2	NE	unione - europeo	N-A	21737.2	6875	2-2
NE	unire - stato	V-O	6798.6	1085	2-2	?	stato - membro	N-N	9243.3	4974	1-3
	candidare - paese	V-O	6444.4	755	1-1	NE	signora - commissario	N-N	7584.9	2012	1-1
CP	diritto - umano	N-A	5050.1	860	4-4		parlamento - europeo	N-A	6520.4	3075	2-2
CP	punto - di - vista	N-P-N	4930.6	558	4-4		emendamento - n	N-N	6339.4	1114	1-1
?	ordine - recare	S-V	4890.0	479	3-1	*	commissione - commissione	N-N	5543.3	227	0-0
CP	paese - terzo	N-A	4358.5	496	4-4		onorevole - collega	A-N	4984.5	871	1-1
NE	unire - nazione	V-O	4190.1	548	2-2	◇	tenere - conto	V-N	4963.2	819	3-3
?	lavoro - svolgere	S-V	4103.1	607	0-3	?	ordine - giorno	N-N	4725.6	1037	4-3
NE	unire - regno	V-O	3810.5	478	2-2	?	ordine - recare	N-V	4716.9	541	3-1
?	mercato - interno	N-A	3735.5	556	3-4		paese - candidare	N-V	4609.9	808	1-1
	presidenza - belga	N-A	3730.3	401	1-1	?	stato - unire	N-V	4463.1	1146	2-1
◇	sviluppo - sostenibile	N-A	3692.3	425	3-3	CP	secondo - luogo	A-N	4219.1	712	4-4
	presidenza - svedese	N-A	3573.2	423	1-1	CP	diritto - umano	N-A	4113.2	901	4-4
CP	libro - bianco	N-A	3516.5	343	4-4	?	giorno - recare	N-V	4030.0	535	0-1
?	posizione - comune	N-A	3282.6	553	1-3	NE	nazione - unire	N-V	4004.3	584	2-2
CP	secondo - luogo	A-N	3151.0	707	4-4		presidenza - svedese	N-A	3981.7	506	1-1
?	diritto - di - uomo	N-P-N	3008.8	510	4-1	CP	punto - vista	N-N	3898.2	756	4-4
?	onorevole - parlamentare	N-A	2976.0	293	3-1	*	unione - commissione	N-N	3875.2	51	0-0
◇	approvare - risoluzione	V-O	2898.8	412	3-3		presidenza - belga	N-A	3627.4	437	1-1
*	diritto - dio	A-N	2719.9	259	0-0	*	commissione - unione	N-N	3569.2	95	0-0
	milione - di - euro	N-P-N	2676.4	377	1-1	*	stato - commissione	N-N	3535.0	94	0-0
◇	base - giuridico	N-A	2669.0	365	3-3	◇	discussione - chiusa	N-N	3508.4	406	3-3
	votazione - svolgere	S-V	2616.7	348	1-1	NE	regno - unire	N-V	3484.0	512	2-2
◇	parlamento - approvare	S-V	2503.7	531	1-1	?	paese - commissione	N-N	3393.9	21	0-1
NE	consiglio - europeo	N-A	2443.0	824	2-2	CP	libro - bianco	N-A	3350.3	352	4-4

Parse-based method

	Key1, Prep, Key2	Type	LLR	F	Labels
CP	essere - umano	N-A	2314.3	398	4-4
CP	società - civile	N-A	2299.9	301	4-4
?	conferenza - intergovernativo	N-A	2284.1	210	1-4
CP	primo - luogo	A-N	2214.5	640	4-4
?	compagnia - aereo	N-A	2196.9	197	3-4
◇	diritto - fondamentale	N-A	2171.4	442	3-3
◇	risolvere - problema	V-O	2121.8	313	3-3
CP	ordine - di - giorno	N-P-N	2119.7	262	4-4
?	processo - decisionale	N-A	2097.1	231	1-4
?	libero - circolazione	A-N	2084.5	193	3-4
◇	carne - bovino	N-A	2060.2	161	3-3
◇	votare - a favore	V-P	2018.8	315	3-3
CP	posto - di - lavoro	N-P-N	1986.4	304	4-4
◇	presidente - in - carica	N-P-N	1965.3	292	3-3
*	dio - cittadino	N-A	1941.4	211	0-0
◇	richiamare - attenzione	V-O	1892.6	181	3-3
?	emendamento - orale	N-A	1863.4	176	1-1
◇	fondo - strutturale	N-A	1774.8	232	3-3
?	banca - centrale	N-A	1773.6	181	2-4
?	sicurezza - alimentare	N-A	1769.3	264	1-3
◇	cogliere - occasione	V-O	1762.5	167	3-3
?	politica - estero	N-A	1718.9	339	3-4
CP	via - di - sviluppo	N-P-N	1689.7	302	4-4

Italian, TS2

?	motivo - principale	N-A	80.6	15	1-3
◇	fermo - condanna	A-N	80.6	8	3-3
?	vincitore - di - premio	N-P-N	80.5	7	3-1

Window method

	Key1, Key2	Type	LLR	F	Labels
?	mercato - interno	N-A	3177.2	580	3-4
CP	primo - luogo	A-N	3105.2	645	4-4
◇	sviluppo - sostenibile	N-A	3011.3	468	3-3
*	commissione - paese	N-N	2956.9	80	0-0
*	commissione - stato	N-N	2952.9	199	0-0
◇	votazione - svolgere	N-V	2948.3	386	3-3
CP	paese - terzo	N-A	2757.7	557	4-4
?	onorevole - parlamentare	N-A	2719.4	331	3-1
?	posizione - comune	N-A	2639.6	565	1-3
?	relazione - onorevole	N-A	2580.5	627	1-0
◇	accogliere - favore	V-N	2455.8	349	3-3
?	commissione - presidente	N-N	2416.6	44	0-1
*	commissione - membro	N-N	2374.1	188	0-0
?	opinione - pubblico	N-A	2317.3	404	3-4
?	diritto - commissione	N-N	2254.0	35	0-1
◇	base - giuridico	N-A	2200.3	392	3-3
◇	diritto - fondamentale	N-A	2171.5	537	3-3
*	unione - unione	N-N	2164.4	53	0-0
?	parlamento - approvare	N-V	2133.5	580	1-1
?	interrogazione - n	N-N	2110.1	354	1-1
◇	approvare - risoluzione	V-N	2109.5	421	3-3
?	unione - consiglio	N-N	2074.4	31	0-1
CP	conferenza - intergovernativo	N-A	2045.8	217	1-4

?	dato - proposta	N-N	92.0	4	0-1
?	discussione - cooperazione	N-N	92.0	5	0-1
◇	cosa - andare	N-V	92.0	45	3-3

Parse-based method

	Key1, Prep, Key2	Type	LLR	F	Labels
?	parlamento - da - relazione	N-P-N	80.5	1	1-0
*	parlamento - con - relazione	N-P-N	80.5	1	0-0
*	parlamento - per - relazione	N-P-N	80.5	1	0-0
?	relazione - in - parlamento	N-P-N	80.5	1	1-0
*	relazione - per - parlamento	N-P-N	80.5	1	0-0
◇	alimento - composto	N-A	80.5	7	3-3
NE	unione - sovietico	N-A	80.4	18	2-2
	norma - comune	N-A	80.4	50	1-1
?	fare - esempio	V-O	80.4	31	3-1
	modifica - costituzionale	N-A	80.4	13	1-1
	governo - cinese	N-A	80.4	15	1-1
	interrogazione - scritto	N-A	80.4	10	1-1
◇	aperto - contrasto	A-N	80.4	7	3-3
?	dovere - a - fatto	V-P-N	80.4	20	1-3
	esortare - governo	V-O	80.3	14	1-1
	creazione - di - agenzia	N-P-N	80.3	18	1-1
?	aspetto - negativo	N-A	80.3	22	3-1
◇	applicare - procedura	V-O	80.3	25	3-3
	deputato - radicale	N-A	80.2	11	1-1
	maggiore - coinvolgimento	A-N	80.2	21	1-1
◇	accordare - priorità	V-O	80.2	12	3-3
	scorso - autunno	A-N	80.1	10	1-1
◇	dotare - di - mezzo	V-P-N	80.1	14	3-3
◇	gentile - parola	A-N	80.1	8	3-3
◇	anello - di - catena	N-P-N	80.1	6	3-3
◇	commissionare - studio	V-O	80.1	7	3-3
	offrire - dal	V-P	80.0	52	1-1
?	formazione - permanente	N-A	80.0	10	3-4

Window method

	Key1, Key2	Type	LLR	F	Labels
*	era - commissione	N-N	92.0	8	0-0
*	situazione - istituzione	N-N	92.0	4	0-0
*	istituzione - situazione	N-N	92.0	4	0-0
*	esportazione - terzo	N-A	92.0	22	0-0
*	linea - modo	N-N	91.9	4	0-0
	anno - impegno	N-N	91.9	15	0-0
*	emendamento - obiettivo	N-N	91.9	11	0-0
*	signora - ancora	N-N	91.9	1	0-0
*	lavoro - partecipazione	N-N	91.9	1	0-0
*	stato - contenuto	N-N	91.9	2	0-0
*	principio - governo	N-N	91.9	3	0-0
?	politica - miglioramento	N-N	91.9	3	1-0
?	questione - importante	N-A	91.9	75	1-3
*	mettere - commissione	V-N	91.9	20	0-0
?	istruzione - stato	N-N	91.9	12	0-1
	azienda - paese	N-N	91.9	6	1-1
*	prevenzione - relazione	N-N	91.9	3	0-0
	sforzo - stato	N-N	91.9	19	1-1
?	politica - giustizia	N-N	91.9	11	0-1
?	paese - risorsa	N-N	91.9	25	0-1
*	consiglio - luce	N-N	91.9	6	0-0
*	onorevole - politica	N-N	91.9	10	0-0
*	politica - seguito	N-N	91.9	1	0-0
	problema - consumatore	N-N	91.9	6	1-1
*	atto - relazione	N-N	91.9	18	0-0
*	fare - controllo	N-N	91.9	2	0-0
*	soluzione - lavoro	N-N	91.9	5	0-0
?	esigenza - unione	N-N	91.9	19	0-1

Parse-based method

Key1, Prep, Key2	Type	LLR	F	Labels
CP				
gara - da - appalto	N-P-N	79.9	5	4-4
? finire - prodotto	V-O	79.9	10	3-4
◇ risposta - per - iscritto	N-P-N	79.9	10	3-3
apprezzare - lavoro	V-O	79.9	19	1-1
anno - passare	S-V	79.9	12	1-1
creare - mercato	V-O	79.8	24	1-1
proprio - territorio	A-N	79.8	21	1-1
soluzione - europeo	N-A	79.8	7	1-1
NE commissione - per - occupazione	N-P-N	79.7	69	2-2
◇ disporre - di - risorsa	V-P-N	79.7	18	3-3
marzo - di - anno	N-P-N	79.7	15	1-1
? caso - particolare	N-A	79.7	17	1-3
CP stato - in - stato	N-P-N	79.7	1	4-4
* stato - di - stato	N-P-N	79.7	1	0-0
legalità - internazionale	N-A	79.7	10	1-1
popolo - algerino	N-A	79.6	10	1-1
? revocare - immunità	V-O	79.6	6	0-3
proposta - a - unione	N-P-N	79.6	1	1-1
* dispositivo - di - dio	N-P-N	79.5	10	0-0

Italian, TS3

Key1, Prep, Key2	Type	LLR	F	Labels
◇ azione - preventivo	N-A	31.0	8	3-3
* simile - premettere	S-V	31.0	2	0-0
◇ eccesso - di - capacità	N-P-N	31.0	5	3-3
? propaganda - elettorale	N-A	31.0	3	3-4
◇ aprire - dialogo	V-O	31.0	8	3-3
trasmissione - di - campione	N-P-N	31.0	3	1-1
tempo - di - volo	N-P-N	31.0	6	1-1

Window method

Key1, Key2	Type	LLR	F	Labels
* commissione - perdita	N-N	91.9	1	0-0
* ministro - punto	N-N	91.9	1	0-0
* progetto - servizio	N-N	91.9	1	0-0
servizio - progetto	N-N	91.9	1	1-1
* agricoltura - relazione	N-N	91.9	9	0-0
* potere - necessario	V-N	91.8	7	0-0
? fondo - accordo	N-N	91.8	8	1-0
* stato - pressione	N-N	91.8	4	0-0
◇ esprimere - auspicio	V-N	91.8	22	3-3
* situazione - o	N-N	91.8	8	0-0
* parlamento - assemblea	N-N	91.8	15	0-0
* tecnologia - unione	N-N	91.8	7	0-0
* collega - programma	N-N	91.8	1	0-0
* programma - collega	N-N	91.8	1	0-0
* ambiente - Europa	N-N	91.8	10	0-0
* commissario - donna	N-N	91.8	1	0-0
diritto - metodo	N-N	91.8	1	0-0
sede - unione	N-N	91.8	10	1-1
* integrazione - relazione	N-N	91.8	2	0-0
* anno - nome	N-N	38.9	2	0-0
* rispetto - applicazione	N-N	38.9	1	0-0
? tempo - intervento	N-N	38.9	4	1-0
* richiesta - azione	N-N	38.9	5	0-0
? assistenza - esterno	N-A	38.9	15	3-1
* potere - anca	N-N	38.9	1	0-0
* polizia - modo	N-N	38.9	3	0-0

Parse-based method

	Key1, Prep, Key2	Type	LLR	F	Labels
	nuovo - carta	A-N	31.0	6	1-1
	controllo - efficace	N-A	31.0	12	1-1
	giunta - in ritardo	N-A	31.0	2	1-1
?	emisfero - sud	N-A	31.0	2	3-2
◇	esprimere - condoglianze	V-O	31.0	5	3-3
	presidente - di - gruppo	N-P-N	31.0	33	1-1
◇	dare - occhiata	V-O	31.0	4	3-3
◇	fondo - destinare	S-V	31.0	7	3-3
◇	fare - balzo	V-O	31.0	5	3-3
	unico - strumento	A-N	31.0	15	1-1
*	foresta - in - comunità	N-P-N	31.0	5	0-0
?	proprio - potere	A-N	31.0	16	3-1
	carattere - peculiare	N-A	31.0	4	1-1
◇	essere - a - altezza	N-P-N	31.0	6	3-3
	principale - fattore	A-N	31.0	8	1-1
?	combattere - contraffazione	V-O	31.0	3	3-1
	obiettivo - occupazionale	N-A	31.0	8	1-1
?	riprendere - filo	V-O	31.0	4	5-3
	popolo - angolano	N-A	31.0	4	1-1
?	misura - vincolante	N-A	31.0	10	3-1
	esortare - assemblea	V-O	31.0	5	1-1
	criminalità - violento	N-A	31.0	4	1-1
?	ora - di - sera	N-P-N	31.0	4	3-1
◇	piantare - albero	V-O	31.0	2	3-3
	finanziare - partito	V-O	31.0	6	1-1
◇	rivolgere - sguardo	V-O	31.0	5	3-3
	misura - previsto	N-A	31.0	15	1-1
	diverso - gruppo	A-N	31.0	15	1-1

Window method

	Key1, Key2	Type	LLR	F	Labels
*	modo - polizia	N-N	38.9	3	0-0
*	essere - fatto	N-N	38.9	3	0-0
?	associazione - paese	N-N	38.9	17	1-0
*	prendere - lavoro	V-N	38.9	10	0-0
*	risultato - decisione	N-N	38.9	8	0-0
*	iniziativa - termine	N-N	38.9	5	0-0
?	egoismo - nazionale	N-A	38.9	7	1-3
*	proposta - dovere	N-N	38.9	1	0-0
*	dovere - proposta	N-N	38.9	1	0-0
*	soluzione - o	N-N	38.9	3	0-0
?	primo - cosa	A-N	38.9	29	4-1
*	fondo - volta	N-N	38.9	1	0-0
	regione - tipo	N-N	38.9	1	0-0
	aspetto - euro	N-N	38.9	5	0-0
?	forza - Europa	N-N	38.9	11	1-0
*	opportunità - governo	N-N	38.9	2	0-0
*	governo - uso	N-N	38.9	2	0-0
*	qualità - fatto	N-N	38.9	2	0-0
*	principio - aspetto	N-N	38.9	4	0-0
*	svedese - consiglio	A-N	38.9	29	0-0
	primo - interrogativo	N-A	38.9	5	1-1
	regime - sistema	N-N	38.9	4	0-0
*	più - intervento	N-N	38.9	17	0-0
◇	tensione - etnico	N-A	38.9	5	3-3
	tipo - iniziativa	N-N	38.9	1	1-1
*	termine - attenzione	N-N	38.9	1	0-0
*	quadro - passo	N-N	38.9	1	0-0
*	dio - popolare	N-V	38.9	9	0-0

Parse-based method

	Key1, Prep, Key2	Type	LLR	F	Labels
?	scorrere - mese	V-O	31.0	6	1-4
?	pezzo - grosso	N-A	31.0	2	5-4
	controparte - russo	N-A	31.0	3	1-1
?	rinnovare - appello	V-O	31.0	5	1-3
?	fondo - di - garanzia	N-P-N	31.0	11	3-4
?	base - statistico	N-A	31.0	8	4-3
?	volo - a - raggio	N-P-N	31.0	3	3-3
◇	corso - di - dibattito	N-P-N	31.0	18	1-4
?	assemblea - manifestare	S-V	30.9	6	1-1
?	economia - reale	N-A	30.9	10	3-1
?	nuovo - frontiera	A-N	30.9	13	3-1
	materiale - pericoloso	N-A	30.9	6	1-1
◇	avviare - azione	V-O	30.9	12	3-3
	osservazione - fatto	N-A	30.9	5	1-1
◇	scarso - entusiasmo	A-N	30.9	4	3-3

Italian, TS4

	Key1, Prep, Key2	Type	LLR	F	Labels
◇	decidere - destino	V-O	12.3	2	3-3
*	poeta - da - lato	N-P-N	12.3	1	0-0
	decidere - parametro	V-O	12.3	2	1-1
*	risparmio - come - imposta	N-P-N	12.3	1	0-0
*	impronta - a - avvenimento	N-P-N	12.3	1	0-0
	incolumità - di - equipaggio	N-P-N	12.3	1	1-1
*	lato - come - appello	N-P-N	12.3	1	0-0
?	licenziamento - bloccare	S-V	12.3	1	1-3
◇	tecnica - sperimentare	S-V	12.3	1	3-3
	medicina - insegnare	S-V	12.3	1	1-1
*	tenore - proibire	S-V	12.3	1	0-0

Window method

	Key1, Key2	Type	LLR	F	Labels
	rispetto - sostegno	N-N	38.9	1	1-1
*	essere - regola	V-N	38.9	65	0-0
*	società - attività	N-N	38.9	4	0-0
?	interrogazione - rispondere	N-V	38.9	8	3-0
?	metodo - materia	N-N	38.9	6	3-1
?	sostegno - ambito	N-N	38.9	11	3-0
*	espressione - politico	N-A	38.9	20	0-0
*	possibile - evitare	N-V	38.9	16	0-0
?	richiesta - essere	N-N	38.9	3	0-1
*	capo - sistema	N-N	38.9	1	0-0
*	persona - fatto	N-N	38.9	7	0-0
?	riconoscimento - problema	N-N	38.9	1	1-3
*	lista - parlamento	N-N	38.9	2	0-0
*	questione - difficoltà	N-N	38.8	5	0-0
*	interesse - esempio	N-N	38.8	3	0-0

	Key1, Key2	Type	LLR	F	Labels
*	richiedere - modo	V-N	24.3	2	0-0
*	donna - ora	N-N	24.3	2	0-0
?	peggiore - ipotesi	A-N	24.3	3	4-1
	distinzione - membro	N-N	24.3	1	1-1
◇	consultazione - popolare	N-A	24.3	7	3-3
*	misura - strada	N-N	24.3	5	0-0
*	zona - esempio	N-N	24.3	1	0-0
	sorvegliare - legittimità	V-N	24.3	3	1-1
*	presenza - più	N-N	24.3	1	0-0
*	più - quota	N-N	24.3	1	0-0
*	più - presenza	N-N	24.3	1	0-0

Parse-based method

	Key1, Prep, Key2	Type	LLR	F	Labels
?	vaccino - sperimentare	S-V	12.3	1	0-3
	ricordo - insegnare	S-V	12.3	1	1-1
	poco - offuscare	S-V	12.3	1	1-1
	finanziamento - adeguare	S-V	12.3	2	1-1
	parlamento - esprimere	S-V	12.3	10	1-1
	industria - investire	S-V	12.3	2	1-1
?	riduzione - di - gettito	N-P-N	12.3	2	1-3
	reagire - a - violazione	V-P-N	12.3	2	1-1
	tema - cadere	S-V	12.3	2	1-1
◇	varare - direttiva	V-O	12.3	4	3-3
	sinonimo - di - accentramento	N-P-N	12.3	1	1-1
*	fare - a - regolamento	V-P-N	12.3	8	0-0
?	depurare - acqua	V-O	12.3	1	3-1
*	sorprendere - leggero	V-O	12.3	1	0-0
?	abbattere - alluvione	V-O	12.3	1	0-3
?	posizione - preminente	N-A	12.3	2	4-3
	finanziare - da - linea	V-P-N	12.3	2	1-1
◇	parte - sostanziale	N-A	12.3	5	3-3
◇	enorme - caos	A-N	12.3	2	3-3
?	importanza - a - stato	N-P-N	12.3	1	1-0
*	animale - tra - stato	N-P-N	12.3	1	0-0
*	animale - in - stato	N-P-N	12.3	1	0-0
◇	rispondere - a - aspirazione	V-P-N	12.3	2	3-3
	relazione - citare	S-V	12.3	8	1-1
◇	rompere - isolamento	V-O	12.3	1	3-3
◇	sbarazzare - eccedenza	V-O	12.3	1	3-3
?	sfociare - fiume	V-O	12.3	1	0-3
*	perseguitare - fama	V-O	12.3	1	0-0
?	forzare - migrazione	V-O	12.3	1	1-3

Window method

	Key1, Key2	Type	LLR	F	Labels
*	competenza - iniziativa	N-N	24.3	4	0-0
*	avere - questione	N-N	24.3	15	0-0
	principio - investimento	N-N	24.3	1	1-1
*	stabilità - tempo	N-N	24.3	2	0-0
	oggetto - grande	N-A	24.3	14	0-0
?	rivolgere - interrogazione	V-N	24.3	14	3-0
*	membro - cattura	N-N	24.3	4	0-0
*	applicazione - rapporto	N-N	24.3	1	0-0
*	appello - materia	N-N	24.3	2	0-0
*	trasparenza - dibattito	N-N	24.3	2	0-0
?	regione - produzione	N-N	24.3	4	0-1
*	agricoltore - informazione	N-N	24.3	1	0-0
*	lavoro - statuto	N-N	24.3	2	0-0
*	sviluppo - lettera	N-N	24.3	1	0-0
*	sviluppo - espressione	N-N	24.3	1	0-0
*	lettera - sviluppo	N-N	24.3	1	0-0
*	compito - commissario	N-N	24.3	3	0-0
*	commissario - compito	N-N	24.3	3	0-0
*	tempo - possibile	N-N	24.3	4	0-0
?	negozio - giuridico	N-A	24.3	4	3-4
?	senso - popolazione	N-N	24.3	2	0-1
?	opinione - azione	N-N	24.3	5	0-0
	giornata - ricordare	N-V	24.3	3	1-1
*	greco - sovvertimento	A-N	24.3	2	0-0
*	vita - rete	N-N	24.3	1	0-0
*	comunità - risorsa	N-N	24.3	2	0-0
*	vittima - base	N-N	24.3	1	0-0
*	occasione - tipo	N-N	24.3	2	0-0
?	tale - democrazia	A-N	24.3	2	0-1

Parse-based method

	Key1, Prep, Key2	Type	LLR	F	Labels
*	fraintendere - risarcimento	V-O	12.3	1	0-0
*	priorità - ovvio	N-Pred-A	12.3	1	0-0
?	raccolta - benvenuto	N-Pred-A	12.3	1	0-1
◇	reazione - immediato	N-Pred-A	12.3	1	3-3
◇	elenco - esaustivo	N-Pred-A	12.3	1	3-3
	sondaggio - tangibile	N-Pred-A	12.3	1	1-1
	dipendenza - assoluto	N-Pred-A	12.3	1	3-3
◇	morte - lento	N-Pred-A	12.3	1	1-3
?	approvazione - maggioritario	N-Pred-A	12.3	1	1-3
?	nozione - effettivo	N-Pred-A	12.3	1	1-3

Italian, TS5

	Key1, Prep, Key2	Type	LLR	F	Labels
?	concludere - terzo	V-O	2.9	1	0-1
	concetto - di - orario	N-P-N	2.9	1	1-1
	anticipare - esigenza	V-O	2.9	1	1-1
◇	notevole - vantaggio	A-N	2.9	2	3-3
	aula - impegnare	S-V	2.9	1	1-1
	prestare - a - produttore	V-P-N	2.9	1	1-1
	prestare - a - orientamento	V-P-N	2.9	1	1-1
?	maternità - per - donna	N-P-N	2.9	1	0-1
*	confrontare - di - sistema	V-P-N	2.9	1	0-0
?	appoggio - sostenere	S-V	2.9	1	0-3
	classificazione - di - opera	N-P-N	2.9	1	1-1
	inaccettabile - forma	A-N	2.9	1	1-1
*	essere - genere	V-O	2.9	1	0-0
?	accelerare - pagamento	V-O	2.9	1	1-3
*	stabilire - gioco	V-O	2.9	1	0-0
?	prassi - stare	S-V	2.9	1	1-0
?	precedere - deputato	V-O	2.9	1	0-1

Window method

	Key1, Key2	Type	LLR	F	Labels
?	pagare - stipendio	V-N	24.3	4	3-0
*	negoziato - rispetto	N-N	24.3	1	0-0
*	spagnolo - parlamento	A-N	24.3	16	0-0
*	gruppo - vantaggio	N-N	24.3	3	0-0
*	automobile - pedone	N-N	24.3	3	0-0
?	fatto - progetto	N-N	24.3	6	0-3
*	regione - possibilità	N-N	24.3	3	0-0
*	modalità - mercato	N-N	24.3	1	0-0
*	regime - regime	N-N	24.3	3	0-0
*	riguardare - aula	V-N	24.3	1	0-0

	Key1, Key2	Type	LLR	F	Labels
?	introdurre - etichettatura	V-N	12.7	4	1-0
	porto - indonesiano	N-A	12.7	2	1-1
*	amministrazione -]	N-N	12.7	1	0-0
*	massimo - veicolo	A-N	12.7	5	0-0
*	aula - soluzione	N-N	12.7	1	0-0
?	denaro - fresco	N-A	12.7	2	1-3
◇	prova - dimostrare	N-V	12.7	5	3-3
*	sanità - futuro	N-N	12.7	1	0-0
*	futuro - sanità	N-N	12.7	1	0-0
*	più - primo	N-A	12.7	6	0-0
*	mediatore - corte	A-N	12.7	2	0-0
?	azione - area	N-N	12.7	4	1-0
*	azione - età	N-N	12.7	1	0-0
?	opportunità - forza	N-N	12.7	1	0-3
?	biglietto - film	N-N	12.7	2	1-0
◇	attenzione - rivolgere	N-V	12.7	3	3-3
◇	concedere - facoltà	V-N	12.7	3	3-3

Parse-based method

	Key1, Prep, Key2	Type	LLR	F	Labels
*	membro - ratificare	S-V	2.9	1	0-0
	membro - dedicare	S-V	2.9	1	1-1
	membro - distribuire	S-V	2.9	1	1-1
?	legge - di - destra	N-P-N	2.9	1	3-1
?	calendario - prevedere	S-V	2.9	1	0-1
	trasformare - gestione	V-O	2.9	1	1-1
	divenire - ostacolo	V-O	2.9	1	1-1
*	interpretare - senso	V-O	2.9	1	0-0
	politica - ampio	N-A	2.9	1	3-3
◇	unione - stesso	N-A	2.9	20	1-1
?	rispondere - secondo	V-P	2.9	1	1-1
	muovere - secondo	V-P	2.9	1	3-1
?	basare - su - impostazione	V-P-N	2.9	1	0-1
?	basare - su - quota	V-P-N	2.9	1	1-1
	normativo - ex	N-A	2.9	1	3-0
?	attuazione - porre	S-V	2.9	1	0-1
?	compito - tradizionale	N-A	2.9	1	1-1
*	importare - di - stampa	V-P-N	2.9	1	0-0
*	importare - di - prova	V-P-N	2.9	1	0-0
*	importare - di - utilizzo	V-P-N	2.9	1	0-0
	concedere - a - impianto	V-P-N	2.9	1	1-1
	richiesta - di - invio	N-P-N	2.9	1	1-1
?	competenza - settoriale	N-A	2.9	1	1-3
*	semplificare - di - consiglio	V-P-N	2.9	1	0-0
	nominare - da - consiglio	V-P-N	2.9	1	1-1
	emanare - da - consiglio	V-P-N	2.9	1	1-1
	menzionare - conoscenza	V-O	2.9	1	1-1
	menzionare - elezione	V-O	2.9	1	1-1

Window method

	Key1, Key2	Type	LLR	F	Labels
?	mancanza - aiuto	N-N	12.7	2	1-0
?	tramite - numero	N-N	12.7	1	0-1
CP	prescindere - fatto	V-N	12.7	8	4-4
*	percentuale - scorsa	A-N	12.7	1	0-0
*	occupato - novecento	A-N	12.7	1	0-0
*	direttivo - trattamento	A-N	12.7	4	0-0
?	aspro - biasimo	A-N	12.7	1	3-1
*	membro - uniforme	N-A	12.7	7	0-0
*	iniziativa - nuova	N-N	12.7	1	0-0
*	candidatura - clamoroso	N-A	12.7	1	0-0
	genitori - desideroso	N-A	12.7	1	1-1
	rapporto - continuo	N-A	12.7	5	1-1
*	negoziato - voto	N-N	12.7	1	0-0
?	quadro - completare	N-V	12.7	5	5-3
*	avere - gestione	V-N	12.7	7	0-0
*	corso - prossimo	N-N	12.7	13	0-0
◇	salita - potere	N-N	12.7	2	3-3
*	direttiva - funzione	N-N	12.7	3	0-0
*	criterio - momento	N-N	12.7	1	0-0
	esistenza - programma	N-N	12.7	1	1-1
	irregolare - caso	A-N	12.7	2	0-0
	bellissimo - paesaggio	A-N	12.7	1	1-1
?	scosso - barbarie	A-N	12.7	1	0-1
*	quadro - libro	N-N	12.7	3	0-0
*	penultimo - individuazione	A-N	12.7	1	0-0
*	competitività - parte	N-N	12.7	1	1-1
*	parte - competitività	N-N	12.7	2	0-0
?	impresa - beneficiario	N-A	12.7	4	3-1

Parse-based method

Key1	Prep, Key2	Type	LLR	F	Labels
CP	giorno - altro - giorno	N-P-N	2.9	6	4-4
CP	giorno - in - giorno	N-P-N	2.9	6	4-4
?	gestione - di - suolo	N-P-N	2.9	1	3-1
	organizzazione - rilevare	S-V	2.9	1	1-1
ID	fatto - parlare	S-V	2.9	1	5-5

Spanish, TS1

Key1	Prep, Key2	Type	LLR	F	Labels
CP	medio - ambiente	N-A	12250.7	1218	4-4
?	parlamento - europeo	N-A	12118.1	2427	2-4
CP	derecho - humano	N-A	8366.0	1370	4-4
◇	tener - en - cuenta	V-P-N	7658.3	966	3-3
?	punto - de - vista	N-P-N	6394.8	825	4-3
?	primero - lugar	A-N	5481.1	1602	4-1
?	millón - de - euro	N-P-N	5181.5	683	1-1
◇	llevar - a - cabo	V-P-N	4480.1	609	3-3
◇	votar - a - favor	V-P-N	4414.9	535	3-3
◇	desempeñar - papel	V-O	4138.6	434	3-3
?	presidencia - sueco	N-A	3990.4	475	1-1
?	dar - gracia	V-O	3874.1	480	3-1
?	desarrollo - sostenible	N-A	3490.7	389	3-4
	posición - común	N-A	3317.5	512	1-1
	presidencia - belga	N-A	3257.0	372	1-1
	nombre - de - grupo	N-P-N	3195.9	588	1-1
?	mismo - tiempo	A-N	3178.3	603	4-3
?	salud - público	N-A	3140.0	436	3-4
◇	debate - cerrar	S-V	3084.6	371	3-3
?	consejo - europeo	N-A	2955.1	749	2-4
CP	libro - blanco	N-A	2939.8	257	4-4

Window method

Key1	Key2	Type	LLR	F	Labels
*	massimo - catrame	A-N	12.7	2	0-0
*	sapere - necessità	V-N	12.7	1	0-0
◇	spendere - soldo	V-N	12.7	3	3-3
*	sostegno - sarà	N-N	12.7	1	0-0
*	tecnologico - mercato	A-N	12.7	6	0-0
CP	medio - ambiente	N-A	9459.5	1289	4-4
?	estado - miembro	N-N	9186.8	4526	1-4
?	parlamento - europeo	N-A	7836.7	2624	2-4
?	primero - lugar	A-N	7446.2	1610	4-1
CP	derecho - humano	N-A	7001.3	1474	4-4
◇	tener - cuenta	V-N	6131.2	1003	3-3
*	comisión - comisión	N-N	5245.3	265	0-0
◇	estimar - colega	V-N	4725.2	547	1-1
◇	llevar - cabo	V-N	4537.6	628	3-3
?	punto - vista	N-N	4207.9	1091	3-3
CP	votar - favor	V-N	4037.1	639	3-1
	orden - día	N-N	3964.6	907	4-4
?	presidencia - sueco	N-A	3958.8	510	1-1
?	dar - gracia	V-N	3774.7	686	3-1
*	segundo - lugar	A-N	3739.9	781	4-1
	país - comisión	N-N	3480.3	28	0-0
	presidencia - belga	N-A	3412.9	420	1-1
◇	desempeñar - papel	V-N	3300.4	441	3-3
?	millón - euro	N-N	3107.3	821	1-1
*	mismo - tiempo	A-N	3075.2	645	4-3
	comisión - país	N-N	3018.5	93	0-0

Parse-based method

	Key1, Prep, Key2	Type	LLR	F	Labels
CP	mercado - interior	N-A	2729.4	381	4-4
◇	aprobar - resolución	V-O	2649.6	374	3-3
CP	orden - de - día	N-P-N	2529.0	294	4-4
	parlamento - aprobar	S-V	2468.3	493	1-1
◇	llamar - atención	V-O	2391.5	228	3-3
?	fundamento - jurídico	N-A	2304.7	278	3-1
?	cualquiera - caso	A-N	2292.6	365	4-1
?	segundo - lugar	A-N	2284.6	780	4-1
CP	sociedad - civil	N-A	2263.2	284	4-4
?	pasar - año	V-O	2059.9	330	0-3
◇	votar - en contra	V-P	1988.8	240	3-3
	nombre - de - comisión	N-P-N	1939.5	646	1-1
?	opinión - público	N-A	1936.0	306	3-4
?	derecho - fundamental	N-A	1917.5	462	3-4
?	fondo - estructural	N-A	1916.8	243	3-4
CP	ser - humano	N-A	1908.5	311	4-4
?	asunto - exterior	N-A	1901.4	358	2-4
◇	realizar - trabajo	V-O	1892.3	326	3-3
?	compañía - aéreo	N-A	1760.6	181	3-4
?	libre - circulación	A-N	1757.7	169	3-4
?	cambio - climático	N-A	1747.9	157	3-4
?	enmienda - oral	N-A	1745.9	170	1-1
CP	medio - de - comunicación	N-P-N	1742.7	177	4-4
?	relacionar - con	V-P	1735.0	491	3-1
?	tribunal - de - cuenta	N-P-N	1699.3	189	2-4
CP	pena - de - muerte	N-P-N	1697.2	152	4-4
◇	votación - tener	S-V	1685.4	307	3-3
◇	presentar - enmienda	V-O	1674.5	395	3-3
?	otro - lado	A-N	1663.1	330	4-3

Window method

	Key1, Key2	Type	LLR	F	Labels
*	estado - comisión	N-N	2995.9	107	0-0
?	desarrollo - sostenible	N-A	2879.3	445	3-4
CP	libro - blanco	N-A	2860.1	271	4-4
	posición - común	N-A	2736.7	524	1-1
?	salud - público	N-A	2693.9	459	3-4
◇	debate - cerrar	N-V	2578.9	372	3-3
?	nombre - grupo	N-N	2546.3	789	1-0
◇	conformidad - orden	N-N	2498.0	518	3-3
CP	mercado - interior	N-A	2466.3	413	4-4
?	señora - señor	N-N	2447.4	327	1-3
◇	acoger - satisfacción	V-N	2439.9	286	3-3
◇	debate - quedar	N-V	2418.6	376	3-3
*	derecho - comisión	N-N	2388.7	49	0-0
*	comisión - estado	N-N	2264.6	257	0-0
	parlamento - aprobar	N-V	2246.1	533	1-1
?	cualquiera - caso	A-N	2238.6	367	4-1
*	Unión Europea - comisión	N-N	2227.7	23	0-0
?	derecho - fundamental	N-A	2227.0	593	3-4
◇	formar - parte	V-N	2195.5	430	3-3
?	otro - parte	A-N	2092.9	699	4-3
?	otro - lado	A-N	2068.2	334	4-3
*	comisión - miembro	N-N	2053.1	197	0-0
◇	tomar - nota	V-N	2051.6	253	3-3
◇	aprobar - resolución	V-N	2039.5	388	3-3
?	fundamento - jurídico	N-A	2027.1	288	3-1
◇	llamar - atención	V-N	2015.3	260	3-3
CP	sociedad - civil	N-A	1982.4	300	4-4
*	comisión - Unión Europea	N-N	1976.7	59	0-0
?	conformidad - día	N-N	1918.5	517	0-3

	Parse-based method						Window method				
	Key1, Prep, Key2	Type	LLR	F	Labels		Key1, Key2	Type	LLR	F	Labels
Spanish, TS2											
?	agente - económico	N-A	72.6	22	1-4	*	mercado - lucha	N-N	82.8	1	0-0
◊	situar - en - plano	V-P-N	72.6	10	3-3	*	lucha - mercado	N-N	82.8	1	0-0
	colega - socialista	N-A	72.6	11	1-1		república - parlamento	N-N	82.7	5	0-0
?	hacer - evaluación	V-O	72.6	22	3-1	*	Unión Europea - delegación	N-N	82.7	1	0-0
	grupo - apoyar	S-V	72.6	20	1-1	*	mecanismo - parlamento	N-N	82.7	3	0-0
?	sacrificio - de - animal	N-P-N	72.5	12	3-1	*	modificación - informe	N-N	82.7	1	0-0
	marcador - resistente	N-A	72.5	4	1-1	*	ámbito - posición	N-N	82.7	4	0-0
	política - energético	N-A	72.5	34	1-1	*	consumidor - materia	N-N	82.7	3	0-0
ID	poner - dedo	V-O	72.5	8	5-5	*	cooperación - condición	N-N	82.7	1	0-0
	mil - de - millón	N-P-N	72.5	28	1-1	?	explotación - agrario	N-A	82.7	17	1-3
	marca - comunitario	N-A	72.5	11	1-1	*	presupuesto - acuerdo	N-N	82.7	6	0-0
?	ministro - de - hacienda	N-P-N	72.5	9	1-4	*	nivel - objetivo	N-N	82.7	7	0-0
?	grupo - de acuerdo	N-Pred-A	72.4	14	1-0	*	cuestión - creación	N-N	82.7	4	0-0
?	campaña - publicitario	N-A	72.4	7	3-4	?	coordinación - propuesta	N-N	82.7	4	1-0
?	trabajo - de - derecho	N-P-N	72.4	1	0-1	*	sustancia - país	N-N	82.7	3	0-0
	dicho - acuerdo	A-N	72.4	39	1-1	*	Unión Europea - estabilidad	N-N	82.7	5	0-0
?	adaptar - a - necesidad	V-P-N	72.3	14	3-1	*	relación - posibilidad	N-N	82.7	8	0-0
	ser - socio	V-O	72.3	22	1-1	*	seguridad - número	N-N	82.7	4	0-0
	mecanismo - defensivo	N-A	72.3	7	1-1	?	asilo - miembro	N-N	82.7	7	0-3
◊	intensificar - lucha	V-O	72.3	10	3-3	?	desarrollo - ampliación	N-N	82.7	4	1-0
?	control - jurisdiccional	N-A	72.3	10	1-4	*	mujer - objetivo	N-N	82.7	5	0-0
	nuevo - gobierno	A-N	72.2	41	1-1	*	hora - seguridad	N-N	82.7	1	0-0
?	red - ferroviario	N-A	72.2	13	3-4	◊	serio - duda	A-N	82.7	17	3-3
?	adopción - de - acervo	N-P-N	72.1	12	3-4	*	transporte - sistema	N-N	82.7	9	0-0
?	Este - último	N-A	72.1	6	3-1	*	materia - resultado	N-N	82.7	3	0-0
ID	cruzar - brazo	V-O	72.1	6	5-5	*	problema - comunidad	N-N	82.7	7	0-0
	bueno - colaboración	A-N	72.1	30	1-1	?	ciudadano - consumidor	N-N	82.6	2	1-3

Parse-based method

	Key1, Prep, Key2	Type	LLR	F	Labels
?	alerta - temprano	N-A	72.1	6	3-1
	texto - legislativo	N-A	72.0	22	1-1
◇	sólido - base	A-N	72.0	9	3-3
◇	consecuencia - nefasto	N-A	72.0	8	3-3
?	ambicioso - programa	A-N	72.0	13	3-1
	ministro - israelí	N-A	72.0	11	1-1
*	ser - por	V-P	72.0	50	0-0
	proyecto - de - directiva	N-P-N	72.0	37	1-1
◇	guardar - minuto	V-O	72.0	7	3-3
?	entendimiento - mutuo	N-A	71.9	7	1-4
◇	invertir - tendencia	V-O	71.9	7	3-3
	situación - cambiar	S-V	71.9	16	1-1
?	persona - minusválido	N-A	71.9	7	3-1
◇	franja - horario	N-A	71.8	4	3-3
?	afectar - país	V-O	71.8	21	3-1
?	región - periférico	N-A	71.8	9	3-1
◇	perder - tiempo	V-O	71.8	18	3-3
◇	dar - respuesta	V-O	71.8	35	3-3
◇	sacrificar - animal	V-O	71.8	8	3-3
	política - europeo	N-A	71.7	106	1-1
◇	suceder - mismo	V-O	71.7	9	1-1
ID	ver - con - ojo	V-P-N	71.7	12	5-5
	dicho - fondo	A-N	71.7	21	1-1

Spanish, TS3

	Key1, Prep, Key2	Type	LLR	F	Labels
*	estrategia - parar	S-V	28.3	12	0-0
	importante - mejora	A-N	28.3	9	1-1
	adhesión - de - Letonia	N-P-N	28.3	3	1-1

Window method

	Key1, Key2	Type	LLR	F	Labels
*	problema - control	N-N	82.6	18	0-0
*	gobierno - momento	N-N	82.6	4	0-0
*	desarrollo - número	N-N	82.6	3	0-0
*	comercio - medida	N-N	82.6	1	0-0
*	problema - creación	N-N	82.6	3	0-0
?	autoridad - español	N-A	82.6	30	1-4
*	país - avance	N-N	82.6	6	0-0
*	sobre - año	N-N	82.6	4	0-0
*	resolución - día	N-N	82.6	5	0-0
*	organización - Europa	N-N	82.6	19	0-0
*	país - estudio	N-N	82.6	4	0-0
?	posición - debate	N-N	82.6	8	0-1
*	parlamento - vía	N-N	82.6	8	0-0
*	ciudadano - protección	N-N	82.6	14	0-0
*	otro - seguridad	N-N	82.6	7	0-0
*	calidad - acuerdo	N-N	82.6	2	0-0
*	procedimiento - acción	N-N	82.6	2	0-0
*	vez - cooperación	N-N	82.6	9	0-0
◇	entidad - crédito	N-N	82.6	21	3-3
*	precio - Unión Europea	N-N	82.6	6	0-0
?	parte - integral	N-A	82.6	17	3-4
◇	tierra - barbecho	N-N	82.6	10	3-3
	medio - marino	N-A	82.6	19	1-1

	Key1, Key2	Type	LLR	F	Labels
*	deber - situación	V-N	35.5	71	0-0
*	solución - tiempo	N-N	35.5	3	0-0
*	artículo - nivel	N-N	35.5	5	0-0

Parse-based method

	Key1, Prep, Key2	Type	LLR	F	Labels
◇	adecuar - medio	V-O	28.3	8	3-3
	crío – de – cerdo	N-P-N	28.3	3	1-1
?	región - insular	N-A	28.3	4	3-1
	continuar - ocupación	V-O	28.3	3	1-1
	aspecto - ecológico	N-A	28.3	9	1-1
?	largo - historia	A-N	28.3	5	3-1
	último - frase	A-N	28.3	9	1-1
?	sufrir – derrota	V-O	28.3	3	3-3
◇	practicar - tortura	V-O	28.2	3	3-1
?	aumentar - beneficio	V-O	28.2	8	3-1
?	bueno - acogida	A-N	28.2	6	3-1
?	instrumento - de - sanción	N-P-N	28.2	6	1-4
◇	manifestar - oposición	V-O	28.2	5	3-3
?	merecer - aplauso	V-O	28.2	3	1-5
	publicar - periódico	V-O	28.2	3	1-1
?	referir - a - papel	V-P-N	28.2	11	1-3
	elección - local	N-A	28.2	8	1-1
?	poner - por	V-P	28.2	2	3-0
◇	establecer - relación	V-O	28.2	13	3-3
?	encargar - agencia	V-O	28.2	4	0-1
?	nota - de - sugerencia	N-P-N	28.2	4	0-3
◇	seguir - tradición	V-O	28.2	5	3-3
?	estado - democrático	N-A	28.2	18	1-4
*	comisión - diputado	N-P-N	28.2	1	0-0
◇	ejercer - profesión	V-O	28.2	4	3-3
	mitad – de – siglo	N-P-N	28.2	4	1-1
?	conclusión - satisfactorio	N-A	28.2	4	1-3
?	consumidor - final	N-A	28.2	6	3-4

Window method

	Key1, Key2	Type	LLR	F	Labels
*	necesidad - animal	N-N	35.5	7	0-0
*	agua - medida	N-N	35.5	3	0-0
?	vitamina - complemento	N-N	35.5	5	1-0
?	abrir - par	V-N	35.5	4	5-3
*	conferencia - reglamento	N-N	35.5	1	0-0
*	mejora - marco	N-N	35.5	2	0-0
*	uso - sector	N-N	35.5	3	0-0
?	anemia - salmón	N-N	35.5	2	1-0
*	restricción - peligroso	N-A	35.5	7	0-0
*	región - producción	N-N	35.5	1	0-0
*	marcha - decisión	N-N	35.5	2	0-0
◇	hacer - progreso	V-N	35.5	36	3-3
?	conclusión – cumbre	N-N	35.5	31	1-0
*	persona - Turquía	N-N	35.5	4	0-0
*	sociedad - consumidor	N-N	35.5	2	0-0
*	relación - bien	N-N	35.5	3	0-0
◇	medida - proponer	N-V	35.5	29	3-3
?	medio - año	A-N	35.5	27	4-1
?	cenar - seta	V-N	35.5	2	0-1
?	energía - alternativo	N-A	35.5	9	3-4
*	compromiso - otro	N-N	35.5	2	0-0
*	parlamento - eliminación	N-N	35.5	2	0-0
◇	ocurrir - frecuencia	V-N	35.5	7	3-3
*	comunidad - número	N-N	35.5	1	0-0
*	tema - candidato	N-N	35.5	2	0-0
?	desarrollo - sesión	N-N	35.5	5	0-1
*	actividad - disposición	N-N	35.5	1	0-0
*	momento - tribunal	N-N	35.5	3	0-0

Parse-based method

	Key1, Prep, Key2	Type	LLR	F	Labels
?	condena - unilateral	N-A	28.2	3	3-1
?	iniciativa - concreto	N-A	28.2	15	1-3
CP	parte - interesado	N-A	28.2	3	4-4
?	necesidad - de - que	N-P-N	28.2	23	0-1
?	cobro - de - recurso	N-P-N	28.2	4	3-1
?	objetivo - cuantitativo	N-A	28.2	6	3-1
?	cuestión - técnico	N-A	28.2	17	1-1
	ocurrir - en	V-P	28.2	43	1-1
?	acabar - año	V-O	28.1	8	0-3
?	armar - enfrentamiento	V-O	28.1	3	3-0
◊	mirar - más allá	V-P	28.1	4	3-3
◊	poner - a - disposición	V-P-N	28.1	4	3-3
?	entidad - bancario	N-A	28.1	4	1-4
	subvención - disminuir	S-V	28.1	3	1-1
	aumentar - competitividad	V-O	28.1	7	3-3
◊	ausencia - total	N-A	28.1	3	3-3
◊	celeridad - posible	N-A	28.1	3	4-3
◊	padecer - consecuencia	V-O	28.1	5	3-3
?	reserva - federal	N-A	28.1	4	2-4

Spanish, TS4

CP	sociedad - de - derecho	N-P-N	18.5	1	4-4
	volver - al	V-P	18.5	9	1-1
	enviar - a - autora	V-P-N	18.5	1	1-1
*	desconcertar - a - avatar	V-P-N	18.5	1	0-0
?	inspeccionar - a - intervalo	V-P-N	18.5	1	1-3
?	neutralizar - a - provocador	V-P-N	18.5	1	3-1
?	vincular - a - genética	V-P-N	18.5	2	0-1
?	desistir - de - reclamación	V-P-N	18.5	1	1-3

Window method

	Key1, Key2	Type	LLR	F	Labels
*	punto - Naciones Unidas	N-N	35.5	1	0-0
*	coste - transfronterizo	N-A	35.5	11	0-0
*	política - personal	N-N	35.5	1	0-0
*	personal - política	N-N	35.5	1	0-0
*	sociedad - orden	N-N	35.5	3	0-0
*	vez - elemento	N-N	35.5	3	0-0
*	mundo - manera	N-N	35.5	4	0-0
?	consejo - general	N-N	35.5	23	0-3
*	existencia - parte	N-N	35.5	1	0-0
*	parte - existencia	N-N	35.5	5	0-0
*	miembro - delincuencia	N-N	35.5	5	0-0
?	propuesta - sobrar	N-V	35.5	69	3-0
*	control - serie	N-N	35.5	1	0-0
?	particular - trabajo	N-N	35.5	6	0-1
?	unión - fuerza	N-N	35.5	5	0-3
	fuerza - unión	N-N	35.5	5	1-1
?	ampliación - libertad	N-N	35.5	2	3-1
*	duda - programa	N-N	35.5	2	0-0
◊	sincero - felicitación	A-N	35.5	4	3-3

*	directiva - ingreso	N-N	22.1	1	0-0
*	detención - derecho	N-N	22.1	3	0-0
*	otra - derecho	N-N	22.1	3	0-0
◊	acuerdo - global	N-A	22.1	19	3-3
*	política - Afganistán	N-N	22.1	2	0-0
?	dictadura - oprimir	N-V	22.1	2	3-1
	reafirmar - compromiso	V-N	22.1	9	1-1
*	acontecimiento - acuerdo	N-N	22.1	2	0-0

Parse-based method

	Key1, Prep, Key2	Type	LLR	F	Labels
?	línea - de - continuidad	N-P-N	18.5	3	5-4
	preparación - de - consejo	N-P-N	18.5	14	1-1
?	beneficiar - de - amnistía	V-P-N	18.5	2	1-3
	título - engañoso	N-A	18.5	2	1-1
◇	conceder - aprobación	V-O	18.5	4	3-3
◇	implantar - sistema	V-O	18.5	4	3-3
?	recibir - invitación	V-O	18.5	4	1-3
	diversidad - de - raza	N-P-N	18.5	2	1-1
?	interesado - principal	N-A	18.5	2	1-4
?	interesado - directo	N-A	18.5	2	3-4
?	giro - histórico	N-A	18.5	2	5-4
◇	pérdida - de - competitividad	N-P-N	18.5	4	3-3
	ser - consecuencia	V-O	18.5	42	1-1
?	esfuerzo - común	N-A	18.5	14	1-4
?	principal - competidor	A-N	18.5	3	1-3
	evitar - multiplicación	V-O	18.5	2	1-1
◇	asunto - tratar	S-V	18.5	6	3-3
	explicación - claro	N-A	18.5	3	1-1
?	punto - de - aplicación	N-P-N	18.5	1	1-4
	aplicación - de - punto	N-P-N	18.5	1	1-1
◇	decir - a - respecto	V-P-N	18.5	9	3-3
?	serie - de - fallo	N-P-N	18.5	4	1-3
◇	sangriento - atentado	A-N	18.5	2	3-3
?	mismo - haber	S-V	18.5	4	4-3
?	año - según - informe	N-P-N	18.5	2	0-0
*	formular - a	V-P	18.5	14	1-1
◇	aceptar - propuesta	V-O	18.5	11	3-3
?	frase - suprimir	S-V	18.5	2	1-3

Window method

	Key1, Key2	Type	LLR	F	Labels
*	cambio - condición	N-N	22.1	5	0-0
*	condición - cambio	N-N	22.1	5	0-0
*	diputado - caso	N-N	22.1	4	0-0
*	gracia - competencia	N-N	22.1	2	0-0
*	aplicación - garantía	N-N	22.1	1	0-0
*	si - salud	N-N	22.1	1	0-0
*	salud - si	N-N	22.1	1	0-0
*	país - altura	N-N	22.1	2	0-0
*	año - innovación	N-N	22.1	1	0-0
*	año - relieve	N-N	22.1	1	0-0
*	innovación - año	N-N	22.1	1	0-0
*	liberación - país	N-N	22.1	1	0-0
*	responsabilidad - serie	N-N	22.1	1	0-0
*	puesto - proyecto	N-N	22.1	2	0-0
?	frenar - propagación	V-N	22.1	3	3-1
?	alianza - terrorismo	N-N	22.1	11	1-3
?	naufragar - costa	V-N	22.1	2	3-1
*	medio - intención	N-N	22.1	2	0-0
*	idea - día	N-N	22.1	1	0-0
◇	posición - exponer	N-V	22.1	9	3-3
?	futuro - conjunto	N-N	22.1	2	1-0
*	reparto - propuesta	N-N	22.1	1	0-0
*	posición - adhesión	N-N	22.1	2	0-0
*	tabaco - Unión Europea	N-N	22.1	1	0-0
?	investigación - nivel	N-N	22.1	18	1-0
*	paso - mercado	N-N	22.1	6	0-0
◇	realizar - valoración	V-N	22.1	9	3-3
*	decisión - inversión	N-N	22.1	3	0-0

Parse-based method

	Key1, Prep, Key2	Type	LLR	F	Labels
?	recordar - colega	V-O	18.5	4	0-1
	turista - procedente	N-A	18.5	2	1-1
	compartir - con	V-P	18.5	29	1-1
	declaración - sorprendente	N-Pred-A	18.5	2	1-1
	comisario - explicar	S-V	18.5	4	1-1
?	mostrar - voluntad	V-O	18.5	5	1-3
?	crisis - inducir	S-V	18.5	2	1-3
	pago - de - deuda	N-P-N	18.5	4	1-1
	recordar - acontecimiento	V-O	18.5	3	1-1
◇	perspectiva - amplio	N-A	18.5	6	3-3
◇	sacar - beneficio	V-O	18.5	4	3-3
?	secretaría - de - comisión	N-P-N	18.5	10	1-3
?	bombardeo - masivo	N-A	18.5	2	1-3
?	norma - de - conducta	N-P-N	18.5	6	4-3

Spanish, TS5

	Key1, Prep, Key2	Type	LLR	F	Labels
	adquisición - hostil	N-A	11.7	1	1-1
?	respaldar - línea	V-O	11.7	5	1-3
?	personal - participante	A-N	11.7	1	0-1
	prestigioso - periodista	A-N	11.7	1	1-1
?	red - de - velocidad	N-P-N	11.7	3	4-1
	combinar - con - reducción	V-P-N	11.7	2	1-1
	ampliar - a - categoría	V-P-N	11.7	2	1-1
?	modo - irresponsable	N-A	11.7	2	1-4
?	inflación - básico	N-A	11.7	2	3-1
?	repercusión - social	N-A	11.7	8	1-4
?	aprovechar - experiencia	V-O	11.7	4	1-3
?	diferente - origen	A-N	11.7	2	1-1

Window method

	Key1, Key2	Type	LLR	F	Labels
?	septiembre - pasado	N-A	22.1	5	1-0
?	reglamento - dibujo	N-N	22.1	5	1-0
◇	falta - realismo	N-N	22.1	5	3-3
*	forma - frontera	N-N	22.1	3	0-0
◇	respetar - obligación	V-N	22.1	13	3-3
*	productor - problema	N-N	22.1	1	0-0
*	forma - consulta	N-N	22.1	2	0-0
?	impacto - negativo	N-A	22.1	3	3-4
*	industria - diputado	N-N	22.1	2	0-0
*	vez - razón	N-N	22.1	11	0-0
*	medida - subvención	N-N	22.1	1	0-0
*	cultivo - medida	N-N	22.1	1	0-0
?	subvención - medida	N-N	22.1	1	0-3
*	opinión - transparencia	N-N	22.1	2	0-0

	Key1, Key2	Type	LLR	F	Labels
*	individuo - afectar	N-V	12.5	1	0-0
*	arancel - irreparable	N-A	12.1	1	0-0
◇	dar - tratamiento	V-N	12.1	13	3-3
◇	libertad - restringir	N-V	12.1	3	3-3
◇	reforma - llevar	N-V	12.1	9	3-3
*	mejora - constante	N-A	12.1	3	0-0
?	decisión - histórico	N-A	12.1	9	3-0
*	deber - punto	V-N	12.1	5	0-0
*	comunidad - retornar	N-V	12.1	2	0-0
◇	discurrir - vía	V-N	12.1	2	3-3
?	capa - grueso	N-A	12.1	1	1-3
	variedad - producto	N-N	12.1	6	1-1

Parse-based method

	Key1, Prep, Key2	Type	LLR	F	Labels
◇	reinar - paz	V-O	11.7	2	3-3
*	futuro - a - país	N-P-N	11.7	1	0-0
◇	abrir - propuesta	V-O	11.7	1	3-3
?	vivir - millón	V-O	11.7	3	0-1
	inocencia - moral	N-A	11.7	1	1-1
	honestidad - moral	N-A	11.7	1	1-1
?	alojamiento - provisional	N-A	11.7	1	1-4
?	vicepresidente - primero	N-A	11.7	1	4-1
◇	imagen - sin - adorno	N-P-N	11.7	1	3-3
?	ilusión - ventaja	N-P-N	11.7	1	1-0
	geografía - de - planeta	N-P-N	11.7	1	1-1
?	dominar - a - los demás	V-P-N	11.7	1	1-3
?	reincorporar - a - agenda	V-P-N	11.7	1	1-3
?	entrever - a - ejecución	V-P-N	11.7	1	0-3
?	poner - instrumento	V-O	11.7	7	0-3
?	aplazar - censo	V-O	11.7	1	1-3
?	responsabilidad - ser	S-V	11.7	15	1-0
?	defensa - requerir	S-V	11.7	2	1-1
?	espectro - otorgar	S-V	11.7	1	0-1
	alcalde - alegar	S-V	11.7	1	1-1
*	anexo - parecer	S-V	11.7	1	0-0
?	aclaración - dar	S-V	11.7	1	0-3
	ganado - cruzar	S-V	11.7	1	1-1
?	insistencia - descubrir	S-V	11.7	1	1-1
	llamado - penalizar	S-V	11.7	1	0-1
	edad - aproximar	S-V	11.7	1	1-1
	duración - penalizar	S-V	11.7	1	1-1

Window method

	Key1, Key2	Type	LLR	F	Labels
◇	anarquía - reinar	N-V	12.1	1	3-3
?	autorización - despegar	N-V	12.1	1	1-3
*	club - siniestro	N-A	12.1	1	0-0
*	estruendo - molestia	N-N	12.1	1	0-0
◇	ritmo - bailar	N-V	12.1	1	3-3
	método - negociación	N-N	12.1	3	1-1
?	control - constitución	N-N	12.1	1	0-1
*	juicio - día	N-N	12.1	1	0-0
?	medicina - consejo	N-N	12.1	1	1-0
?	desvanecer - golpe	V-N	12.1	1	1-0
?	consejo - medicina	N-N	12.1	1	1-0
*	sobre - este	N-A	12.1	4	0-0
*	italiano - bistec	N-N	12.1	1	0-0
?	frontera - vida	N-N	12.1	2	0-3
*	actriz - italiano	N-N	12.1	1	0-0
*	África - decrecer	N-V	12.1	1	0-0
*	bienestar - entrometer	N-V	12.1	1	0-0
*	segundo - consejo	N-N	12.1	1	0-0
*	vida - frontera	N-N	12.1	2	0-0
*	plan - minorista	N-A	12.1	2	0-0
*	urgencia - punto	N-N	12.1	4	0-0
?	izquierda - italiano	N-A	12.1	3	1-5
*	lucha - materia	N-N	12.1	1	0-0
?	importancia - línea	N-N	12.1	3	1-0
*	materia - policía	N-N	12.1	1	0-0
*	incumplimiento - comunitario	N-A	12.1	5	0-0
*	valor - transparencia	N-N	12.1	3	0-0

Parse-based method

	Key1, Prep, Key2	Type	LLR	F	Labels
?	potencia - extranjero	N-A	11.7	2	1-4
	informe - interesante	N-A	11.7	4	1-1
	preocupación - real	N-A	11.7	4	1-1
	cielo - soportar	S-V	11.7	1	1-1
?	conductor - avisar	S-V	11.7	1	0-1
?	conductor - descansar	S-V	11.7	1	0-1
◇	fiebre - contagiar	S-V	11.7	1	3-3
*	fiebre - inscribir	S-V	11.7	1	0-0
*	sede - responsabilizar	S-V	11.7	1	0-0
?	centro - derrumbar	S-V	11.7	1	0-3
?	materia - controvertir	S-V	11.7	1	1-3

Window method

	Key1, Key2	Type	LLR	F	Labels
*	interés - tanto	N-N	12.1	1	0-0
	endémico - mundo	A-N	12.1	2	1-1
*	rabia - bueno	N-A	12.1	2	0-0
	sanción - proporcionar	N-V	12.1	4	1-1
*	alcohólico - niño	A-N	12.1	2	0-0
*	abrumador - niño	A-N	12.1	2	0-0
*	autorización - afectar	N-V	11.5	1	0-0
?	compromiso - real	N-A	12.1	10	3-1
?	red - penal	N-A	12.1	7	0-1
?	aprender - brote	V-N	12.1	2	0-1
?	autoridad - evolución	N-N	12.1	1	0-1

E.2 Results

Graphical display of the results obtained in Experiment 2 (Section 4.4.5).

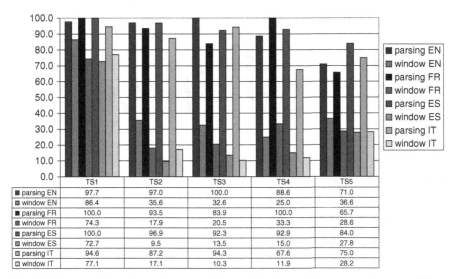

	TS1	TS2	TS3	TS4	TS5
■ parsing EN	97.7	97.0	100.0	88.6	71.0
▫ window EN	86.4	35.6	32.6	25.0	36.6
■ parsing FR	100.0	93.5	83.9	100.0	65.7
▪ window FR	74.3	17.9	20.5	33.3	28.6
■ parsing ES	100.0	96.9	92.3	92.9	84.0
▫ window ES	72.7	9.5	13.5	15.0	27.8
▫ parsing IT	94.6	87.2	94.3	67.6	75.0
▫ window IT	77.1	17.1	10.3	11.9	28.2

Fig. E.1 Results of Experiment 2: grammatical precision for each language and test set (EN = English, FR = French, ES = Spanish, IT = Italian)

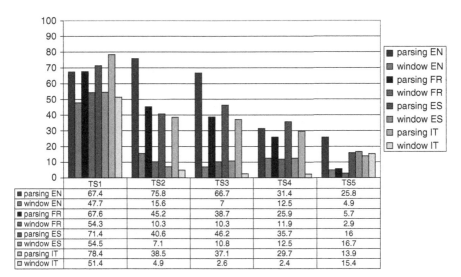

	TS1	TS2	TS3	TS4	TS5
■ parsing EN	67.4	75.8	66.7	31.4	25.8
▫ window EN	47.7	15.6	7	12.5	4.9
■ parsing FR	67.6	45.2	38.7	25.9	5.7
▪ window FR	54.3	10.3	10.3	11.9	2.9
■ parsing ES	71.4	40.6	46.2	35.7	16
▫ window ES	54.5	7.1	10.8	12.5	16.7
▫ parsing IT	78.4	38.5	37.1	29.7	13.9
▫ window IT	51.4	4.9	2.6	2.4	15.4

Fig. E.2 Results of Experiment 2: MWE precision for each language and test set (EN = English, FR = French, ES = Spanish, IT = Italian)

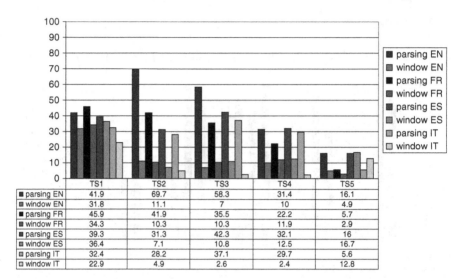

	TS1	TS2	TS3	TS4	TS5
■ parsing EN	41.9	69.7	58.3	31.4	16.1
▨ window EN	31.8	11.1	7	10	4.9
■ parsing FR	45.9	41.9	35.5	22.2	5.7
▨ window FR	34.3	10.3	10.3	11.9	2.9
▨ parsing ES	39.3	31.3	42.3	32.1	16
▨ window ES	36.4	7.1	10.8	12.5	16.7
▨ parsing IT	32.4	28.2	37.1	29.7	5.6
▢ window IT	22.9	4.9	2.6	2.4	12.8

Fig. E.3 Results of Experiment 2: collocational precision for each language and test set (*EN* = English, *FR* = French, *ES* = Spanish, *IT* = Italian)

Appendix F
Output Comparison

Output comparison for the parse-based method (P) and sliding window method (W) in Experiment 2 (Section 4.4.5): *Percentage (/P)* = percentage of pair types in the output of P satisfying the criterion in the first column; *Percentage (/W)* = same interpretation for W; *Common* = number of pair types common to P and W that satisfy the criterion in the first column; *Common (/P)* = ratio of common items relative to the entire output of P; *Common (/W)* = same interpretation for W; ρ = Spearman's ρ correlation coefficient on the intersection.

	Language	Percentage (/P)	Percentage (/W)	Common	Common (/P) (%)	Common (/W) (%)	ρ
All	EN	100.00	100.00	237565	75.59	16.53	0.477
	FR	100.00	100.00	228373	73.48	16.09	0.521
	IT	100.00	100.00	260434	79.58	19.07	0.471
	ES	100.00	100.00	247983	80.81	18.02	0.480
	Avg	100.00	100.00	243588.8	77.36	17.43	0.487
Rank $\leq$ 1,000	EN	0.32	0.07	315	0.10	0.02	0.597
	FR	0.32	0.07	293	0.09	0.02	0.710
	IT	0.31	0.07	300	0.09	0.02	0.476
	ES	0.33	0.07	308	0.10	0.02	0.708
	Avg	0.32	0.07	304.0	0.10	0.02	0.623
Rank $\leq$ 2,000	EN	0.64	0.14	535	0.17	0.04	0.612
	FR	0.64	0.14	541	0.17	0.04	0.486
	IT	0.61	0.15	545	0.17	0.04	0.441
	ES	0.65	0.15	551	0.18	0.04	0.550
	Avg	0.64	0.14	543.0	0.17	0.04	0.522
Rank $\leq$ 5,000	EN	1.59	0.35	1088	0.35	0.08	0.532
	FR	1.61	0.35	1195	0.38	0.08	0.509
	IT	1.53	0.37	1327	0.41	0.10	0.592
	ES	1.63	0.36	1159	0.38	0.08	0.421
	Avg	1.59	0.36	1192.3	0.38	0.09	0.513
Rank $\leq$ 10,000	EN	3.18	0.70	2030	0.65	0.14	0.406
	FR	3.22	0.70	2318	0.75	0.16	0.553
	IT	3.06	0.73	2601	0.79	0.19	0.918
	ES	3.26	0.73	2133	0.70	0.16	0.418
	Avg	3.18	0.71	2270.5	0.72	0.16	0.574

	Language	Percentage (/P)	Percentage (/W)	Common	Common (/P) (%)	Common (/W) (%)	ρ
LLR > 1,000	EN	0.02	0.01	40	0.01	0.00	0.734
	FR	0.04	0.01	57	0.02	0.00	0.792
	IT	0.04	0.02	71	0.02	0.01	0.841
	ES	0.04	0.01	77	0.03	0.01	0.868
	Avg	0.03	0.01	61.3	0.02	0.00	0.809
LLR > 100	EN	0.62	0.63	1206	0.38	0.08	0.692
	FR	0.84	0.69	1496	0.48	0.11	0.621
	IT	0.81	0.86	1704	0.52	0.12	0.482
	ES	0.74	0.74	1426	0.46	0.10	0.658
	Avg	0.75	0.73	1458.0	0.46	0.10	0.613
LLR > 10	EN	16.00	13.14	22352	7.11	1.56	0.594
	FR	16.98	13.13	23457	7.55	1.65	0.655
	IT	15.51	12.90	24507	7.49	1.79	0.611
	ES	14.57	12.79	21033	6.85	1.53	0.627
	Avg	15.76	12.99	22837.3	7.25	1.63	0.622
f > 100	EN	0.12	0.06	187	0.06	0.01	0.870
	FR	0.15	0.08	224	0.07	0.02	0.834
	IT	0.12	0.11	279	0.09	0.02	0.900
	ES	0.15	0.07	247	0.08	0.02	0.849
	Avg	0.13	0.08	234.3	0.07	0.02	0.863
f > 10	EN	2.55	2.08	5212	1.66	0.36	0.796
	FR	2.78	2.19	5542	1.78	0.39	0.747
	IT	2.78	2.86	6698	2.05	0.49	0.749
	ES	3.10	2.56	6204	2.02	0.45	0.731
	Avg	2.80	2.42	5914.0	1.88	0.42	0.756
f > 3	EN	9.35	9.34	20639	6.57	1.44	0.662
	FR	10.21	9.66	22036	7.09	1.55	0.641
	IT	10.02	11.65	25280	7.72	1.85	0.640
	ES	10.97	11.19	24251	7.90	1.76	0.614
	Avg	10.14	10.46	23051.5	7.32	1.65	0.639

References

Alonso Ramos M (2004) Elaboración del diccionario de colocaciones del español y sus aplicaciones. In: Bataner P, de Cesaris J (eds) De Lexicografia. Actes del I Simposium internacional de Lexicografía, IULA y Edicions Petició, Barcelona, pp 149–162

Alshawi H, Carter D (1994) Training and scaling preference functions for disambiguation. Computational Linguistics 20(4):635–648

Archer V (2006) Acquisition semi-automatique de collocations à partir de corpus monolingues et multilingues comparables. In: Proceedings of Rencontre des Etudiants Chercheurs en Informatique pour le Traitement Automatique des Langues (RECITAL 2006), Leuven, Belgique

Artstein R, Poesio M (2008) Inter-coder agreement for computational linguistics. Computational Linguistics 34(4):555–596

Bahns J (1993) Lexical collocations: a contrastive view. ELT Journal 1(47):56–63

Baker CF, Fillmore CJ, Lowe JB (1998) The Berkeley FrameNet project. In: Proceedings of the COLING-ACL, Montreal, Canada, pp 86–90

Baldwin T, Kim SN (2010) Multiword expressions. In: Indurkhya N, Damerau FJ (eds) Handbook of Natural Language Processing, Second Edition, CRC Press, Taylor and Francis Group, Boca Raton, FL

Baldwin T, Bannard C, Tanaka T, Widdows D (2003) An empirical model of multiword expression decomposability. In: Bond F, Korhonen A, McCarthy D, Villavicencio A (eds) Proceedings of the ACL 2003 Workshop on Multiword Expressions: Analysis, Acquisition and Treatment, Sapporo, Japan, pp 89–96

Baldwin T, Beavers J, van der Beek L, Bond F, Flickinger D, Sag IA (2006) In search of a systematic treatment of determinerless PPs. In: Saint-Dizier P (ed) The Syntax and Semantics of Prepositions, Springer, Dordrecht

Ballestros L, Croft WB (1996) Dictionary-based methods for cross-lingual information retrieval. In: Proceedings of the 7th International DEXA Conference in Database and Expert Systems Applications, Zurich, Switzerland, pp 791–801

Bally C (1909) Traité de stylistique française. Klincksieck, Paris

Bally C (1951) Traité de stylistique française. Klincksieck, Paris

Banerjee S, Pedersen T (2003) The design, implementation, and use of the Ngram Statistic Package. In: Proceedings of the 4th International Conference on Intelligent Text Processing and Computational Linguistics, Mexico City, Mexico

Bannard C (2005) Learning about the meaning of verb-particle constructions from corpora. Computer Speech and Language 19(4):467–478

Barnbrook G (1996) Language and Computers: A Practical Introduction to the Computer Analysis of Language. Edinburgh University Press, Edinburgh

Baroni M, Evert S (2008) Statistical methods for corpus exploitation. In: Lüdeling A, Kytö M (eds) Corpus Linguistics. An International Handbook, Mouton de Gruyter, Berlin, pp 777–803

Bartsch S (2004) Structural and Functional Properties of Collocations in English. A Corpus Study of Lexical and Pragmatic Constraints on Lexical Cooccurrence. Gunter Narr Verlag, Tübingen

Basili R, Pazienza MT, Velardi P (1994) A "not-so-shallow" parser for collocational analysis. In: Proceedings of the 15th Conference on Computational Linguistics, Kyoto, Japan, pp 447–453

Beauchesne J (2001) Dictionnaire des cooccurrences. Guérin, Montréal

Benson M (1990) Collocations and general-purpose dictionaries. International Journal of Lexicography 3(1):23–35

Benson M, Benson E, Ilson R (1986a) The BBI Dictionary of English Word Combinations. John Benjamins, Amsterdam/Philadelphia

Benson M, Benson E, Ilson R (1986b) Lexicographic Description of English. John Benjamins, Amsterdam/Philadelphia

Berry-Rogghe GLM (1973) The computation of collocations and their relevance to lexical studies. In: Aitken AJ, Bailey RW, Hamilton-Smith N (eds) The Computer and Literary Studies, Edinburgh University Press, Edinburgh, pp 103–112

Berthouzoz C, Merlo P (1997) Statistical ambiguity resolution for principle-based parsing. In: Nicolov N, Mitkov R (eds) Recent Advances in Natural Language Processing: Selected Papers from RANLP'97, Current Issues in Linguistic Theory, John Benjamins, Amsterdam/Philadelphia

Blaheta D, Johnson M (2001) Unsupervised learning of multi-word verbs. In: Proceedings of the ACL Workshop on Collocation: Computational Extraction, Analysis and Exploitation, Toulouse, France, pp 54–60

Boitet C, Mangeot M, Sérasset G (2002) The PAPILLON Project: Cooperatively building a multilingual lexical database to derive open source dictionaries and lexicons. In: Proceedings of the 2nd Workshop on NLP and XML (NLPXML-2002), Taipei, Taiwan

Bolshakov IA, Gelbukh AF (2001) A very large database of collocations and semantic links. In: NLDB '00: Proceedings of the 5th International Conference on Applications of Natural Language to Information Systems-Revised Papers, Springer, London, UK, pp 103–114

Bourigault D (1992a) LEXTER, vers un outil linguistique d'aide à l'acquisition des connaissances. In: Actes des 3èmes Journées d'acquisition des Connaissances, Dourdan, France

Bourigault D (1992b) Surface grammatical analysis for the extraction of terminological noun phrases. In: Proceedings of the 15th International Conference on Computational Linguistics, Nantes, France, pp 977–981

Bourigault D (2005) Les Voisins de Le Monde. http://w3.erss.univ-tlse2.fr/voisinsdelemonde/, accessed June, 2010

Breidt E (1993) Extraction of V-N-collocations from text corpora: A feasibility study for German. In: Proceedings of the Workshop on Very Large Corpora: Academic and Industrial Perspectives, Columbus, OH, USA, pp 74–83

Bresnan J (2001) Lexical Functional Syntax. Blackwell, Oxford

Brown PF, Pietra SAD, Pietra VJD, Mercer RL (1991) Word-sense disambiguation using statistical methods. In: Proceedings of the 29th Annual Meeting of the Association for Computational Linguistics (ACL 1991), Berkeley, CA, USA, pp 264–270

Calzolari N, Bindi R (1990) Acquisition of lexical information from a large textual Italian corpus. In: Proceedings of the 13th International Conference on Computational Linguistics, Helsinki, Finland, pp 54–59

de Caseli HM, Ramisch C, das Graças Volpe Nunes M, Villavicencio A (2010) Alignment-based extraction of multiword expressions. Language Resources and Evaluation Special Issue on Multiword Expressions: Hard Going or Plain Sailing 44(1–2):59–77

Charest S, Brunelle E, Fontaine J, Pelletier B (2007) Élaboration automatique d'un dictionnaire de cooccurrences grand public. In: Actes de la 14e conférence sur le Traitement Automatique des Langues Naturelles (TALN 2007), Toulouse, France, pp 283–292

Chomsky N (1995) The Minimalist Program. MIT Press, Cambridge, MA

Choueka Y (1988) Looking for needles in a haystack, or locating interesting collocational expressions in large textual databases. In: Proceedings of the International Conference on User-Oriented Content-Based Text and Image Handling, Cambridge, MA, USA, pp 609–623

Choueka Y, Klein S, Neuwitz E (1983) Automatic retrieval of frequent idiomatic and collocational expressions in a large corpus. Journal of the Association for Literary and Linguistic Computing 4(1):34–38

Church K, Hanks P (1990) Word association norms, mutual information, and lexicography. Computational Linguistics 16(1):22–29

Church K, Gale W, Hanks P, Hindle D (1989) Parsing, word associations and typical predicate-argument relations. In: Proceedings of the International Workshop on Parsing Technologies, Carnegie Mellon University, Pittsburgh, PA, pp 103–112

Church K, Gale W, Hanks P, Hindle D (1991) Using statistics in lexical analysis. In: Zernik U (ed) Lexical Acquisition: Exploiting On-Line Resources to Build a Lexicon, Lawrence Erlbaum, Hillsdale, NJ, pp 115–164

Church KW, Hanks P (1989) Word association norms, mutual information, and lexicography. In: Proceedings of the 27th Annual Meeting of the Association for Computational Linguistics, Association for Computational Linguistics, Vancouver, BC, pp 76–83

Cohen J (1960) A coefficient of agreement for nominal scales. Educational and Psychological Measurement 20:37–46

Cook P, Fazly A, Stevenson S (2008) The VNC-tokens dataset. In: Proceedings of the LREC Workshop Towards a Shared Task for Multiword Expressions (MWE 2008), Marrakech, Morocco, pp 19–22

Coseriu E (1967) Lexikalische Solidaritäten. Poetica (1):293–303

Cowie AP (1978) The place of illustrative material and collocations in the design of a learner's dictionary. In: Strevens P (ed) In Honour of A.S. Hornby, Oxford University Press, Oxford, pp 127–139

Cowie AP (1998) Phraseology. Theory, Analysis, and Applications. Claredon Press, Oxford

Cruse DA (1986) Lexical Semantics. Cambridge University Press, Cambridge

Culicover P, Jackendoff R (2005) Simpler Syntax. Oxford University Press, Oxford

Dagan I, Church K (1994) *Termight*: Identifying and translating technical terminology. In: Proceedings of the 4th Conference on Applied Natural Language Processing (ANLP), Stuttgart, Germany, pp 34–40

Daille B (1994) Approche mixte pour l'extraction automatique de terminologie: statistiques lexicales et filtres linguistiques. PhD thesis, Université Paris 7

Diab MT, Bhutada P (2009) Verb noun construction MWE token supervised classification. In: 2009 Workshop on Multiword Expressions: Identification, Interpretation, Disambiguation, Applications, Suntec, Singapore, pp 17–22

Dias G (2003) Multiword unit hybrid extraction. In: Proceedings of the ACL Workshop on Multiword Expressions, Sapporo, Japan, pp 41–48

Dunning T (1993) Accurate methods for the statistics of surprise and coincidence. Computational Linguistics 19(1):61–74

van der Eijk P (1993) Automating the acquisition of bilingual terminology. In: Proceedings of the 6th Conference on European Chapter of the Association for Computational Linguistics, Utrecht, The Netherlands, pp 113–119

Erman B, Warren B (2000) The idiom principle and the open choice principle. Text 20(1):29–62

Evert S (2004a) Significance tests for the evaluation of ranking methods. In: Proceedings of Coling 2004, Geneva, Switzerland, pp 945–951

Evert S (2004b) The statistics of word cooccurrences: Word pairs and collocations. PhD thesis, University of Stuttgart

Evert S (2008a) Corpora and collocations. In: Lüdeling A, Kytö M (eds) Corpus Linguistics. An International Handbook, Mouton de Gruyter, Berlin

Evert S (2008b) A lexicographic evaluation of German adjective-noun collocations. In: Proceedings of the LREC Workshop Towards a Shared Task for Multiword Expressions (MWE 2008), Marrakech, Morocco

Evert S, Kermes H (2002) The influence of linguistic preprocessing on candidate data. In: Proceedings of Workshop on Computational Approaches to Collocations (Colloc02), Vienna, Austria

Evert S, Kermes H (2003) Experiments on candidate data for collocation extraction. In: Companion Volume to the Proceedings of the 10th Conference of the European Chapter of the Association for Computational Linguistics (EACL'03), Budapest, Hungary, pp 83–86

Evert S, Krenn B (2001) Methods for the qualitative evaluation of lexical association measures. In: Proceedings of the 39th Annual Meeting of the Association for Computational Linguistics, Toulouse, France, pp 188–195

Evert S, Krenn B (2005) Using small random samples for the manual evaluation of statistical association measures. Computer Speech & Language 19(4):450–466

Evert S, Heid U, Spranger K (2004) Identifying morphosyntactic preferences in collocations. In: Proceedings of the 4th International Conference on Language Resources and Evaluation (LREC 2004), Lisbon, Portugal, pp 907–910

Fazly A (2007) Automatic acquisition of lexical knowledge about multiword predicates. PhD thesis, University of Toronto

Fazly A, Stevenson S (2007) Distinguishing subtypes of multiword expressions using linguistically-motivated statistical measures. In: Proceedings of the Workshop on A Broader Perspective on Multiword Expressions, Prague, Czech Republic, pp 9–16

Ferret O (2002) Using collocations for topic segmentation and link detection. In: Proceedings of the 19th International Conference on Computational Linguistics (COLING 2002), Taipei, Taiwan, pp 260–266

Ferret O (2003) Filtrage thématique d'un réseau de collocations. In: Proceedings of TALN 2003, Batz-sur-Mer, France, pp 347–352

Ferret O, Zock M (2006) Enhancing electronic dictionaries with an index based on associations. In: Proceedings of the 21st International Conference on Computational Linguistics and 44th Annual Meeting of the ACL, Sydney, Australia, pp 281–288

Fillmore C, Kay P, O'Connor C (1988) Regularity and idiomaticity in grammatical constructions: The case of *let alone*. Language 64(3):501–538

Fillmore CJ (1982) Frame semantics. In: Linguistics in the Morning Calm, Hanshin Publishing Co., Seoul, pp 111–137

Firth JR (1957) Papers in Linguistics 1934-1951. Oxford University Press, Oxford

Firth JR (1968) A synopsis of linguistic theory, 1930–1955. In: Palmer F (ed) Selected papers of J. R. Firth, 1952–1959, Indiana University Press, Bloomington, IN, pp 168–205

Fleiss JL (1981) Measuring nominal scale agreement among many raters. Psychological Bulletin 76:378–382

Fontenelle T (1992) Collocation acquisition from a corpus or from a dictionary: A comparison. Proceedings I-II Papers submitted to the 5th EURALEX International Congress on Lexicography in Tampere, Tampere, Finland, pp 221–228

Fontenelle T (1997a) Turning a Bilingual Dictionary into a Lexical-Semantic Database. Max Niemeyer Verlag, Tübingen

Fontenelle T (1997b) Using a bilingual dictionary to create semantic networks. International Journal of Lexicography 10(4):276–303

Fontenelle T (1999) Semantic resources for word sense disambiguation: A *sine qua non*? Linguistica e Filologia (9):25–43, dipartimento di Linguistica e Letterature Comparate, Università degli Studi di Bergamo

Fontenelle T (2001) Collocation modelling: From lexical functions to frame semantics. In: Proceedings of the ACL Workshop on Collocation: Computational Extraction, Analysis and Exploitation, Toulouse, France, pp 1–7

Francis G (1993) A corpus-driven approach to grammar: Principles, methods and examples. In: Baker M, Francis G, Tognini-Bonelli E (eds) Text and Technology: In Honour of John Sinclair, John Benjamins, Amsterdam, pp 137–156

Frantzi KT, Ananiadou S, Mima H (2000) Automatic recognition of multi-word terms: The C-value/NC-value method. International Journal on Digital Libraries 2(3):115–130

Fritzinger F, Weller M, Heid U (2010) A survey of idiomatic Preposition-Noun-Verb triples on token level. In: Proceedings of the 7th Conference on International Language Resources and Evaluation (LREC'10), Valletta, Malta

Fur DL, Freund Y, Trouillez E, Dilger M (2007) Dictionnaire des combinaisons de mots: les synonymes en contexte. Le Robert, Paris

Gildea D, Palmer M (2002) The necessity of parsing for predicate argument recognition. In: Proceedings of 40th Annual Meeting of the Association for Computational Linguistics, Philadelphia, PA, USA, pp 239–246

Gitsaki C (1996) The development of ESL collocational knowledge. PhD thesis, University of Queensland

Goldman JP, Nerima L, Wehrli E (2001) Collocation extraction using a syntactic parser. In: Proceedings of the ACL Workshop on Collocation: Computational Extraction, Analysis and Exploitation, Toulouse, France, pp 61–66

Grefenstette G, Teufel S (1995) Corpus-based method for automatic identification of support verbs for nominalizations. In: Proceedings of the 7th Conference of the European Chapter of the Association for Computational Linguistics, Dublin, Ireland, pp 98–103

Grégoire N, Evert S, Krenn B (eds) (2008) Proceedings of the LREC Workshop Towards a Shared Task for Multiword Expressions (MWE 2008). European Language Resources Association (ELRA), Marrakech, Morocco

Gross G (1996) Les expressions figées en français. OPHRYS, Paris

Gross M (1984) Lexicon-grammar and the syntactic analysis of French. In: Proceedings of the 10th International Conference on Computational Linguistics and 22nd Annual Meeting of the Association for Computational Linguistics, Morristown, NJ, USA, pp 275–282

Grossmann F, Tutin A (eds) (2003) Les Collocations. Analyse et traitement. Éditions De Werelt, Amsterdam

Hajič J (2000) Morphological tagging: Data vs. dictionaries. In: Proceedings of the 6th Applied Natural Language Processing and the 1st NAACL Conference, Seattle, WA, USA, pp 94–101

Halliday MAK, Hasan R (1976) Cohesion in English. Longman, London

Hargreaves P (2000) Collocation and testing. In: Lewis M (ed) Teaching Collocations, Language Teaching Publications, Hove

Hausmann FJ (1979) Un dictionnaire des collocations est-il possible? Travaux de littérature et de linguistique de l'Université de Strasbourg 17(1):187–195

Hausmann FJ (1985) Kollokationen im deutschen Wörterbuch. Ein Beitrag zur Theorie des lexikographischen Beispiels. In: Bergenholtz H, Mugdan J (eds) Lexikographie und Grammatik. Akten des Essener Kolloquiums zur Grammatik im Wörterbuch, Lexicographica. Series Major 3, pp 118–129

Hausmann FJ (1989) Le dictionnaire de collocations. In: Hausmann F, Reichmann O, Wiegand H, Zgusta L (eds) Wörterbücher: Ein internationales Handbuch zur Lexicographie. Dictionaries, Dictionnaires, de Gruyter, Berlin, pp 1010–1019

Hausmann FJ (2004) Was sind eigentlich Kollokationen? In: Steyer K (ed) Wortverbindungen – mehr oder weniger fest. Jahrbuch des Instituts für Deutsche Sprache 2003, de Gruyter, Berlin, pp 309–334

Heid U (1994) On ways words work together – research topics in lexical combinatorics. In: Proceedings of the 6th Euralex International Congress on Lexicography (EURALEX '94), Amsterdam, The Netherlands, pp 226–257

Heid U, Raab S (1989) Collocations in multilingual generation. In: Proceeding of the 4th Conference of the European Chapter of the Association for Computational Linguistics (EACL'89), Manchester, England, pp 130–136

Heid U, Weller M (2008) Tools for collocation extraction: Preferences for active vs. passive. In: Proceedings of the 6th International Language Resources and Evaluation (LREC'08), Marrakech, Morocco

Heylen D, Maxwell KG, Verhagen M (1994) Lexical functions and machine translation. In: Proceedings of the 15th International Conference on Computational Linguistics (COLING 1994), Kyoto, Japan, pp 1240–1244

Hill J, Lewis M (eds) (1997) The LTP Dictionary of Selected Collocations. Language Teaching Publications, Hove

Hindle D, Rooth M (1993) Structural ambiguity and lexical relations. Computational Linguistics 19(1):103–120

Hoey M (1991) Patterns of Lexis in Text. Oxford University Press, Oxford

Hoey M (1997) From concordance to text structure: New uses for computer corpora. In: Melia J, Lewandoska B (eds) Proceedings of Practical Applications of Language Corpora (PALC 1997), Lodz, Poland, pp 2–23

Hoey M (2000) A world beyond collocation: New perspectives on vocabulary teaching. In: Lewis M (ed) Teaching Collocations, Language Teaching Publications, Hove

Hornby A, Gatenby E, Wakefield H (1942) Idiomatic and Syntactic English Dictionary (ISED). Kaitakusha, Tokyo

Hornby AS, Cowie AP, Lewis JW (1948a) Oxford Advanced Learner's Dictionary of Current English. Oxford University Press, London

Hornby AS, Gatenby EV, Wakefield H (1948b) A Learner's Dictionary of Current English. Oxford University Press, London

Hornby AS, Gatenby EV, Wakefield H (1952) The Advanced Learner's Dictionary of Current English. Oxford University Press, London

Howarth P, Nesi H (1996) The teaching of collocations in EAP. Technical report, University of Leeds

Huang CR, Kilgarriff A, Wu Y, Chiu CM, Smith S, Rychly P, Bai MH, Chen KJ (2005) Chinese Sketch Engine and the extraction of grammatical collocations. In: Proceedings of the 4th SIGHAN Workshop on Chinese Language Processing, Jeju Island, Korea, pp 48–55

Hull DA, Grefenstette G (1998) Querying across languages: A dictionary-based approach to multilingual information retrieval. In: Jones KS, Willett P (eds) Readings in Information Retrieval, Morgan Kaufmann, San Francisco, CA, pp 484–492

Hunston S, Francis G (1998) Verbs observed: A corpus-driven pedagogic grammar. Applied Linguistics 19(1):45–72

Hunston S, Francis G, Manning E (1997) Grammar and vocabulary: Showing the connections. English Language Teaching Journal 3(51):208–215

Ikehara S, Shirai S, Kawaoka T (1995) Automatic extraction of uninterrupted collocations by n-gram statistics. In: Proceedings of First Annual Meeting of the Association for Natural Language Processing, Tokyo, Japan, pp 313–316

Jackendoff R (1997) The Architecture of the Language Faculty. MIT Press, Cambridge, MA

Jacquemin C, Klavans JL, Tzoukermann E (1997) Expansion of multi-word terms for indexing and retrieval using morphology and syntax. In: Proceedings of the 35th Annual Meeting on Association for Computational Linguistics, Morristown, NJ, USA, pp 24–31

Justeson JS, Katz SM (1995) Technical terminology: Some linguistic properties and an algorithm for identification in text. Natural Language Engineering 1(1):9–27

Kahane S, Polguère A (2001) Formal foundations of lexical functions. In: Proceedings of the ACL Workshop on Collocation: Computational Extraction, Analysis and Exploitation, Toulouse, France, pp 8–15

Keller F, Lapata M (2003) Using the web to obtain frequencies for unseen bigrams. Computational Linguistics 29(3):459–484

Kermes H, Heid U (2003) Using chunked corpora for the acquisition of collocations and idiomatic expressions. In: Kiefer F, Pajzs J (eds) Proceedings of the 7th Conference on Computational Lexicography and Corpus Research, Research Institute for Linguistics, Hungarian Academy of Sciences, Budapest, Hungary

Kilgarriff A (1996) Which words are particularly characteristic of a text? A survey of statistical approaches. In: Proceedings of AISB Workshop on Language Engineering for Document Analysis and Recognition, Sussex, UK, pp 33–40

Kilgarriff A, Tugwell D (2001) WORD SKETCH: Extraction and display of significant collocations for lexicography. In: Proceedings of the ACL Workshop on Collocation: Computational Extraction, Analysis and Exploitation, Toulouse, France, pp 32–38

Kilgarriff A, Rychly P, Smrz P, Tugwell D (2004) The Sketch Engine. In: Proceedings of the 11th EURALEX International Congress, Lorient, France, pp 105–116

Kilgarriff A, Kovář V, Krek S, Srdanović I, Tiberius C (2010) A quantitative evaluation of word sketches. In: Proceedings of the 14th EURALEX International Congress, Leeuwarden, The Netherlands

Kim S, Yang Z, Song M, Ahn JH (1999) Retrieving collocations from Korean text. In: Proceedings of the 1999 Joint SIGDAT Conference on Empirical Methods in Natural Language Processing and Very Large Corpora, College Park, MD, USA, pp 71–81

Kim S, Yoon J, Song M (2001) Automatic extraction of collocations from Korean text. Computers and the Humanities 35(3):273–297

Kitamura M, Matsumoto Y (1996) Automatic extraction of word sequence correspondences in parallel corpora. In: Proceedings of the 4th Workshop on Very Large Corpora, Copenhagen, Denmark, pp 79–87

Kjellmer G (1987) Aspects of English collocations. In: Meijs W (ed) Corpus Linguistics and Beyond, Rodopi, Amsterdam, pp 133–140

Kjellmer G (1990) Patterns of collocability. In: Aarts J, Meijs W (eds) Theory and practice in Corpus Linguistics, Rodopi B.V., Amsterdam, pp 163–178

Kjellmer G (1991) A mint of phrases. In: Aijmer K, Altenberg B (eds) English Corpus Linguistics. Studies in Honour of Jan Svartvik, Longman, London/New York, pp 111–127

Kjellmer G (1994) A Dictionary of English Collocations. Claredon Press, Oxford

Koehn P (2005) Europarl: A parallel corpus for statistical machine translation. In: Proceedings of the 10th Machine Translation Summit (MT Summit X), Phuket, Thailand, pp 79–86

Krenn B (2000a) Collocation mining: Exploiting corpora for collocation identification and representation. In: Proceedings of KONVENS 2000, Ilmenau, Germany, pp 209–214

Krenn B (2000b) The Usual Suspects: Data-Oriented Models for Identification and Representation of Lexical Collocations, vol 7. German Research Center for Artificial Intelligence and Saarland University Dissertations in Computational Linguistics and Language Technology, Saarbrücken, Germany

Krenn B (2008) Description of evaluation resource – German PP-verb data. In: Proceedings of the LREC Workshop Towards a Shared Task for Multiword Expressions (MWE 2008), Marrakech, Morocco

Krenn B, Evert S (2001) Can we do better than frequency? A case study on extracting PP-verb collocations. In: Proceedings of the ACL Workshop on Collocation: Computational Extraction, Analysis and Exploitation, Toulouse, France, pp 39–46

Krenn B, Evert S, Zinsmeister H (2004) Determining intercoder agreement for a collocation identification task. In: Proceedings of KONVENS 2004, Vienna, Austria

Kupiec J (1993) An algorithm for finding noun phrase correspondences in bilingual corpora. In: Proceedings of the 31st Annual Meeting of the Association for Computational Linguistics, Columbus, OH, USA, pp 17–22

Kurz D, Xu F (2002) Text mining for the extraction of domain relevant terms and term collocations. In: Proceedings of the International Workshop on Computational Approaches to Collocations, Vienna, Austria

Lafon P (1984) Dépouillements et statistiques en lexicométrie. Slatkine – Champion, Genève/Paris

Landis J, Koch G (1977) The measurement of observer agreement for categorical data. Biometrics 33:159–174

Lea D, Runcie M (eds) (2002) Oxford Collocations Dictionary for Students of English. Oxford University Press, Oxford

Lehr A (1996) Germanistische Linguistik: Kollokationen und maschinenlesbare Korpora, vol 168. Niemeyer, Tübingen

Leoni de Leon JA (2008) Modèle d'analyse lexico-syntaxique des locutions espagnoles. PhD thesis, University of Geneva

Lewis M (2000) Teaching Collocations. Further Developments in the Lexical Approach. Language Teaching Publications, Hove

L'Homme MC (2003) Combinaisons lexicales spécialisées (CLS) : Description lexicographique et intégration aux banques de terminologie. In: Grossmann F, Tutin A (eds) Les collocations: analyse et traitement, Editions De Werelt, Amsterdam, pp 89–103

Lin D (1998) Extracting collocations from text corpora. In: First Workshop on Computational Terminology, Montreal, Canada, pp 57–63

Lin D (1999) Automatic identification of non-compositional phrases. In: Proceedings of the 37th Annual Meeting of the Association for Computational Linguistics on Computational Linguistics, Morristown, NJ, USA, pp 317–324

Louw B (1993) Irony in the text or insincerity in the writer? The diagnostic potential of semantic prosodies. In: Baker M, Francis G, Tognini-Bonelli E (eds) Text and Technology: In Honour of John Sinclair, John Benjamins, Amsterdam, pp 157–176

Lu Q, Li Y, Xu R (2004) Improving Xtract for Chinese collocation extraction. In: Proceedings of IEEE International Conference on Natural Language Processing and Knowledge Engineering, Beijing, China, pp 333–338

Lü Y, Zhou M (2004) Collocation translation acquisition using monolingual corpora. In: Proceedings of the 42nd Meeting of the Association for Computational Linguistics (ACL'04), Barcelona, Spain, pp 167–174

Maingay S, Tribble C (1993) Longman Language Activator Workbook. Longman, Harlow

Makkai A (1972) Idiom Structure in English. Mouton, The Hague

Mangeot M (2006) Papillon project: Retrospective and perspectives. In: Proceedings of the LREC 2006 Workshop on Acquiring and Representing Multilingual, Specialized Lexicons: The Case of Biomedicine, Genoa, Italy

Manning CD, Schütze H (1999) Foundations of Statistical Natural Language Processing. MIT Press, Cambridge, MA

Maynard D, Ananiadou S (1999) A linguistic approach to terminological context clustering. In: Proceedings of Natural Language Pacific Rim Symposium 99, Beijing, China

McCarthy D, Keller B, Carroll J (2003) Detecting a continuum of compositionality in phrasal verbs. In: Proceedings of the ACL 2003 Workshop on Multiword Expressions: Analysis, Acquisition and Treatment, Sapporo, Japan, pp 73–80

McCarthy D, Venkatapathy S, Joshi A (2007) Detecting compositionality of verb-object combinations using selectional preferences. In: Proceedings of the 2007 Joint Conference on Empirical Methods in Natural Language Processing and Computational Natural Language Learning (EMNLP-CoNLL), Prague, Czech Republic, pp 369–379

McKeown KR, Radev DR (2000) Collocations. In: Dale R, Moisl H, Somers H (eds) A Handbook of Natural Language Processing, Marcel Dekker, New York, NY, pp 507–523

Melamed ID (1997) A portable algorithm for mapping bitext correspondence. In: Proceedings of the 35th Conference of the Association for Computational Linguistics (ACL'97), Madrid, Spain, pp 305–312

Mel'čuk I (1998) Collocations and lexical functions. In: Cowie AP (ed) Phraseology. Theory, Analysis, and Applications, Claredon Press, Oxford, pp 23–53

Mel'čuk I (2003) Collocations: définition, rôle et utilité. In: Grossmann F, Tutin A (eds) Les collocations: analyse et traitement, Editions De Werelt, Amsterdam, pp 23–32

Mel'čuk et al I (1984, 1988, 1992, 1999) Dictionnaire explicatif et combinatoire du français contemporain. Recherches léxico-sémantiques. Presses de l'Université de Montréal, Montréal

Meunier F, Granger S (eds) (2008) Phraseology in Foreign Language and Teaching. John Benjamins, Amsterdam/Philadelphia

Michelbacher L, Evert S, Schütze H (2007) Asymmetric association measures. In: Proceedings of the International Conference on Recent Advances in Natural Language Processing (RANLP 2007), Borovetz, Bulgaria

Michiels A (2000) New developments in the DEFI Matcher. International Journal of Lexicography 13(3):151–167

Mille S, Wanner L (2008) Making text resources accessible to the reader: The case of patent claims. In: Proceedings of the 6th International Language Resources and Evaluation (LREC'08), Marrakech, Morocco

Moon R (1998) Fixed Expressions and Idioms in English: A Corpus-Based Approach. Claredon Press Oxford, Oxford

Nerima L, Seretan V, Wehrli E (2003) Creating a multilingual collocation dictionary from large text corpora. In: Companion Volume to the Proceedings of the 10th Conference of the European Chapter of the Association for Computational Linguistics (EACL'03), Budapest, Hungary, pp 131–134

Nivre J (2006) Inductive Dependency Parsing (Text, Speech and Language Technology). Springer-Verlag New York, Inc., Secaucus, NJ

Oakes MP (1998) Statistics for Corpus Linguistics. Edinburgh University Press, Edinburgh

O'Dell F, McCarthy M (2008) English Collocations in Use: Advanced. Cambridge University Press, Cambridge

Orliac B (2006) Un outil d'extraction de collocations spécialisées basé sur les fonctions lexicales. Terminology 12(2):261–280

Orliac B, Dillinger M (2003) Collocation extraction for machine translation. In: Proceedings of Machine Translation Summit IX, New Orleans, LA, USA, pp 292–298

Padó S, Lapata M (2007) Dependency-based construction of semantic space models. Computational Linguistics 33(2):161–199

Pantel P, Lin D (2000) An unsupervised approach to prepositional phrase attachment using contextually similar words. In: Proceedings of the 38th Annual Meeting of the Association for Computational Linguistics, Hong Kong, China, pp 101–108

Pawley A, Syder FH (1983) Two puzzles for linguistic theory: nativelike selection and nativelike fluency. In: Richards J, Schmidt R (eds) Language and Communication, Longman, London, pp 191–227

Pearce D (2001a) Synonymy in collocation extraction. In: Proceedings of the NAACL Workshop on WordNet and Other Lexical Resources: Applications, Extensions and Customizations, Pittsburgh, PA, USA, pp 41–46

Pearce D (2001b) Using conceptual similarity for collocation extraction. In: Proceedings of the 4th UK Special Interest Group for Computational Linguistics (CLUK4), Sheffield, UK, pp 34–42

Pearce D (2002) A comparative evaluation of collocation extraction techniques. In: Proceedings of the 3rd International Conference on Language Resources and Evaluation, Las Palmas, Spain, pp 1530–1536

Pecina P (2005) An extensive empirical study of collocation extraction methods. In: Proceedings of the ACL Student Research Workshop, Ann Arbor, MI, USA, pp 13–18

Pecina P (2008a) Lexical association measures: Collocation extraction. PhD thesis, Charles University in Prague

Pecina P (2008b) A machine learning approach to multiword expression extraction. In: Proceedings of the LREC Workshop Towards a Shared Task for Multiword Expressions (MWE 2008), Marrakech, Morocco, pp 54–57

Pecina P (2010) Lexical association measures and collocation extraction. Language Resources and Evaluation 1(44):137–158

Pedersen T (1996) Fishing for exactness. In: Proceedings of the South Central SAS User's Group Conference (SCSUG-96), Austin, TX, USA, pp 188–200

Piao SS, Rayson P, Archera D, McEnery T (2005) Comparing and combining a semantic tagger and a statistical tool for MWE extraction. Computer Speech and Language Special Issue on Multiword Expressions 19(4):378–397

Piao SS, Rayson P, Mudraya O, Wilson A, Garside R (2006) Measuring MWE compositionality using semantic annotation. In: Proceedings of the Workshop on Multiword Expressions: Identifying and Exploiting Underlying Properties, Sydney, Australia, pp 2–11

Polguère A (2000) Towards a theoretically-motivated general public dictionary of semantic derivations and collocations for French. In: Proceedings of the 9th EURALEX International Congress, EURALEX 2000, Stuttgart, Germany, pp 517–527

Procter P (ed) (1987) Longman Dictionary of Contemporary English. Longman, Harlow, London

Rajman M, Besançon R (1998) Text mining – Knowledge extraction from unstructured textual data. In: Proceedings of the 6th Conference of International Federation of Classification Societies (IFCS-98), Roma, Italy, pp 473–480

Ramisch C, Schreiner P, Idiart M, Villavicencio A (2008) An evaluation of methods for the extraction of multiword expressions. In: Proceedings of the LREC Workshop Towards a Shared Task for Multiword Expressions (MWE 2008), Marrakech, Morocco

Ramos MA, Wanner L (2007) Collocation chains: How to deal with them? In: Gerdes K, Reuther T, Wanner L (eds) Proceedings of the 3rd International Conference on Meaning-Text Theory, Wiener Slawistischer Almanach Sonderband 69, Munich and Vienna

Ramos MA, Rambow O, Wanner L (2008) Using semantically annotated corpora to build collocation resources. In: Proceedings of the 6th International Language Resources and Evaluation (LREC'08), Marrakech, Morocco

Ratnaparkhi A (1998) Statistical models for unsupervised prepositional phrase attachment. In: Proceedings of the 36th Annual Meeting of the Association for Computational Linguistics and 17th International Conference on Computational Linguistics, Montreal, QC, Canada, pp 1079–1085

Rayson P, Piao S, Sharoff S, Evert S, Moirón BV (2010) Multiword expressions: hard going or plain sailing? Language Resources and Evaluation Special Issue on Multiword Expressions: Hard Going or Plain Sailing 44(1–2):1–25

Renouf A, Sinclair J (1991) Collocational frameworks in English. In: Aijmer K, Altenberg B (eds) English Corpus Linguistics. Studies in Honour of Jan Svartvik, Longman, London/New York

Ritz J (2006) Collocation extraction: Needs, feeds and results of an extraction system for German. In: Proceedings of the Workshop on Multi-Word-Expressions in a Multilingual Context at the 11th Conference of the European Chapter of the Association for Computational Linguistics, Trento, Italy, pp 41–48

Rögnvaldsson E (2010) Collocations in the minimalist framework. Lambda (18):107–118

Sag IA, Baldwin T, Bond F, Copestake A, Flickinger D (2002) Multiword expressions: A pain in the neck for NLP. In: Proceedings of the 3rd International Conference on Intelligent Text Processing and Computational Linguistics (CICLING 2002), Mexico City, Mexico, pp 1–15

Santos Pereira LA, Mendes A, Braasch A, Povlsen C (2002) An electronic dictionary of collocations for European Portuguese: Methodology, results and applications. In: Braasch A, Povlsen C (eds) Proceedings of the 10th Euralex International Congress (EURALEX 2002), Copenhagen, Denmark, pp 841–849

Schone P, Jurafsky D (2001) Is knowledge-free induction of multiword unit dictionary headwords a solved problem? In: Proceedings of Empirical Methods in Natural Language Processing, Pittsburgh, PA, USA, pp 100–108

Schulte im Walde S (2003) A collocation database for German verbs and nouns. In: Kiefer F, Pajzs J (eds) Proceedings of the 7th Conference on Computational Lexicography and Corpus Research, Research Institute for Linguistics, Hungarian Academy of Sciences, Budapest, Hungary

Selva T, Verlinde S, Binon J (2002) Le DAFLES, un nouveau dictionnaire électronique pour apprenants du français. In: Braasch A, Povlsen C (eds) Proceedings of the 10th Euralex International Congress (EURALEX 2002), Copenhagen, Denmark, pp 199–208

Sérasset G (2004) A generic collaborative platform for multilingual lexical database development. In: Sérasset G, Armstrong S, Boitet C, Popescu-Belis A, Tufis D (eds) Proceedings of the Workshop on Multilingual Linguistic Ressources (MLR2004), Geneva, Switzerland, pp 73–79

Seretan V (2008) Collocation extraction based on syntactic parsing. PhD thesis, University of Geneva

Seretan V (2009) An integrated environment for extracting and translating collocations. In: Mahlberg M, González-Díaz V, Smith C (eds) Proceedings of the Corpus Linguistics Conference CL2009, Liverpool, UK

Seretan V, Wehrli E (2006) Multilingual collocation extraction: Issues and solutions. In: Proceedings of COLING/ACL Workshop on Multilingual Language Resources and Interoperability, Sydney, Australia, pp 40–49

Seretan V, Wehrli E (2007) Collocation translation based on sentence alignment and parsing. In: Actes de la 14e conférence sur le Traitement Automatique des Langues Naturelles (TALN 2007), Toulouse, France, pp 401–410

Seretan V, Wehrli E (2009) Multilingual collocation extraction with a syntactic parser. Language Resources and Evaluation 43(1):71–85

Seretan V, Nerima L, Wehrli E (2004) A tool for multi-word collocation extraction and visualization in multilingual corpora. In: Proceedings of the 11th EURALEX International Congress, EURALEX 2004, Lorient, France, pp 755–766

Silberztein M (1993) Dictionnaires électroniques et analyse automatique de textes. Le système INTEX. Masson, Paris

Sinclair J (1991) Corpus, Concordance, Collocation. Oxford University Press, Oxford

Sinclair J (1995) Collins Cobuild English Dictionary. Harper Collins, London

Smadja F (1993) Retrieving collocations from text: Xtract. Computational Linguistics 19(1):143–177

Smadja F, McKeown K, Hatzivassiloglou V (1996) Translating collocations for bilingual lexicons: A statistical approach. Computational Linguistics 22(1):1–38

Spina S (2010) The Dictionary of Italian Collocations: Design and integration in an online learning environment. In: Proceedings of the 7th Conference on International Language Resources and Evaluation (LREC'10), Valletta, Malta

Stone M, Doran C (1996) Paying heed to collocations. In: Proceedings of the 8th International Workshop on Natural Language Generation, Herstmonceux, Sussex, England, pp 91–100

Stubbs M (1995) Corpus evidence for norms of lexical collocation. In: Cook G, Seidlhofer B (eds) Principle & Practice in Applied Linguistics. Studies in Honour of H.G. Widdowson, Oxford University Press, Oxford

Stubbs M (2002) Words and Phrases: Corpus Studies of Lexical Semantics. Blackwell, Oxford

Thanopoulos A, Fakotakis N, Kokkinakis G (2002) Comparative evaluation of collocation extraction metrics. In: Proceedings of the 3rd International Conference on Language Resources and Evaluation, Las Palmas, Spain, pp 620–625

Todiraşcu A, Tufiş D, Heid U, Gledhill C, Ştefănescu D, Weller M, Rousselot F (2008) A hybrid approach to extracting and classifying verb+noun constructions. In: Proceedings of the 6th International Language Resources and Evaluation (LREC'08), Marrakech, Morocco

Tutin A (2004) Pour une modélisation dynamique des collocations dans les textes. In: Proceedings of the 11th EURALEX International Congress, Lorient, France, pp 207–219

Tutin A (2005) Annotating lexical functions in corpora: Showing collocations in context. In: Proceedings of the 2nd International Conference on the Meaning-Text Theory, Moscow, Russia

Venkatapathy S, Joshi AK (2005) Relative compositionality of multi-word expressions: A study of verb-noun (V-N) collocations. In: Natural Language Processing - IJCNLP 2005, Lecture Notes in Computer Science, vol 3651, Springer, Berlin/Heidelberg, pp 553–564

Vetulani G, Vetulani Z, Obrebski T (2008) Verb-noun collocation SyntLex dictionary: Corpus-based approach. In: Proceedings of the 6th International Language Resources and Evaluation (LREC'08), Marrakech, Morocco

Villada Moirón Bn, Tiedemann J (2006) Identifying idiomatic expressions using automatic word-alignment. In: Proceedings of the Workshop on Multi-Word-Expressions in a Multilingual Context), Trento, Italy, pp 33–40

Villada Moirón MBn (2005) Data-driven identification of fixed expressions and their modifiability. PhD thesis, University of Groningen

Villavicencio A, Bond F, Korhonen A, McCarthy D (2005) Introduction to the special issue on multiword expressions: Having a crack at a hard nut. Computer Speech and Language Special Issue on Multiword Expressions 19(4):365–377

Volk M (2002) Using the Web as a corpus for linguistic research. In: Pajusalu R, Hennoste T (eds) Catcher of the Meaning. A festschrift for Professor Haldur Õim, Publications of the Department of General Linguistics 3, University of Tartu, Estonia

Wanner L (1997) Exploring lexical resources for text generation in a systemic functional language model. PhD thesis, University of the Saarland, Saarbrücken

Wanner L, Bohnet B, Giereth M (2006) Making sense of collocations. Computer Speech & Language 20(4):609–624

Wehrli E (1997) L'analyse syntaxique des langues naturelles: Problèmes et méthodes. Masson, Paris

Wehrli E (2000) Parsing and collocations. In: Christodoulakis D (ed) Natural Language Processing, Springer, Berlin, pp 272–282

Wehrli E (2004) Un modèle multilingue d'analyse syntaxique. In: Auchlin A, Burger M, Filliettaz L, Grobet A, Moeschler J, Perrin L, Rossari C, de Saussure L (eds) Structures et discours - Mélanges offerts à Eddy Roulet, Éditions Nota bene, Québec, pp 311–329

Wehrli E (2007) Fips, a "deep" linguistic multilingual parser. In: ACL 2007 Workshop on Deep Linguistic Processing, Prague, Czech Republic, pp 120–127

Wehrli E, Nerima L, Scherrer Y (2009) Deep linguistic multilingual translation and bilingual dictionaries. In: Proceedings of the Fourth Workshop on Statistical Machine Translation, Association for Computational Linguistics, Athens, Greece, pp 90–94

Weller M, Heid U (2010) Extraction of German multiword expressions from parsed corpora using context features. In: Proceedings of the 7th Conference on International Language Resources and Evaluation (LREC'10), Valletta, Malta

Wermter J, Hahn U (2004) Collocation extraction based on modifiability statistics. In: Proceedings of the 20th International Conference on Computational Linguistics (COLING 2004), Geneva, Switzerland, pp 980–986

Wermter J, Hahn U (2006) You can't beat frequency (unless you use linguistic knowledge) – a qualitative evaluation of association measures for collocation and term extraction. In: Proceedings of the 21st International Conference on Computational Linguistics and 44th Annual Meeting of the Association for Computational Linguistics, Sydney, Australia, pp 785–792

Williams G (2002) In search of representativity in specialised corpora: Categorisation through collocation. International Journal of Corpus Linguistics 7(1):43–64

van der Wouden T (1997) Negative Contexts. Collocation, Polarity, and Multiple Negation. Routledge, London, New York

van der Wouden T (2001) Collocational behaviour in non content words. In: Proceedings of the ACL Workshop on Collocation: Computational Extraction, Analysis and Exploitation, Toulouse, France, pp 16–23

Wu D (1994) Aligning a parallel English-Chinese corpus statistically with lexical criteria. In: Proceedings of the 32nd Annual Meeting of the Association for Computational Linguistics (ACL '94), Las Cruces, NM, USA, pp 80–87

Wu H, Zhou M (2003) Synonymous collocation extraction using translation information. In: Proceeding of the Annual Meeting of the Association for Computational Linguistics (ACL 2003), Sapporo, Japan, pp 120–127

Yang S (2003) Machine Learning for collocation identification. In: International Conference on Natural Language Processing and Knowledge Engineering Proceedings (NPLKE), Beijing, China

Yarowsky D (1993) One sense per collocation. In: Proceedings of ARPA Human Language Technology Workshop, Princeton, NJ, USA, pp 266–271

Yarowsky D (1995) Unsupervised word sense disambiguation rivaling supervised methods. In: Proceedings of the 33rd Annual Meeting of the Association for Computational Linguistics (ACL 1995), Cambridge, MA, USA, pp 189–196

Zaiu Inkpen D, Hirst G (2002) Acquiring collocations for lexical choice between near-synonyms. In: Proceedings of the ACL-02 Workshop on Unsupervised Lexical Acquisition, Philadephia, PA, USA, pp 67–76

Zajac R, Lange E, Yang J (2003) Customizing complex lexical entries for high-quality MT. In: Proceedings of the 9th Machine Translation Summit, New Orleans, LA, USA, pp 433–438

Zeevat H (1995) Idiomatic blocking and the Elsewhere principle. In: Everaert M, van der Linden EJ, Schenk A, Schreuder R (eds) Idioms: Structural and Psychological Perspectives, Lawrence Erlbaum Associates, Hillsdale, NJ and Hove, UK, pp 301–316

Zinglé H, Brobeck-Zinglé ML (2003) Dictionnaire combinatoire du français: expressions, locutions et constructions. La Maison du Dictionnaire, Paris

Zinsmeister H, Heid U (2002) Collocations of complex words: Implications for the acquisition with a stochastic grammar. In: Proceedings of Workshop on Computational Approaches to Collocations (Colloc02), Vienna, Austria

Zinsmeister H, Heid U (2003) Significant triples: Adjective+Noun+Verb combinations. In: Proceedings of the 7th Conference on Computational Lexicography and Text Research (Complex 2003), Budapest, Hungary

Zinsmeister H, Heid U (2004) Collocations of complex nouns: Evidence for lexicalisation. In: Proceedings of KONVENS 2004, Vienna, Austria

Index